4.00 - Strand 3-67 (Steffin)

The Aristocratic Journey

MARGARET HUNTER
BEFORE HER MARRIAGE TO
CAPTAIN BASIL HALL

From a miniature by W. J. Thomas, reproduced by courtesy of her granddaughter,
Margaret, Lady Parsons

The Aristocratic Journey

by margaret (Hunter) Hall

Being the Outspoken LETTERS
OF MRS. BASIL HALL *Written
during a Fourteen Months'
Sojourn in America 1827–1828*

Prefaced and Edited
by
UNA POPE-HENNESSY

ILLUSTRATED

NEW YORK   G. P. PUTNAM'S SONS   LONDON
The Knickerbocker Press
1931

Made in the United States of America

19506

CONTENTS

v

CONTENTS

vi

ILLUSTRATIONS

The Aristocratic Journey

PREFACE

THE writer of these Letters, Margaret Hunter, was born on the day of George Washington's death, and twenty-six years later married Basil Hall, grandson of the Lord Selkirk whose silver plate had been raided and rendered back by Paul Jones. Fantastic though it would be to lay hold of these family traditions as pointers of destiny their mere existence caused the girl to realize America as something actually connected with her personal life. Basil Hall, himself a sailor, talked to her frequently of his experiences in New York and Boston and of the boyhood friends he had made among officers of the United States Navy in the halcyon years when Americans were permitted to use the British fortresses of Gibraltar and Malta as bases for fighting the Bashaw of Tripoli. In this way the fame of Decatur became known to her as well as that of Somers, "whose name passed into a battle-cry in the American Marine." When, in 1827, Captain Hall suggested to his wife that they, together with their child, should make a tour through the United States, she welcomed the project. The letters printed in this volume are her running commentary on the visit. They are intimate and outspoken, for they were written to her sister Jane with whom in the past she had shared coach journeys over the Pyrenees and voyages to Corunna when as girls they had travelled to join their father, Sir John Hunter, British Consul-General in Spain.

In the year 1815 both girls had taken very kindly to life in Madrid where they made many diplomatic friends and acquired, amongst other accomplishments, the art of valsing. When they returned home to Edinburgh the dance was still unknown there, and they were requested one night to dance it together at the As-

3

sembly Rooms. So much interest was taken in this display that ladies stood on chairs to see over the heads of the people in front of them. Spain, in a sense, set for Margaret Hall the standard of life abroad, and memories of those delightful days impaired her enjoyment of the drabber entertainments of the New World. Balls in America were compared with balls in Madrid, American partners with Spanish cavaliers, American clumsiness with Spanish agility. The scintillating receptions after the victory of Waterloo, the bejewelled, exquisite women gowned in bright satins and shimmering brocades, the elegant diplomats beribboned and bestarred—the total restored array of monarchical splendour had put into the girl's impressionable mind a definite picture of what life in a capital city should be, and Washington suffered by the comparison. Sixty years later when she lay dying, her last words were of bells ringing in Madrid.

Having no public in her mind when she wrote her letters from the United States, Mrs. Hall simply described men and things as they seemed to her and as she wished her correspondent to see them. If the letters are in many respects hostile to America and full of a type of criticism belonging to the age of patronage, it must be remembered that they were written artlessly and from the point of view of an elegant lady who has suddenly dropped into a society that nothing in her past experience has fitted her to appraise leniently or sympathetically. Every divergence from the polite code of her own set is pilloried and few allowances made for deviations in custom arising out of the makeshift nature of transatlantic social usage. Americans, it was observed, ate "pease" with their knives, but it must have been difficult to do anything else in a country of two-pronged forks. They arranged their first and second courses simultaneously along two sides of the table, but any other arrangement in a practically servantless land would have obliged the diners to discomforting movement. It was noted that those at table helped themselves with the same spoon to different dishes, but then they had to wash up for themselves. Men were always chewing tobacco and ejecting its juice, but what other way had they of deriving

comfort from nicotine when "segars" were costly, snuff an aristocratic abomination, and suitable pipes not to be obtained?

Many of the habits of the Americans that were so distasteful
to Mrs. Hall arose through shortages of some sort due to the conditions under which they lived, but it was not her habit to look beneath the surface of things, and she had a way of sizing up such
evidences of adaptability as inferiorities. Apart from these fashionable and feminine shortcomings, Mrs. Hall's descriptions of men,
manners, hostelries, and means of travel are probably more detailed
and more accurate than those of any other traveller in the America
of her day. Her very alertness in pouncing so often and unerr-
ingly on every distinguishing variation from typical European
behaviour made her a faithful if, indeed, an unpleasing chronicler
of the incidents of the foreigner's experience in the United States
a century ago.

Mrs. Hall, though she was pleased to be treated as a true "azure
blue" by professors in New York, made no claim to special intel-
lectual attainments and found her chief pleasure in society. It is
amusing to note in her letters how much more enjoyment it gave
her to meet Scotch people than any other folk. She discovers them
everywhere, from Canada to New Orleans, with never-failing delight. She did not really share her husband's enthusiasm for visiting institutions, but being anxious to see whatever was "characteristic" of the country she accompanied him to Penitentiaries and
many places of detention for deaf, dumb, and lunatics, as well as
to numerous schools. This she called "doing up the Lions." Captain Hall's special hobbies, geology, astronomy, philology, and book-
publishing, held no attractions for her, and from first to last she
behaved as a woman of *ton,* conscious of her success with Ministers, Secretaries of Legation, and Scotchmen generally, but she
remained unable or unwilling to charm Americans.

In appearance Mrs. Hall was of middle height, fair, with blue
eyes and a merry expression of face. She had a passion for dress
and though not beautiful was vivacious and attractive. She talked
well, her hair was modishly arranged in ringlets, her Polish cloak,

her bonnets, and her evening gowns were in the latest fashion, while her *parure* of blue topazes was the envy of all beholders. Having a good ear and being musical she picked up languages easily. In France she was taken for a Frenchwoman, in Spain she learned to speak admirable Spanish, and in America her English was found so pure and so correct that many persons assumed she must be an American.

The baby, Eliza, who accompanied her parents on their tour was fifteen months old when they landed in New York. Many warning voices had been lifted up in Edinburgh against the folly of dragging a child on such a journey and exposing it to the vicissitudes of climate, insect bites, and unsuitable food; but Eliza was carried off and survived the experiment, though members of the family thought, when she died at the age of thirty, that it must in some way have weakened her constitution. True, she was sheltered against avoidable hardship by her nurse, the imperturbable Mrs. Cownie from Forfar, but there were days when nothing more suitable for "the wee lambie" was forthcoming than milkless tea or coffee, broiled ham or hung beef, while on board ship, in alleviation of her violent and continuous seasickness she was given mugs of ale. There were days, too, when her fat legs were "mangled" by mosquitoes and her chubby face and fingers disfigured by strange blisters "like strawberries." Notwithstanding these manifold afflictions Eliza was always laughing and high-spirited, and her company gave the liveliest pleasure to her parents. In letter after letter Mrs. Hall repeats how thankful they are not to have heeded the advice of the wiseacres at home. The only regret they harboured was that she might not in after years be able to recall her unique experience.

Both Captain and Mrs. Hall disapproved on principle of everything that America presented of equality and fraternity and were completely out of their bearings in a society unmapped by class distinctions. They held democracy to be a demoralizing blight from which, however, it was always possible a country might recover. Mrs. Hall made no attempt to understand the great experiment of a self-governing people spread before her eyes, and the uniform impartiality of the want of sympathy displayed by her with all popular modifications of life, gave a sharply objective quality to her outlook which renders it invaluable to any one wishing to study the social conditions of that day. Some of her generalizations are interesting, notably those she makes on the contrast between accommodation, prices, and manners in the Slave States and accommodation, prices, and manners in the Free States. Her characterization of cities like Boston, New York, Philadelphia, Baltimore, and Washington are especially acute.

The Halls went to America armed with over a hundred letters of introduction and picked up many more as they went along. They dined with the Daniel Websters in Boston, with De Witt Clinton at Albany, with William Astor in New York, with Joseph Bonaparte at Point Breeze, with John Quincy Adams at the White House. Gilbert Stuart told them anecdotes about his sitter, George Washington, and described his meeting with Voltaire at the house of David Hume in Edinburgh. They conversed with Washington Allston, the artist, through an evening "six Havannahs" long. They met Prescott, Bancroft, Jared Sparks, and many other well-known people. To launch them in Washington society the British Minister sent round their visiting cards with his own to members of the Government and *Corps Diplomatique*. No two persons had a better chance of seeing what there was to be seen in America, and no two people made more exhaustive notes on what they saw there. Captain Hall, who was already well known for a book on South America, wrote another on the United States, which gained for him further celebrity in England and considerable notoriety in America. Before undertaking the American trip Captain Hall had learnt to manipulate the *camera lucida* in order to be able to take sketches of the places that interested him. The illustrations in this volume are examples of his industry.

Mrs. Hall's letters are a triumph of effortless observation, though in every case (and this may be said of all of us), her understanding was limited by her disapprovals. For example, she hated the Catholic Church and alluded to its ceremonies as "mockery" and "mummery"; she despised the Quakers, and for her, their religious performances were nothing but "absurdities." There is no reason, however, to take any of Mrs. Hall's opinions on serious subjects seriously; she was not a philosopher. Her merit lies in her instinct for minute observation and description, by means of which she was able to give a more complete picture of American ways of life than is obtainable from any other tourist of that date. The letters to a greater or less degree mirror the propensity of all English travellers and reveal the secret of their unpopularity with foreigners. They evince an almost fatuously superior attitude to any life other than that they are familiar with, and superiority is irritating to those exposed to its incidence no matter how humble or insensitive they may be.

Admiration of the old superstructure of society in Europe was not peculiar to Mrs. Hall. The England and Scotland of her day were imbued with it as with a religion, and nothing short of the World War three generations later availed to shake the foundations of this creed. When rationing and other disagreeable economies became necessary the superstructure tottered, for a duchess could get no more butter or meat than a scullery maid. Formal entertaining and formal manners were annihilated at one blow. People who lived in the grand traditional way awoke to find butlers and footmen turning magically into batmen and machine-gunners, or maids throwing down their dust-pans to make bombs. Improvisations of all kinds became obligatory, and a queer independence was forced upon every one as guests carried their own bread-cards or sugar about with them. Class distinctions became blurred and almost obliterated when substitutes had to be found for persons as well as things. England unconsciously was more and more assimilated to America as a country of makeshifts. In fact, it was only war on a national scale that made it possible for English people to begin to understand America, her many trials, triumphs, and mistakes.

Renan once said: "Despite the miracles of grace one is always of one's age." Mrs. Hall was typically of her age. Bred and brought up in the "Athens of the North" most other places, always excepting London, Paris, and Madrid, were little better than a wilderness for her and, to her prejudiced mind, America was the worst wilderness of all.

UNA POPE-HENNESSY.

LETTER I

LIFE ON THE OCEAN WAVE

Before engaging passages for New York Captain Hall made enquiry into the comparative merits of English and American ships, for he wished his wife to travel as comfortably as possible. In the shipping advertisements boats were variously described as "first-rate hotels upon the water" and "floating palaces." He found, however, that on English boats the ladies were "cocked up at the nether end of the ship" and that on the American boats they were placed at "the centre of motion," a merciful and considerate arrangement which decided him in favor of the foreign packet. He, therefore, took passages for his party on the sailing ship *Florida,* due to leave Liverpool for New York on April 15, 1827. Mrs. Hall's first letter is written four days later from Cork.

OFF CORK, April 19, 1827.

MY DEAREST JANE,

Here we are becalmed or pretty nearly so, which is more favourable for writing a letter than for getting to New York, but for the present I have so completely recovered from my sickness that the life we are spending is really very agreeable. This is a lovely afternoon, so mild and sweet. Just as the party in the Gentlemen's Cabin had finished dinner notice was given that a fishing boat was along side. There was a general rush on deck, and I had by that time got so much better that I joined the party and found them bargaining for twelve fine cod. The fishermen were all complete Paddies, and we were much amused talking to them, and Eliza was as much interested in the whole scene as any of us. Yesterday, in spite of all my good resolutions and struggles, I was the first to give in, but in place of making myself worse by going below, I had a comfortable bed arranged on a settee on deck, and when it became too cold to admit my remaining longer there, I lay down on the sofa in the Ladies' Cabin, as I wished not to go to bed till my usual hour, ten o'clock. I slept well, but the exertion of dressing this morning of course made me sick again. However, after I did make the exertion, I felt the advantage of lying on deck rather than remaining below all day. Unfortunately Mrs. Cownie became sick to-day. I had become sanguine about her keeping up, she had held out so well, but that was too much to expect. She is lying on the sofa in the Ladies' Cabin more dead than alive, and Basil has had to act the part of nurse to us all. Meantime Eliza has been as good and as merry as usual and great friends with everyone on board. At nine we have breakfast, at half past twelve, luncheon, at four, dinner, at seven, tea and I hear a great jingling of glasses and spoons between nine and ten. The only sort of occupation I have been at all able for, was reading an American novel, *A Peep at the Pilgrims*. And so good-night to you, for it gets rather cold and I must go below, which is by no means so favourable for my writing.

April 24:—Many days, you see, have elapsed without my having the power of writing, and I now feel by no means confident that the attempt will be successful. On the evening of the nineteenth there was a most discomposing swell which lasted the whole night, and on the next day there was so much motion that neither Mrs. Cownie nor I could raise our heads from our pillows, so you may believe that Basil had his hands full enough, for altho' Eliza was frequently very sick, she would by no means consent to be still, and nothing pleased her except being continually walked about, and by night Basil said he was sure his arms were black and blue. He was a good nurse before this apprenticeship, but his experience on board will enable him to be upper nurse in a "Nobleman's or Gentleman's Family"! The sufferings that one endures on board ship are very well to laugh at after they are over, but—they are no laughing matter at the time, tho' I must say that occasionally in spite of sickness and misery I could not help laughing at the extremely ludicrous appearance we made. I was extended at one end of a hard, hair-sofa in the Ladies' Cabin, (Oh, dear, dear, how I did wish for one day of my own charming sofas in St. Colm Street!) at the other end of the same sofa, half lying half sitting was Mrs. Cownie, now and then making a desperate effort to tie one of Chicky's strings, and then as suddenly grasping the bason. We have made some alteration in our accommodation. We have given Mrs. Cownie and Eliza our State Room and we sleep on the floor in the Ladies' Cabin. It is an unspeakable comfort that there is but one other lady, Miss Wright, on board, and she is really as good as none. She seldom stirs out of her own cabin. Except the variety of being better or worse we have had little to relieve the monotony of our lives, and yet it is astonishing how quickly time has passed; not a thing have I done except listen for the half hour bells, which are the greatest comfort, every half hour that passes is so much taken from the period of our discomfort. The passengers in general are not sick, but they all lead as idle a life as could well be and without their four or five meals a day would find it hard work to kill the time. There is an occasional game of chess, some playing on the flute, a great deal of shooting with the rifle, and yesterday, being the King's birthday, the Captain sported champagne, and the gentlemen fired a *feu de joie* with rifle and pistols.

I find Eliza's dress and my own the very thing it ought to be, her little stuff frock is most serviceable, and the duffle pelisse which was got at your suggestion is equally useful. My own cloak of shepherd's plaid is never off except at night when it lies above me, for the weather is still cold. A soft bonnet, too, is a luxury without which no one ought to go to sea. I have found mine so comfortable, I can lie down with it on at all times and places, and Eliza's nankeen one has the same advantages. My bones are so sore with lying so much on the hard beds and sofas that I can scarcely walk yet, even with assistance, partly from weakness and very much from want of sea legs.

APRIL 25:—I wish you could see the picturesque group seated

12

on a mattress on the floor in the Ladies' Cabin, Mrs. Cownie, Eliza, and myself, mixed up with a medley of bricks, backgammon men, plums, thimbles, thread and many other things too numerous to mention. A ship is a capital preparation for America if there is as much equality in society as we are told, for here are Mrs. Cownie and I cheek by jowl all day long, always dining together and pressing each other to a little bit of this or a little drop of that. I shall really feel quite strange when I come to sit down to dinner without my maid. I find that altho' I can eat very well sometimes when sitting on the ground I cannot encounter the smell in the cabin, just as you and I used to find, you may remember, going out to Corunna, when we demolished such quantities of beef-steaks and porter seated on the floor behind the curtain that screened us from everyone else!

On Wednesday night a gale sprung up, which continued all Thursday and totally disabled all the sick ones of the party, amongst whom are preeminent myself and Mrs. Cownie, not forgetting Eliza who has been undoubtedly the most sick person on board. Not a thing has remained on her stomach for several days except a glass of ale. She does not eat anything, but the delight expressed in her face as she leans back her head, closes her eyes, and applies her mouth like a leech to a mug of any kind of liquid, is quite amusing. We shipped many a sea on Thursday, and I had the full benefit of one as I lay on the sofa in the evening, immediately under the skylight. The dead-lights were in all day to prevent the sea from breaking into the cabin. I used to stand in great awe of the dead-lights and to suppose that when they were put up it was a sort of announcement that we were speedily going to the bottom. However, I find there is nothing so ominous about them, and that they are merely to prevent the sea from getting into the cabin. Yesterday, Saturday, was very uncomfortable; there was a nasty, cross sea which was extremely disagreeable, but to my infinite satisfaction I learned that we had accomplished more than half our voyage. To-day we have had first a calm and now a contrary wind with a fog, the sort of weather that is always met with near the banks of Newfoundland, as we are now. We all assembled in the Cabin an hour ago and the Captain read us a sermon. Last Sunday was too rough for any notice to be taken of it. I hope we shall spend but one more Sunday on board. I am most thoroughly tired of sea life.

MAY 2:—Well, ten days more I trust will land us in the United States; we are two thirds of the way. Eliza has become such friends with all the gentlemen and sailors upon deck that she will not come from them even to Mrs. Cownie. She feels they can amuse her by carrying her about, which she is aware Mrs. Cownie does not. I am sorry that we were not at New York by the first of May to see the universal *flitting* which I am told takes place on that day, the people are so extremely locomotive in their habits that they seldom remain longer than a year in a house. This is very characteristic of their constant wish to better themselves.

MAY 3:—We have seen an ice island, which is something to have seen, as it was at a sufficient distance to take away all sense of danger and in broad daylight. About half past five this morning I heard the Captain calling to Basil, which gave me rather a start, as last night the wind blew very fresh and I knew there was sufficient fear of encountering the ice to cause the Captain to shorten sail very much. However, in a minute or two Basil came back to tell me that there was an ice island in sight, so I got up, dressed myself after a fashion, and joined the very queer looking group on deck. The ice was a very beautiful object, in shape and size very much like to the Bass. It was about a mile and a half or two miles distant, and the sun shone brightly upon it, and the waves broke over it in great style. Even poor little Miss Wright came creeping out of her nest to see the show. She has been in mortal dread of the ice for nearly a week past, and last night she consulted Basil as to whether she ought to go to sleep or not, which he strongly advised her doing, and promised to give her timely notice in case of any danger. I was amused when I remember my own resolutions about dressing and the gown that I kept out for a dinner dress, but so different is the reality that I am well content if I can get my clothes huddled on in the course of the day, and with my large cloak to hide all deficiencies I am obliged to dispense with all that is not absolutely necessary to make them hold on. I hope we shall find warm baths at New York; that will be a luxury beyond all price.

We are all in spirits again, getting on beautifully, and in paradise compared to our situation some days ago. Our comforts are daily decreasing, the soda water is all done and so are the crackers, little biscuits of which Eliza is particularly fond. It is very hard upon we sick females that so many liquids should fail us, for the thirst that we suffer from is quite intolerable.

MAY 8:—During the last few days we have had time to arrange our letters of introduction and to insert them in a book, along with notes as to the connections between the persons the letters are from and those they are to, which, considering that we have upwards of a hundred already and will probably acquire more as we go along, is very necessary, for one, of course, forgets all the circumstances, and then when you come to be asked by any one about their brother or uncle or cousin, you are at a loss to know who is meant. Now by having this book to refer to before sending our letters of introduction at the different places, we shall inform ourselves of all that we have been told about the people. Then we have another book in which is noted everything that we are to go to see at each place, the best inns and boarding houses, and a variety of other memorandums. I think we shall find them both very useful.

MAY 14:—All sorts of preparations for landing are going forward, packing amongst the passengers, whilst the Captain is making out a list of the baggage and writing down the names and ages of the ladies and gentlemen on board. Eliza is in such spirits that one would imagine that she knew how near the land we are. We have much need to land, the clean towels are done. I must say we have been rather skimpily stocked in many ways and had we had an average passage, which is considered thirty-six days, we should have been very ill off indeed. Should you by any chance know of anyone who proposes making this voyage, advise them by all means to provide themselves with raspberry vinegar and lemon sirop and any other little luxuries of the kind that they can think of, not to be put into requisition until the ship's stores are done. Some towels, too, would not be amiss, as for the chloride of lime, which is recommended as taking away bad smells, I think the smell of itself is infinitely more disgusting than anything it is made use of to cure, that I do not recommend it to anyone.

MAY 15:—Whilst we were at dinner the pilot came on board, a very consequential looking person indeed. Next came a Revenue Cutter along side to look at the Manifest and see that all was right, and half an hour ago came one of the owners of the ship. In the boat with the owner was a large branch of dogwood, a wild flower very like the wild rose. We seized upon it with avidity as the first green thing we had seen for so long. Most of the passengers go on shore to-night, but we shall sleep here and go quietly on shore to-morrow in peace and comfort. The last person who came on board brought Basil a letter from Mr. Wilkes recommending us to go to the American Hotel, which is newly established. We grudge sadly going towards New York in the dark, for we are told that the approach is very pretty.

Ever, my dearest Jane, affectionately

yours,

MARGARET HALL.

LETTER II

NEW YORK CITY

As the *Florida* arrived in harbour after sunset on May the fifteenth, the Halls arranged to wait until next morning before going on shore. By 8:30 A.M. on the sixteenth Mrs. Hall was ensconced in a sitting room at the new American Hotel looking out on Broadway. Pen in hand, she sat down to write her first impressions of New York. Callers soon interrupted her— Mr. Wilkes, Dr. Hosack, Mr. Philip Hone, and Dr. Mitchell all proffered entertainment. Nineteen new visitors on the second day rather hindered the flow of narrative. A busy fortnight was spent in seeing "the lions," such as the House of Refuge, the Almshouse, the Female High School, the African School, the Supreme Court, the National Gallery, and the Penitentiary. The dullness of the sight-seeing was enlivened by much dancing of quadrilles. "I shall be danced to death in this grave country," where "the very professors of colleges join in the amusement."

THE AMERICAN HOTEL
NEW YORK, May 16, 1827.

MY DEAREST JANE,

At length we are really once more on land, and as happy to find ourselves there as poor mortals who have been pretty constantly wretched for the last four weeks may be supposed to be. There was no sleep to be had last night, such a noise of passengers talking and ship putting to rights, that by six o'clock I was right glad to get up and go on deck to refresh my eyes with the sight of houses. Finding ourselves so early astir we thought it as well to get ready at once and come on shore for breakfast, and we were the more resolved to this as a gentleman who had come on board told us that Mr. Wilkes had taken apartments for us at this hotel. The sun shone so bright that we felt ashamed to expose ourselves in our ship-dresses, and therefore we dressed ourselves creditably, got a coach, and drove here. There is an odd mixture in one's

17

feeling in landing in New York. There is so much that is English, the signs, the language, and at the same time everything wears a foreign aspect, the hackney coach had green silk curtains instead of windows. We met several covered-waggon sort of things outside of which was written in large letters "ICE" and many other trivial circumstances which, tho' nothing in description, make you feel that you are from home.

Whilst writing, breakfast made its appearance, a most ample one; beefsteak, mutton chops, shad (a sort of fish somewhat resembling flounder), mackerel, omelet and eggs, besides tea, toast, and rolls, all excellent as far as we put it to the trial. We had scarcely finished breakfast when Mr. Wilkes came to call. He sat for a considerable time with us, and now he and Basil are gone out together. We are to dine with him to-day. He is a very frank, pleasing person, and seems to have quite taken us in hand. This hotel is quite new, and the change from the dirt of the ship to the cleanliness here is quite refreshing. The sitting room in which I now am is as nicely furnished as any hotel in England, and the bedrooms look clean and comfortable, tho' the portion of furniture in them is not so great as we should find at home. The Master of the House is a quiet, civil sort of person, apparently very desirous to please and to accommodate us in every way, and, as yet, we have had no reason to complain of the attendance.

When I brought Eliza on deck this morning, she was at first quite bewildered at the variety of objects that she saw until the sight of a cart and horse quite roused her up, and I thought she would have sprung out of my arms to catch them. She has enjoyed looking out of the window amazingly and hearing the racket of the carriages, which is almost as great as in any frequented street in London. The entrance to the Hotel is from the Park, but most of the windows look into Broadway which is the Bond Street of New York. Almost all the boarding houses are in Broadway, also the principal shops. I am sitting in expectation of a visit from Mr. Wilkes's daughters, but whether they are single or married, I have yet to learn.

MAY 17:—This is such a busy place that I feel as if I had no time to write, and our visitors begin at so early an hour that even our morning is not our own, but I am charmed with New York, and we shall require to be resolute in leaving it soon in order to have plenty of time for our summer tour. It is hot already, but nothing to what it will be. Yesterday Mr. Wilkes returned in the course of the day and brought with him his two daughters, Mrs. Colden and Miss Wilkes, and also the elder Mrs. Colden, mother-in-law to the other and to whose husband we brought a letter. The younger Mrs. Colden is very handsome indeed, and both she and her sister are extremely pleasing. We dined with them and met also Mr. David Colden, (husband to the aforementioned handsome lady), Mr. Horace Wilkes, the youngest son, and Mrs. MacAdam, aunt to Miss Wilkes and aunt-in-law to the Road Maker. She is ninety-two years old and has all her faculties as entire as any of us. They are altogether a delightful family, so very kind and such a degree of heartiness about them I feel already quite at home and shall be very happy to return to New York——Altho' I began writing more than an hour ago we have had such a multitude of visitors that this is all the length I have got. First of all came Dr. Mitchell, one of the leading men of the place, rather an oddity, I conjecture, and perhaps a bit of a bore. Yesterday we had Dr. Hosack, another of the principal, scientific persons, next we had Mr. David Colden, and then Captain Leslie, an old South American friend of Basil's. We have also had Mr. Buchanan, the English Consul, Mr. Philip Hone, the late Mayor, who came to invite us to a ball to-morrow evening, and one or two others. But to return to our yesterday's dinner. Mr. and Mrs. Cadwallader Colden, father and mother to Mr. Wilkes's son-in-law, came in the evening, also a young Mr. Charles Wilkes, nephew to the other and his wife. I had heard so much in England about the overloaded tables in America that I was surprised to see the table at Mr. Wilkes's smaller than it would have been for the same party at home, neither were things in the same keeping at all. We had plenty of French wine but no covers to the dishes and not set down with much nicety. The tarts, the fruit, and the cheese were all placed on the table at the same time, and the table cloth was not removed. Altogether, the style was more foreign than English.

We walked home from Mr. Wilkes's and enjoyed the cool air amazingly. They have not yet lighted their streets with gas, though they use it in the principal shops. The oil lamps make a very miserable show, nevertheless the economical people of this good town make a bargain to have a smaller quantity of oil during the period of moonlight——I have just been interrupted by a visit from Captain Barclay of the British Navy and his wife. She is an American, but a handsome specimen. We have been very much struck with the beauty of the women in general. Their features are so delicate; they dress magnificently. I never in my life saw so many fine bonnets as from my window yesterday. Talking of that I had a curious little trait of American curiosity this morning. Mrs. Cownie had the Imperial[1] open arranging the things when a lady came into the room and, on seeing the hats and bonnets, acted as if they were for sale. I came in sight at the moment and I suppose scared her away, but presently she returned and begged Mrs. Cownie just to let her look at the pink hat!

Basil is gone with young Mr. Wilkes and Mr. Denison to the Navy Yard, they are to be back by three, which is the public dinner hour. We have a private parlour and might breakfast and dine in it if we chose, but as we wish to see the people of the country in every way we prefer the public table. Mrs. Wilkes is as quiet a soul as can be, with a double dose of the nasal twang which they have one and all, more or less. When I heard people in England counterfeit the American *snivel* I thought they surely caricatured, but the original goes far beyond any imitation I ever heard.

MAY 18:—Yesterday, whilst Basil was out, I had nineteen visitors, besides those who had called previously. Mr. Denison and he did not return from the Navy Yard until after the company had sat down to dinner, however, we went to the public table and

---

[1] A travelling trunk.

found a party of eighteen or twenty, all eating with their knives, which is a most universal practice here.

We took a very long walk after dinner. We first went down to the Battery where there is a very delightful walk along the river side, and after walking a good deal about that part of the town we finished by calling at Mr. Colden's. You must understand that the two Mr. and Mrs. Coldens live together in the house next to Mr. Wilkes. The elder gentleman is a remarkably clever man. He was formerly Mayor of New York and is a great patron and promoter of all charitable and useful institutions. He took us to-day to one of the most interesting I have ever seen, the House of Refuge where boys convicted of crime are sent, instead of to the other prison where they are exposed to the influence and bad example of older criminals, and from whence they generally come out worse than they went in. They are taught some trade, either shoemakers, or chair-makers, or nail-makers, and when their conduct has been blameless for a sufficient length of time, they are bound as apprentices or sent into the country, which is preferred, as it effectually removes them from their former associates. The whole establishment is well arranged, clean and comfortable, and so well ventilated. The Superintendent is a Methodist, a very pleasing person, whose manners are admirably adapted for the situation he holds; they are so kind, and, I should think, calculated to inspire the boys with respect and confidence. The House has been established nearly three years, during which time there have been only four boys returned whose conduct did not give satisfaction. There is a similar establishment for girls, but, as yet, there are only twenty. The ladies take as great charge of it as the gentlemen do of the other. We went next to the Alms House and Penitentiary, but, as it was very hot and I was afraid of fatiguing myself too much before the ball this evening, I contented myself with merely walking through one of the wards, where I saw a set of very old women. From thence we went to the High School, which is framed pretty much in the mould of the High School in Edinburgh. In one room there was a Spanish Class, as that is considered useful for boys who are to be brought up as merchants, owing to the commerce with South America.

Last night when we came home we were told that a gentleman of the name of Livingstone had called and was then in the public reading room. We sent to say that we would be happy to see him, and presently our Edinburgh acquaintance walked in. I suppose you remember him, a tall, good looking young man. He is now married, has several children, and is entirely settled in the country about twenty miles from this town. He is extremely desirous that we should see something of the country life amongst the gentleman farmers and country gentlemen of this side of the water, but as we are equally anxious to see it we shall probably go to his house on Thursday next for two or three days, on our way to Albany. Amongst my visitors yesterday were Miss Douglas, and Mrs. James Monroe, sister to Miss Douglas, whom we knew in Edinburgh. In Edinburgh people, whilst they laughed at Miss Douglas, chose to set it down as a matter of course that she was a facsimile of all the code in New York and belonging to the very first society here, but the state of the case is that the whole family are quizzed here and thought quite as strange as we could think them. They are by no means popular and are most prodigiously vulgar, and their low origin is constantly mentioned as the cause of this vulgarity. They are very rich, however, and entertain in great style, we are told. We are to dine with them upon Thursday next and expect an immense feast. We dine to-morrow and Sunday at Mrs. Colden's, to-morrow with a party and Sunday after dinner we go to the Chapel of the House of Refuge. I am filing all our notes of invitation and suchlike and shall also keep the visiting cards.

Eliza is growing funnier every day and laughs with such glee at her own jokes. It is quite enlivening. I shall be made so vain about her, she is so much admired and petted by everyone and she is certainly a delightful child to carry about in this way, she is always so pleased with strangers.

MAY 19:—I feel a little tired to-day, owing to being late up last night. We did not come home from Mr. Hone's till nearly one o'clock. We went at half past nine and found a terribly formal circle of ladies and a group of gentlemen in the middle of the room. There were two large rooms open, communicating by folding doors and handsomely furnished and lighted. Quadrilles were danced in both rooms, the same set with very slight variation that is danced in Edinburgh. I danced once, for it would be thought quite strange here that any married lady should decline dancing. They marry so very young, generally about sixteen or seventeen, that they would have no enjoyment at all if they ceased to dance on that account. Between the dances we had a song or two from a Madame Mallibran. She was a Madame Garcia and is here thought the most surprising singer that ever was heard. I should think that in London she would be considered third, fourth, or fifth rate. And the most disagreeable part of the manners of the Americans is that you are called upon to admire and be surprised to such a degree that by the time I came home, I was perfectly worn out. Another thing, too, which is very puzzling is the constant appeal that is made whether their manners and society are not exactly the same as those in London. What can I say? I can't tell people who are doing their best to amuse and please me that they are not within a hundred degrees of the polish and refinement of English society; the very question shows their deficiency, for what can be more ill-bred than to ask anyone what they think of yourself, and it is, in fact, neither more nor less. I am extremely interested by seeing and hearing the progress of their institutions, their desire to acquire knowledge, and the quiet, sensible, and at the same time enthusiastic conversation of clever men upon the state of the country, and the many improvements, but when they come to light ballroom conversation nothing can be so ponderous, and, as for an attempt at a joke, the weight of it is enough to crush you to atoms. The women do not bear the test of evening dress. They have no air, and, tho' they have plenty of good clothes on, the taste is not good. There was too great a mixture of flowers and pearls and different kinds of ornaments in the hair. They hold themselves ill, I saw but one person who danced well. We had tables laid out with refreshments of all kinds and a quantity of ice and champagne. They attacked the *victuals* with prodigious avidity.

MAY 20:—One of the things that Basil has been most desirous of seeing at New York is a fire, and as one or two occur generally every week he would have been very unlucky had he not been gratified in this respect. Since we arrived there have been three, the latter part of one he saw on Friday evening, but early this morning he had the good fortune to see a magnificent one. Before two o'clock there was an alarm of fire. I awoke fancying I was still at sea and that the ship was on fire. Basil got up and dressed, but on going to the door found that it was a false alarm. I had slept most uncomfortably for a short time when again I heard the people running along the street calling out, "Fire! Fire! Fire!" all in the same tone, the engines rattling as fast as they could be carried, whilst every church bell in the place began to toll. I was prepared to expect all this noise and hubbub in the event of such an occurrence, nevertheless, I could hardly persuade myself that the whole town was not in flames. Basil again dressed, and this time he was repaid for his trouble and saw a most magnificent fire. He came back at six o'clock, quite pleased with his good fortune. The number of wooden houses is the cause of so many fires here, but they do not occur in the more respectable parts of the town. They happen so frequently that we found that what we thought so much of had not excited the least sensation!

Basil has been this morning to one of the Episcopalian Churches. I sent Mrs. Cownie to Church, also, and staid at home with Eliza. We made out all our visits yesterday, which, considering that we had at most doors to wait five minutes till the negro servant thought fit to attend to us and another five before the ladies made their appearance, was no slight task. The American women I suspect to be a good deal like Spaniards, very gaily dressed when they have notice to prepare but, when taken unawares, not always tidy and nice like English women. We dined at Mr. Colden's, where besides

An American Stage-Coach

Drawn with the Camera Lucida by Captⁿ. B. Hall. R.N

Engraved by W. H. Lizars

Mr. and Miss Wilkes we had Mrs. Clinton, wife to the Governor of the Sate of New York, her mother, her two step-daughters, and her son. The Governor was engaged to dinner but had promised to join us after dinner, which I was sorry he did not, as I have not yet seen him. Mrs. Clinton is abundantly vulgar and amused us by the violence of her Republican principles, declaring that she did not consider herself above the poorest person in the community and that there is the most perfect equality amongst Americans. Mr. Colden laughed at the sentiment as much as we did, and agreed with me that altho' there may be an equality of rights you must create human nature afresh before you can expect that one man is not to value himself above another on account of his wealth or talents or something of that kind. At the same time that Mrs. Clinton made all her professions of humility and equality it was easy to see that she was not a little proud of her station as wife of the Governor, and I was quite angry with the way in which she quite decidedly took rank over her old mother.

The Coldens and the Wilkeses I like better the more I see of them. Mr. Wilkes is quite delightful. He is an Englishman and it is impossible not to feel one's national pride gratified by the most agreeable and gentlemanlike man we have yet met.

MAY 21 :—We have been to-day with Mr. Collins, a Quaker, to two schools; the female High School on the same plan as that for the boys, and the African school, which is the most interesting I have yet seen. The boys are all black, that is to say they must all have come of black blood, tho' they are of all shades, but it has been found not at all to answer to mix them along with white children. Up to a certain age the boys are all the greatest of friends and make no distinction of colour, but after that the poor blacks feel themselves badly looked down upon, and their spirit is quite broken by feeling themselves despised. The teacher of the African school has a most admirable method of exercising the boys so as to show whether they really do understand what they have been taught, and the result of what we heard to-day was most satisfactory. He is quite an enthusiast, but what surprised us most was a certain style of drollery and fun that ran through his whole system. We imagined that we had at length found a Yankee who could joke, but alas! on questioning some of the boys we learnt that he is an Englishman.

MAY 22:—We went to the Supreme Court in the morning in expectation of hearing one of their most eminent lawyers, Mr. Emmet, brother to the hero of Washington Irving's story of the *Broken Heart,* but we were disappointed. The Chief Justice and the two judges had much the appearance of Methodist Ministers, with sleek, smooth hair and black coats. I must say I thought the absence of wigs and gowns took much from the appearance of dignity, but no doubt the judgement is not influenced by those outward circumstances. We did not hear anything and therefore soon came away to the American Academy of Fine Arts, but I suppose there was never anything seen in the way of arts less fine, such daubs to be sure, and even the most superior men in the place are so little acquainted with anything better in that way, that they think these vile things beautiful. At the National Gallery neither was there anything much better except the casts from fine statues. We also went to the Panorama of Athens, the same that was in England, and to the Lyceum, which finished our sight seeing for the day, and now we are waiting for Miss Wilkes to call to take us to dinner at Miss Douglas's.

We have delayed our departure from New York till Monday, we find so many temptations to remain that really it is difficult to tear ourselves away. There never were people so petted and made of as we are; we have the whole town at our command. The people leave their business and everything to attend to our slightest wish. Basil has just been remarking to me what I already felt, that we have all at once been translated to the highest rank, for were we a Duke and Duchess we could not be more attended to. We were told by someone before we came here that ladies were very little attended to, and that altho' Basil might be asked out, I would not, instead of which I have been taken as much notice of even by the *learned* men as if I were azure blue.

I shall be danced to death in this grave country, where the very Professors of the Colleges join in the amusement, so that there is no hope whatever of getting into a society which would consider itself too dignified to adopt so frivolous an occupation. I danced last night with Professor Benwick who belongs to Columbia College, and who I should have imagined as little a dancing man as Professor Jameson or Mr. Pillans, but I found I was quite mistaken in my calculations. We had a very grand party at Miss Douglas's, but she is the vulgarest of all human beings. Basil was bored beyond endurance. She bestowed all her tediousness on him and the most provoking part of it is that the old woman sets up for English, not American, and truth to tell she is much more like a vulgar Englishwoman than anything American I have ever seen, for with all their want of polish and refinement they are not vulgar. It appears that want of leisure is what prevents them from becoming polished, they are so constantly hard at work with real business that they have no time to think of the little minor things that constitute refinement. At the same time they are all sufficiently educated and have a want of selfishness that makes them desirous to please. They are a very odd mixture of English and French character, not French *manners* at all certainly, but that boasting self-praise and exaggeration that they indulge in is very French. I wish I could by any means convey to you an idea of them, but I fear you must take a trip across the Atlantic to accomplish this.

We are frequently obliged to ask the way from one place to another as we walk along, and I never say anything like the perfect civility with which we were answered by all ranks. There is less loud talking or swearing or mirth either in the streets than in England, much less liveliness, but much less misery too, for there is not a beggar to be seen. The Douglases are most unpopular, the Coldens will not visit them, and Ann Wilkes went there yesterday merely out of compassion to us. The constant reproach upon them is that they stand for nothing except their wealth, which in this *aristocratic* country does not go down at all. Mrs. James Monroe, the married one, is a very good humoured person, but Miss Margaret Douglas is particularly disagreeable, and I can perceive that she purposes to torment me with civility. She presses me to shop, to *roide,* to go to the Play with her, but all in vain, for I will not do any of all that.

MAY 24:—We had a grand party last night at Dr. Hosack's and more dancing, but we made our escape early, for we cannot stand so much dissipation. It was the same sort of party as at Mr. Hone's, but considerably more crowded. The ladies looked infinitely better than when I saw them before in the evening. We had previously dined with sixteen people at Mr. Wilkes's, and by and by I must mention that altho' the family dinners are not over large, they give prodigious feasts when they have company. We have now been at three large dinner parties, and yesterday, for instance, there were seven dishes down each side of the table, besides the top and bottom dishes being twice removed, and that is no more than we had both at Mr. Colden's and at Mrs. Douglas's. They have no meat along with the sweet things, but a most profuse supply of puddings, pies, jellies, sweetmeats, and immense *pillars* of ice, after which there are pine apples and all manner of dessert. In the evening, too, there is a quantity of ice. The cookery is very inferior indeed and the arrangements are not in good keeping, in short, they are far behind everything that relates to elegance, but they are so hospitable and kind that I feel unwilling even to make the remark.

We have just returned from a very delightful drive in Long Island which is quite the garden of New York. It is, I believe, about one hundred and fifty miles long, but two thirds of it is still covered with forest. The part through which we drove is prettily wooded and has altogether an English appearance, altho' the trees are very small. We went along the water side and returned by a road inland. I did not see a single stone or brick house, all were of wood, and so clean and nice they looked, with little verandahs in front, and sometimes all round. The Steam Boat in which we crossed is larger than those on the Dundee ferry, and we crossed with a speed that I never sailed with before.

MAY 27:—Yesterday morning we set off at eight o'clock and crossed the ferry to Paulus Hook, in New Jersey, our party filled two carriages and consisted of Mr. and Mrs. Wilkes, Mr. and Mrs. David Colden, Mr., Mrs., and Miss Macready. We drove through a most beautiful, Yorkshire-looking country, almost entirely pasture, for the vicinity of this great town makes the land too valuable to be appropriated to corn. We passed through Newark and Belleville to Aquacanoc. The road all along was lined with weeping willows and acacia trees covered with flower. The wild cherry too was covered with blossoms, and everything still looks fresh and green. The road was close to the river and as thickly strewed with neat houses as any flourishing county in England, but the trees are very inferior to what I expected to see. I had formed a wrong estimate of them from hearing so much of American forests, not considering that in a forest they are so crowded together that they have no room to be fine, and that where the land has been cleared the trees were looked upon as the greatest impediment to improvement and cultivation, and were cut down without either mercy or judgement, and it is only of late years that people have begun to plant, at least such is the case here, but I may very probably see finer ones elsewhere. We dined at Aquacanoc, and a very poor dinner we had, to the great mortification of our American friends who were much vexed that our first experience of the country inns should be so bad. However, we did not complain and shall be quite contented if we meet with nothing worse in the course of our travels. After dinner we drove six miles further to Paterson, a manufacturing town which has sprung up within the last dozen years in consequence of the convenient supply of water for the various mills, but this barbarous application of the water has very much impaired what we went to see, the Falls of the Passaic. They are still, however, well worth visiting, and the scenery round is very beautiful, but I have no genius for description. There is a very curious cleft in the rock down which the water falls, and which was delightful food for Basil to speculate as to the great wave and the deluge! When we returned to the Inn for tea we found Mr. and Mrs. Colden had rode out to join us, and we spent the rest of the evening most agreeably as in a warm climate, walking on the bridge or sitting with all the windows and doors around us open, drinking quantities of iced lemonade and hot tea. It is quite a Cockney place and crowded with Saturday and Sunday visitors. This morning after breakfast we walked to the opposite side of the Fall and sat for two or three hours under the shade of the trees conversing with Mr. Wilkes and Mr. Colden, who have always something to say worth listening to. Mr. Colden is one of the cleverest men in this country and most willing to impart his information. We dined at Paterson and did not set off on our return home till half past three, as we wished to avoid the heat of the day. We came back by a shorter road to vary the scene and got home about eight o'clock. We found Eliza in perfect health and I do think she is happy now to see us when we return home after being away any time. To-night I found her fretting very much for her supper, but the moment I took her she became as funny as possible. Her most newly acquired accomplishment is *kissing* and there never was anything so sweet as her little kisses. Adieu, my dearest Jane, believe me ever affectionately yours,

MARGARET HALL.

LETTER III

THE HUDSON, ALBANY, STOCKBRIDGE

Captain Hall and his party left New York by May the 29th by steamboat and disembarked at Calendar on the Hudson in order to stay for two nights with an old friend, Mr. Livingstone, who took them to see half-built Sing-Sing. From Calendar they went to West Point, which interested Mrs. Hall less than watching the antics of Eliza. Their next port of call was Catskill, and thence they jolted up to Pine Orchard to an hotel kept by an Englishman and "therefore" comfortable. On arriving at Albany they deposited Eliza and Mrs. Cownie in the charge of Mr. Cruttenden, the hotel keeper, while they made a flying visit to another English friend living at Stockbridge. On the return journey to Albany they inspected the Shaker Settlement at Lebanon Springs.

WEST POINT, May 30, 1827.

My DEAREST JANE,

We left New York according to our intention on Tuesday morning, the twenty-ninth. We were unlucky in having rainy weather and a small, stuffy, steamy steamboat, being the only one on the river which is in the habit of stopping at Mr. Livingstone's wharf at Calendar, which is the name of his farm. The distance from New York is only twenty-three miles, and as we had started at eight o'clock we reached our destination at eleven. About half an hour before landing the clouds rolled away and the rain ceased, leaving the air most delightfully fresh. On the wharf we found Mr. Livingstone's carriage waiting to carry us to the house about a quarter of a mile off at the top of a steep hill, the road along which wound so as to keep us always in sight of the beautiful Hudson and its wooded hills, at the bottom of which are innumerable villages and single houses. Indeed, the whole length that we have yet come reminds us of the banks of the Clyde or Loch Lomond

31

or any other of the most populous parts of Scotland. The numerous steamboats and sailing sloops, too, is another feature of resemblance in the landscape, and the frequent stops to take in or let out passengers proves that the banks of the Hudson are to the New Yorkers in point of summer resort what the banks of the Clyde are to the citizens of Glasgow. Mr. Livingstone's house is like all the country houses I have yet seen on this side of the Atlantic, of wood with a wide verandah in front. There is not the slightest attempt at dressing up the grounds about the door, the grass is allowed to grow up half as high as a man, and except a few honeysuckles amongst the rails, there is not a flower near the house. The public rooms were particularly comfortable, covered with mats instead of carpets, and most effectually kept cool by the outward air and the light being excluded.

Yesterday Basil and I accompanied by Mr. Livingstone took a drive of ten miles to see the new State Prison of Sing Sing, as it is called, tho' it is situated close to the village of Sparta. Basil had a letter to the superintendent, Captain Lynds, with whom we had a great deal of interesting conversation. He has the entire management of the establishment at present and is building the Prison by means of the convicts. There are two hundred now there, who live in that part of the building which is finished, whilst they are employed in finishing the rest. When finished it is calculated to hold eight hundred. The two hundred now there are under the charge of ten superintendents and ten Military Guards, four of whom at a time are sentinels, stationed at the brow of the hill above the hollow in which is the prison, with loaded muskets, and this number is found quite sufficient to keep those below in order. At night they are shut up, each in a separate cell, and during the day they are not allowed to speak at all to each other, which effectually prevents their being able to form any plot or plan of escape. It is about two years and a half since Captain Lynds landed where he now is, and during that length of time only one man has contrived to escape. In spite of this it was some time before I could divest myself of a certain feeling of fear when I found myself surrounded by such a set of wretches. I felt that the physical force was on their side, and that few or none of them felt any moral obligation to desist from doing us any mischief that might be in their power. I was aware that this was false reasoning, as I have not heard so many discussions upon discipline to so little advantage as not to know that it does not require numbers to enforce it effectually, but for all this, just at first I must confess I felt *queerish*. There is one very excellent regulation; in every cell there is a Bible and no other book is allowed, so that they are driven of necessity to read the Bible if they read at all. There are prayers every evening and Church service every Sunday and the Chaplain who attends has the power to converse with and to catechize the men. A prison is at best a very disagreeable sight to see, but as I am on the plan of seeing everything at present, I do not choose to give way to my repugnance and so lose the opportunities I have of seeing such things to advantage.

Our drive led through what Washington Irving has made classic ground by his story of *Sleepy Hollow*. The first village we passed through was Tarry Town, which he says was so named by the good wives of the Dutch settlers in that part of the country from the tendency that their husbands had to tarry there on market days. We passed also the Church and the Pond which have acquired celebrity from the same source, and about three miles to the right of where we were is Sleepy Hollow itself, still noted for Legends of Ghosts and Hobgoblins. The characters in the story are founded upon reality and Brom Bones is still extant.

There is another circumstance of more melancholy interest connected with our yesterday's drive; it is the scene of Major André's capture. The American Revolutionary War is a subject of so little interest now-a-days that it is quite possible many of the present generation may never have heard of him. I remember breaking my heart over his fate some years ago, in Miss Seward's letters. He was sent to communicate with General Arnold who had been bribed over to British interests and to betray his own country. Suspicion of this had got abroad and on his return to the river side to embark in the vessel which lay in waiting for him, he was seized and I believe that his own questions betrayed him, for at first his captors had no idea who he was. We passed the very spot where his horse was drinking in a little brook at the moment he was made prisoner. He was hanged at Tapaan, a small town immediately opposite to Mr. Livingstone's house. He was buried about a mile from thence, but three or four years ago his remains were moved to England. I am told that his fate caused as much consternation in America as it did in England. Not a dry eye was found amongst those whose duty obliged them to be present at his execution, and the signing of his death warrant is said to have been the most painful duty that Washington had to perform, but he was a spy to all intents and purposes, and the severity was considered indispensable. General Arnold died broken-hearted in England, thoroughly despised by the English as well as by his own countrymen.

MAY 31 :—We did not leave Mr. Livingstone's this morning till eleven o'clock and got to West Point at three. Nice, short, little trips those are for poor Chick, who flourishes upon them amazingly and is quite enchanted with the novelty of all she sees. She has a particular taste for steam engines, which you know she has by inheritance. I do not pretend to be an impartial judge, but I must say she seems to take much more notice of what is around her than other children of her own age. To-day there was a child of seventeen months old on board (two months older than Eliza) a fine like child, too, but she sat on her mother's or the maid's knee quite quiet and contented the whole day without attempting to get off, instead of which my little Miss trotted away as hard as she could go, pulling Mrs. Cownie or me after her and poked into every corner of the steamboat, opened every door and every box that she could lift the lid off, and, in short, did not rest until she had made a complete examination of everything she could get at, and had so thoroughly wearied herself that she slept sound for two hours on her back on the deck.

CATSKILL, JUNE 1:—If you saw the drawing of the Catskill scenery hung up in this room and read the flaming puff descriptive of it, you would blush to acknowledge that you never before heard of such a place, and really I am surprised on looking round the banks of this river that till six months ago I scarcely knew of its existence. We left West Point to-day about twelve o'clock, by one of the steamboats going up from New York to Albany.

The scenery is beautiful. We got out of the Highlands eight miles above West Point, altho' soon after that we came in sight of much higher mountains than any of the Highlands. The steam vessel we came in is the most magnificent thing of its kind I have yet seen. The deck is about one hundred and fifty feet long, and below there are excellent cabins, one very large in the centre where the meals are laid out, and at one end is the Ladies' Cabin and the other end the Gentlemen's, all three magnificently furnished and the dinner the best and the most neatly served that I have seen in any hotel in this country. You may imagine how spacious the accommodation is when altho' a hundred covers were laid for dinner and made use of, there never appeared to be more than twenty persons on board. The wind and tide were both against us, but we were exactly five hours and three quarters coming from West Point to Catskill, a distance of fifty-nine miles, in the course of which we stopped five or six times to take in or put out passengers.

The company on board the steam vessels is much the same I think as what is to be met with in similar conveyances on the Clyde, I mean the mass of the company, for on the Clyde you would certainly meet more ladies occasionally and especially more gentlemen, which article I must confess to be rare in this country, tho' I beg that you will not bring me into disgrace by whispering that I have said so. I cannot deny the fact that I have not yet seen *one* American gentleman. Mr. Colden perhaps may be called so, but he is a gentleman not of the last century but of two or three centuries back and never speaks to me without calling me Madam. As for the young men, they Ma'am and Sir in a most appalling manner, and one and all, male and female, eat invariably and indefatigably with their knives. It goes rather against one's feelings to see a prettily dressed, nice-looking, young woman ladling rice pudding into her mouth with the point of a great knife, and yesterday to my great horror I saw a nursery maid feeding an infant of seventeen months in the same way. I must own the woman deserved credit for her dexterity in not cutting the child's mouth.

PINE ORCHARD ON THE CATSKILL MOUNTAINS, JUNE 3:—We jolted up here yesterday at the rate of four hours to thirteen miles and quite fast enough for the sake of one's bones, for such a road for ruts and holes and all manner of conveniences for shaking poor mortals to pieces I have not travelled over since I crossed the Pyrenees. We left the village of Catskill at ten o'clock in a large, lumbering stage with a seat at each side and one in the middle meant to stow eight persons, but as the fashionable season for visiting this place is not yet arrived, and the Stages consequently do not ply regularly, we engaged one of the said machines for our own use, giving a seat also to an old lawyer who had no other way of ascending the mountain. We had four horses to draw this vehicle and required them all, some parts of the road were extremely steep and indeed no part of it at all would be agreeable to a nervous lady. There is absolutely nothing to prevent the carriage from rolling down the precipice, but the horses are so well used to the ascent that there is no danger whatever. We rejoice exceedingly that we are here without the annoyance of hosts of tourists, and another advantage of coming thus early is that we see everything in the first freshness of green, and I never saw anything more lovely than the variety of tints of green over the mountains interpersed with a profusion of rich, pink honeysuckle. From the front of this house we have a view of the Hudson to the extent of seventy miles, altho' on account of the great height on which we stand it does not appear to be more than five or six. The immense plain below us is as much cultivated as Yorkshire and studded all over with houses and villages.

This house was established by a company but is kept by an Englishman (Webb), which, had you been upwards of a fortnight in America as I have been, you would not require to be told. Everything is so neat and nice and comfortable, plenty of silver forks, a luxury not to be met with at the best inns in this country, a dinner cooked by Mrs. Webb herself who has fortunately no cook at present, consequently we are spared the extraordinary rivers of butter and oceans of grease which belong to American cookery. Everything in short partaking in some degree of that refinement that becomes a second nature to English persons, who if they have never been deprived of them are not aware how necessary they are to their comfort and will probably be apt to think that they would never miss such and such things, and that they do not care for luxuries and many more such remarks, not considering that a bason to yourself is a luxury or a three-pronged fork (two-pronged being all that we are indulged with in this uncivilised country). It is, however, a very good country in spite of all this, but I am not in the smallest danger of becoming a citizen of the United States.

By the by, I do not think I have yet mentioned one very striking peculiarity of the Americans, which is, I believe, universal, the extreme quickness with which they eat. We find ourselves continually left far in the rear, and Mr. Webb, who was for some time a waiter in one of the principal hotels in New York, told us that he has frequently seen fifty persons sit down to dinner and in a quarter of an hour every one of them had left the room. At those large public tables they do not waste those precious moments upon little luxuries of change of plates or knives and think nothing of lifting a spoon from the potatoes and diving straightway into the pudding.

ALBANY, N. Y., JUNE 5:—We came down yesterday morning from the Catskill mountains to the village and arrived upon a training of militia, such a set! O dear, I never saw such *gaucherie* in my life. They hold themselves precisely *inverse* from the carriage of English Militiamen. Their chests one and all are *concave* instead of *convex* and this applies to every American of the male species that I have yet seen. They have not an idea of straightening their legs when marching, and shouldered their arms as often on the wrong as the right one. They are called out twice a year, besides the general review in the autumn or the *fall* as that season is universally called in this country. Basil dined with some of those gentlemen at the public table, but Eliza and I preferred a quiet meal. There was no boat last night to Albany, but, being tired of the drumming of the militia, in the cool of the evening we drove five miles further to Athens, a pretty little village, and there crossed the ferry to Hudson. Classical names abound along the route that we are now going to travel. You see we have already been both at Sparta and Athens. Hudson is a remarkably pretty, clean town with macadamised streets, the first we have seen in the Union. After bespeaking our rooms Basil and I went out, taking Eliza with us on purpose to leave Mrs. Cownie more at leisure to make her preparations for the night. We wandered to a grassy knoll on a sort of common where cows and pigs were grazing, and rested ourselves on the ground whilst Eliza trotted round us trying to attract the pigs whom she loves as she does all animals, and imitating their grunts most admirably. I never saw her more attractive. The sequel to her walk was that she laughed herself to sleep at her own joke, thrusting her toes into Mrs. Cownie's mouth!

The steamboat that would first call at Hudson in the morning, we were told, came there about five o'clock and thinking that a more agreeable time for travel than later in the day we were roused up soon after four. Eliza was so sound asleep that it occurred to us it was the greatest pity to awake her, accordingly there was no attempt made to dress her, so she was wrapped up in a cloak, and Mrs. Cownie carried her a good half mile down to the wharf. Here we found that we were considerably too early, so, still rolled up in her cloak, she was laid upon a table in the receiving house connected with the Ferry. There was ringing of bells and slamming of doors, but Eliza never stirred. In half an hour the boat came up, she was carried through all the noise and confusion attendant upon all such conveyances, and laid on a bed in the Ladies' Cabin, and never woke throughout all this till we had gone three or four miles up the Hudson.

STOCKBRIDGE, MASS., JUNE 8:—We left Albany yesterday at twelve o'clock, and altho' the whole distance was but thirty-eight miles we did not reach the end of our journey till nine in the evening. Five miles from here we left the stage and came on in "a wagon," as all open carriages that we have yet seen in this country are called. They are in appearance rude enough, wood without any covering or lining, but they are by no means uncomfortable except as regards getting in and out which is "considerable of a difficulty" as they say here. We learnt on arriving that Mr. Ashburner was confined to his room by illness. His eldest son and two daughters met us at the door and welcomed Basil as an old friend. Mrs. Ashburner is a pretty-looking, quiet, inoffensive person, who does not seem to interfere with them at all. We sat upwards of an hour with them before going to bed, and then as usual asked the breakfast hour, which as they had been alluding to their very early hours, Basil said in joke he supposed was between six and seven, but what was my horror and astonishment when Miss Ashburner answered, "No, between five and six." I am very anxious to accommodate myself to the habits of the country I am in, but really to get up at half past four without any absolute necessity is an effort beyond my nature, and I showed my reluctance so plainly that they named eight, which was an indulgence equal to twelve in England. I remarked that if half past five was the breakfast hour they dined at ten. "O no," said one of the young ladies rather indignant at my supposing that they could be such Goths, "we do not dine till," (I thought she was going to say three or four), "between twelve and one." By eight we were ready and found that most of the family had fortified themselves against such an extraordinary change of hours by an early breakfast. Mr. Ashburner came down when we had done. He is more like a death's head than anything I have seen for a long time, but he is a man of a good deal of general information and consequent variety of topics of conversation, which is rarely to be met with among persons in this country.

I had a nice little letter from Mr. Vaughan yesterday in which he desired to be particularly remembered to Mama and you. He says Washington is a most detestable place of residence; in winter, whilst Congress is sitting, those parts of the town scattered here and there which are finished are crowded to excess, and in summer they are abandoned by the principal "Members of the Government" and left to a small circle of miserably paid persons belonging to public offices. This accounts for the dislike that all the English Ministers have to accept the situation.

JUNE 10:—I feel quite hopeless of being able to give you any idea of the extraordinary exhibition we witnessed to-day and which Basil, who has seen a good many varieties of religious ceremonies, declares to be the strangest way of worshipping God that ever fell under his notice. I do not believe you ever heard of a sect of Quakers denominated Shakers; I know I never did till I came to this country where there are several establishments of them. The principal one is at Lebanon, about twenty-five miles from here and only two miles from Lebanon Springs, a fashionable watering place in this State. We had resolved to return to Albany by that road, and, accordingly, in Mr. Ashburner's waggon and accompanied by George and Anne Ashburner, we set out from Stockbridge yesterday between three and four o'clock. I ought first to tell you what I know of the faith and forms of the Shakers. Their founder was a woman of the name of Ann Lee, whom they call Mother. She was, as far as I can understand, perfectly mad from fanaticism, at least it is charitable to suppose her so, for if she had her senses she was profane to a degree in accepting homage as if she were a divine person, which her followers believed her to have been, and that in her was a second manifestation of the coming of Christ. She was persecuted in England for her religious opinions, and, in consequence, made her escape to this country where very shortly she was joined by many

others as wild as herself. They now, of course, get leave to do
as they please and are an exceedingly orderly and quiet part of
the community, neat to a degree in their houses and persons.
They do not allow of marriages, and married persons who join
them must dissolve their connection. Unfortunately a thunder-
storm detained us so long on the road that by the time we reached
the village we had only time to go into the Shop, or Store, as
they call it, to buy a few little knick-knacks of their making. We
wished much to have seen one of their houses, but by this time
it was sunset, at which hour on Saturday night they have a meeting, so we were obliged to drive on to the Springs for the night.
To-day we again went to the village at half past ten to see their
service. The Church is a large handsome room eighty-four feet
by ninety, with the best kept and most beautifully polished floor
I have seen in this country, and in the corners are *spitting boxes*
that the boards may be preserved from such contamination. A
place is set apart for strangers, the ladies and gentlemen sitting
separately. There were few of the Shakers assembled when we
went in, but very shortly they all arrived, the females ranged
themselves on one side and the males on the other on benches.
Everything was done with the greatest quietness, the women
walked on their toes, seemingly afraid to make even the noise of
moving to their places. After sitting for a few moments, the
whole assembly rose up and one of the men gave a short discourse
on the reason of their meeting, namely to worship God, and spoke
of the great privilege they were allowed in meeting for that
purpose. They all sung a hymn and when that was finished they
all knelt and sung another. This went on for some time, an
occasional discourse, or rather a conversation, for many spoke,
both males and females, and now and then a hymn. So far all
was well, nothing ridiculous was said and no absurd thing was
done, but by and by the person who had first spoken and seemed
to be a kind of leader said, "Now let us refresh our souls with
a little exercise," upon which there was a general throwing off
of coats on the part of the men, the women only put aside their

pocket handkerchieves, which they had hitherto held over the left arm, and to work they went with one accord, singing or rather screaming, tunes of a kind of jig time, at the same time walking round the room with a swinging step somewhat between a walk and a dance and flapping their hand with a penguin kind of motion. At the end of the first act of this folly there was a universal clapping of hands like the applause in a theatre, and to work they went again occasionally stopping for a few minutes, discoursing a little on the merits of Mother, as they call Ann Lee, and then starting off on a new song led by any of the party, male or female. Occasionally they stamped violently with their feet in the course of their march and sometimes with their hands. At length they ceased and again resumed their seats on the benches, when the orator who had spoken most stepped forward and addressed the strangers whom he laboured to convince that the Shakers are the elect people of God, and tried to prove that being concerned in the Government of the World or in the increase of its population or, in short, having anything whatever to do with it, is against the spirit of Christianity, for that Christ had nothing to do with any of those things, and a great deal more he said that I cannot repeat, but after another hymn or two notice was given that it was time for the meeting to break up and each one to return to his own residence.

Basil was spoken to by one of the men as we left the Church, and this made him suppose that he might converse with any of them, so he walked after a man who was going up the hill and began with, "May I speak a few moments with you?" The person addressed made no answer, but took to his heels and ran as fast as he could, and we then learnt that they do not choose to be spoken to on Sunday. The women are the ugliest set of females I ever saw gathered together, perhaps their particularly unbecoming dress added to the plainness of their appearance, it seems to be adapted to make them look as ugly as art can possibly devise in the Quaker fashion, only totally devoid of any of the *trigness* which generally accompanies the dress of that order, for their petticoats are long and trolloping, and there is nothing to mark the waist. They are however, most scrupulously clean.

We came on to Albany after dinner and found dear little Eliza very well indeed and delighted to see us. Mrs. Cownie took her to Church yesterday, but she shows little symptom of early piety, and not being contented at being indecorous enough to dance and talk herself she did her utmost to shake the gravity of a pew full of ladies behind her, holding out her hand to them and crying, "How do? How do?" She very soon succeeded in her endeavours, and at length when the organ began to play her delight was so great and so loudly expressed that Mrs. Cownie was obliged to bring her away.

JUNE 11:—We were hard at work all yesterday writing, and fortunately were left undisturbed the whole morning except by a visit from the Governor who came to offer everything to our service, even one of his aide-de-camps to go all over the country with us if we chose. We meant to have set out to-morrow, but some acquaintances in Albany have persuaded us to delay another day to go with them to-morrow to the Shakers' village of Niskayuna that we may have an opportunity of seeing them at their daily occupations. To-day we have had so many visitors that we have not got on with our letters till after dinner, but here we dine at two o'clock so there is plenty of time after all. We have met with a variety of dinner hours in this country, the latest five, the most frequent three. The latest breakfast hour I have heard of, except at Mr. Livingstone's, is eight, a more common one is seven and sometimes six. I don't like their early hours at all, but really it is the next thing to impossible to get any breakfast later than eight, although we try it when we breakfast alone.

Ever affectionately yours,

MARGARET HALL.

LETTER IV

ALBANY TO NIAGARA

This letter was begun at Schenectady and continued at Utica where, to Mrs.
Hall's delight, they fell in with an English party and could once again enjoy
the lively, animated conversation they had been "so long deprived of".
Syracuse and Auburn formed part of the itinerary, and a halt was made
at Cayuga to enable Captain Hall to draw the long bridge across the Lake.
At Canandaigua, another stopping place, they were lucky enough to find a
. Scotchman "strikingly like Sir Walter Scott," who asked them to stay.
Thence they proceeded to the village of Rochester where Captain Hall
made several sketches. From Rochester they took the road to Lockport and
from Lockport to Niagara.

SCHENECTADY, June 16, 1827.

My Dearest Jane,

On the thirteenth, still at Albany, we went to breakfast at
Mr. Cooper's. After breakfast they took us a drive of six miles to
Niskayuna to see the Shakers, who, after the melancholy and de-
mure physiognomy I had seen those of the same sect wear on
Friday, I was surprised to find a very conversible set of people, and
some very pretty women amongst the females. The cleanliness and
nicety of their establishment is much cried up in this country, but
it did not strike me as so worthy of admiration as any cottage in
England. They took us through every part of their houses. There
are about a hundred of them at Niskayuna, or one family. It was
perhaps as well to go and see them at their daily occupations, for
once, as we had seen them on Sunday at their absurdities, but I
hardly think they were worth the trouble of a dusty drive of sixteen
miles on a hot day. We dined at Mr. Cooper's at the very late hour

44

of half past four, with the mayor and a son-in-law of Mr. Cooper, Professor Knot of the Union College at Schenectady.

On the fourteenth we left Albany, visited the Arsenal, and then drove to Troy where to my great amusement I discovered in the parlour a satin piece worked, I suppose, by one of the young ladies of the house, the subject of which was the parting between Hector and Andromache. Young Astyanax cut a distinguished figure in the group! Few travellers think of getting on the Canal at Albany, there are so many locks between that and Schenectady that the whole day is occupied by what is done by land in two or three hours. This (Schenectady) being therefore the starting and the landing point, it is a very busy scene, and we found the inn door and the Canal Bridge close by thronged with stages ready to start on the arrival of the packet from the west, and almost as much competition to secure passengers as there is on a similar occasion in England. All night, too, there were coaches setting off, to the great discomposure of sleep. Yesterday we walked up after breakfast to the College to call upon Mr. and Mrs. Knot, and whilst Basil went over the college and to one of the classes with the Professor I sat with the lady. They have been married only a few months, and have a delightful house in the College, which commands an extensive view of the rich plain below.

We wished to try a little Canal travelling, and chose yesterday afternoon, being cloudy, for that purpose. We dined and embarked into the packet at two o'clock to go a distance of six or seven and twenty miles, which we did not get to the end of till ten o'clock, our rate of going being about three miles an hour, but we did not tire, the scenery the whole way was so enchanting, indeed all my epithets of admiration are completely worn out in this country, and as that strain is always mightily tiresome to the reader, I feel half inclined to promise that instead of mentioning what is beautiful I shall only give notice when I see anything that is ugly.

We thought at one time of going on from here to Utica, twenty-two miles off by the Canal boat, but the hour of her arrival here is so uncertain that we have decided on going by land in preference.

The greatest inconvenience from travelling in that way arises from the numerous bridges, which are so low that at each it is necessary to come off the top of the boat. There are only two tolerable sized cabins likewise, but except at tea I did not go into them, it was so close and hot.

UTICA, June 18:—The section of the country along which we have travelled is called the "German Flats," and is entirely a German settlement. The inhabitants speak English, but imperfectly. The names, too, are all German. We changed horses at Heikimer and passed through Frankfort. It was a lovely evening, and dear little Eliza slept the first seven miles of our journey, and the remaining fifteen was as fresh and in as high spirits as if she had not stirred from home. We did not reach Utica till near ten o'clock, the first person we espied in the lobby of the inn was an Englishman. He introduced himself to us on board the Canal boat as having recently arrived from England and showed unequivocal symptoms of wishing to thrust himself into an intimacy and to join us. Now it forms no part of our plan to let anyone join us, it would form too great a restraint on the irregularity and uncertainty of our movements, but this man had nothing to recommend him, a dull, silly, commonplace, sort of noodle. I certainly never in my life worked so hard to keep any one back, for he did not possess sense sufficient to take a hint easily. Just at the same time we met another Englishman of a very different stamp. We were sitting at tea in the public room, where everyone takes all their meals, when a gentleman walked in apologising for the intrusion, which together with his manners and appearance showed very plainly that he did not belong to this country. He proved to be Mr. Jackson, the King's Commissioner, who came out to Washington some four years ago to settle about some money that was to be paid to the American Government for slaves taken during the war. He formed one of an English party that we had at dinner. The meeting was most agreeable, an English party being what we have been so long deprived of, and the difference between the liveliness and animated

46

conversation of the English end of the table contrasted with the silence of the American meal was very striking. We parted after dinner. Basil and I and Mr. Jackson went to the Episcopalian Church. I had sent Mrs. Cownie to Church in the morning, and she not having ascertained the road very accurately found herself in the Roman Catholic Chapel. Out of that, however, she speedily made her exit and stumbled upon a Swedes' Meeting, I should imagine by her description, but I dare say if she had gone into the Presbyterian Church she would have been as much scandalised as Basil was to hear an organ!

It was a rainy, stormy, miserably cold day, but after some deliberation Basil and I determined to go to Trenton Falls. When we arrived at the Inn, which is three miles from the village of the same name, we found the landlord and a solitary guest enjoying an excellent wood fire, which we too were happy to draw our chairs close to, and ordered one to be lighted in our bed room.

SYRACUSE, JUNE 19:—I got so sleepy last night that I was obliged to leave the Trenton Falls to take care of themselves, and, for that matter, I might do the same to-night, both from a like cause and also that really description of scenery does not lie in my way, but I may just mention that we spent five hours amongst the Falls most agreeably. There are four of them. I had heard much of the difficulty, I might almost say, the danger of the walk, tho' I could discover neither the one nor the other, tho' perhaps some whose heads are less strong might find the view of the gulf beneath with a ledge to walk on not two feet wide rather terrific. However, in the narrowest places there is an iron chain along the rock to lay hold of. It is not above a few years since those falls became known to any except those who resided in the neighbourhood, and they were almost inaccessible until Mr. Sherman, the landlord of the inn, facilitated the descent by ladders and otherwise rendered visiting them convenient and comfortable. They are by far the most striking falls we have yet seen in this country and reminded us both of the Falls of the Clyde, with

47

this difference, that they are on an infinitely greater scale. By the time we returned to the house for dinner a large party of tourists had assembled. Mr. Sherman, as is the fashion in this country, (at least we have found it so, beginning with Albany) took the head of the table. He is a man of a good deal of information, and has a small collection of petrifactions and other queer things in which I take no interest and, therefore, cannot pretend to tell you anything of, for I made my escape in the midst of a lecture he was delivering, quite with the air of a Professor, on Trilobites and other curiosities of his museum. He is a bit of a geologist too, and Basil and he had some conversation on the subject of the Great Wave, which I am sure you must have heard him upon, to the great amusement but I don't think much to the edification of the rest of the party. We left this morning, the nineteenth, at nine o'clock and have travelled fifty miles in quite a different style of country from any that we have before seen, much more recently cleared and by far the greater part of it still forest. We accidentally saw every stage of the clearing, for just as we passed one part of the road a tree was felled and on each side all along were those only just cut down or fields of wheat, barley, or Indian corn filled with the stumps, for they plough round them and let them remain in the fields till they rot, when they become good manure. In some places they have a machine by which they extract the stumps, but this is not generally considered a good plan as it leaves immense holes in the ground and turns up worse soil. We saw Indians to-day for the first time, of the Oneida tribe. We saw them about seventeen miles from Utica where they have a reservation, that is to say, when their lands were purchased from them by the United States, they reserved a portion to dwell in.

There is a strange jumble of countries in the names of the places we passed through to-day. To begin with, Utica. We changed horses at Manchester, Vernon, and Lenox, where we dined, and then went on to Chittenengo, Manlius Fourcorners, alias Fayetteville, and so on to Syracuse, and now I must go to try a Syracusian bed.

AUBURN, JUNE 21:—A gentleman whom we met yesterday gave an explanation of the names of the places on this road, which to some extent does away with the absurdity. They were lands which were given to the officers and soldiers who fought in the War of Independence as a reward for their services, a sort of pension, and the Commissioners who had the charge of dividing them gave them those military Roman names that they now bear. Syracuse owes its existence entirely to the Canal. In 1820 the only buildings on the site where it now stands were an old house, a Mill, and a tavern. In 1827 there is a population of fifteen hundred inhabitants, two large churches, a very pretty flourishing village indeed, and a splendid inn which is not yet finished. This is only one of the towns and villages which date their birth or increase from the circumstance of the Canal running through them. Every one of those villages, however small, prints one newspaper at least.

Yesterday was a day of incessant rain, but good enough for our purpose, which was to see the salt works at Saliva and Geddesborough, about a mile from Syracuse. Basil had a letter from Governor Clinton to a Mr. Moses Barnet, which facilitated our seeing the works. I paddled along in a pair of india rubber shoes which Mrs. Ford, the wife of a gentleman who accompanied us, lent to me. They are very much worn here in wet weather and are excellent for the purpose, being quite impervious to wet. By the time we left Syracuse at four o'clock the rain had ceased, and we had a very pleasant drive of twenty-four miles, changing horses at Camillas and Elbridge, passing through Brutus, and arrived at Auburn at nine o'clock. We never average more than five miles an hour. We often drive faster than that, but they take so long changing horses, besides stopping to water them at least once in every stage, tho' they are never more than eight, nine, or ten miles long, so that there is a great deal of time lost, and this is not because of the heat of the weather, for we have been most fortunate in this respect.

We are going by and by to see the Prison, which used formerly to be the State Prison, but that is now removed to Sing Sing, of which I wrote to you in my last letter, and whether we move at all to-day or where we shall go to, remains a matter of most complete uncertainty. We stop always when we are tired and never set off till we are quite disposed to do so, and Eliza laughs and crows and enjoys every new thing she sees and makes us feel more thankful every day that we did not leave her behind. It had been a loss we never could have made up had we deprived ourselves of the delight of seeing her daily advancement, and she is becoming so fond both of her Papa and myself. I wish you could see her after a day's journey or even in the carriage playing so nicely or watching the cows and the pigs. This is a delightful country for her to travel in, we never go a quarter of a mile without meeting one horse at least and frequently villages and consequently innumerable animals of all kinds, so that Eliza is never at a loss for amusement. In this room hangs one of the only two prints to be seen in every inn, great and small: the one is General Washington holding in one hand a roll of paper and in the other, extended in a position which indicates what the Americans would call a very lengthy speech, at least that is my feeling of the matter, but perhaps this arises from my being thoroughly sickened of the eternal picture; the other, which is that which at this moment has raised my ire, is General La Fayette in a brown wig and greatcoat, looking like a farmer on a cold day. I dare say you don't know that La Fayette served under Washington in the War of Independence, to which the French Government lent its aid, little thinking that by so doing they were bringing an old house about their ears, for I believe it was the American Revolution that led to that in France. Whether or not La Fayette's services made him worthy of all the *éclat* and rejoicing with which he was received on revisiting this country a few years ago, I know not, but the result of that war was so glorious to this country that every circumstance or person in any way connected with it is remembered with enthusiasm, and accordingly when General La Fayette came to America four years ago he was received everywhere as if he had been the Saviour of the Country.

ROCHESTER, JUNE 26:—While at Auburn we went to see the Prison, but unfortunately Judge Power, the keeper of it, was absent, and altho' Mr. Curtis, the Chaplain, had every inclination to make up for him he has been but a short time there and is therefore not calculated to tell us much about it. It is under the same regulations as the prison at Sing Sing, perfect silence and separate cells at night instead of the large rooms, as used to be the place of keeping the convicts. We travelled only eight miles on the twenty-first to Cayuga at the end of a lake of the same name, across which there is a bridge of upwards of a mile in length, of wood, as all the bridges with a very few exceptions, are. Both Basil and I felt a little sceptical as to the length and fancied that our friends applied their usual habits of amplification to it, but a walk across it convinced us that they did not overshoot the mark. He measured it and I found it a much longer walk than I expected. The shores of the lake are low and have not that picturesque beauty, at least not that part we saw, but it is forty miles long, and there may be variety in the scenery that we did not see.

Cayuga has quite a country inn, but very comfortable in all save that we were on the point of being obliged to sleep on feather beds, however, we managed to get rid of them by spreading one or two thick coverlids on the top of the straw palliasse, which makes a very comfortable bed. Anything, in short, is better than feathers, and it seems strange that in a country where there is so hot a summer they should not universally use mattresses, but they have not learnt yet to adapt comforts suitable to the different seasons. Their houses seem to be built expressly for summer without the slightest reference to the six months' winter that they suffer. They are all of wood except in some of the large towns, have no window shutters, very few window curtains, and are so ill-furnished about the floors and windows that the wind blows through them, as we have found, even in the middle of June.

We left Cayuga at eight o'clock in the morning of the twenty-second, a stormy day with frequent showers, saw the Seneca hills, or rather rapids, and stopped at Waterloo to have one of our horses shod. The name tells you that it has sprung up within twelve years. It is a pretty little place containing two or three churches. We have not passed a single village, however small, where there is not at least one church, often more, and of a size that shows they are built with an eye to the fast increasing population, and we are told by all those who know that the first thing that is thought of when any village is begun is having a church. The next place we came to after Waterloo was Geneva, at the head of the Seneca Lake, and so named by Mr. Williamson, brother to Lord Balgray, who settled that part of the country and gave the name of Geneva from a resemblance in situation to the original Geneva. It is a most beautiful village laid out with great taste and contains two splendid hotels. In the neighborhood the lands which belonged to Sir William Pulteney and are now the property of his heir. The weather has been cold and stormy all the morning and only cleared up for a little, while we were at Geneva. When we set off again after dinner the rain and wind came on more violently than before, and after we reached Canandaigua we could hardly keep ourselves warm with all our cloaks and coats. When we stopped at the Inn the Landlord produced a letter which contained a request from Mr. and Mrs. Greig immediately on our arrival at Canandaigua that we would go to their house and make it our home during our stay in the place. This was an invitation not to be refused, and without loss of time we drove there and found Mr. and Mrs. Greig seated close to a blazing wood fire, the most charming sight to poor cold travellers. The sound of Mr. Greig's Scotch voice too added to the charm, and the appearance of the house altogether with its beautiful flower pots at the door and jars and plates filled with

Drawn with the Camera Lucida by Capt.ⁿ B. Hall R.N.

Engraved by W. H. Lizars

THE BRIDGE ACROSS LAKE CAYUGA

flowers in the drawing room, besides innumerable prettily bound books, was more like home than anything that we have seen on this side of the Atlantic. I do not know whether Mrs. Greig learnt all this taste in England, for she is American, but certainly her house in every respect is by far the nicest I have seen in this western world. Both she and her husband are kind to the greatest degree and very agreeable. He is strikingly like Sir Walter Scott both in appearance and voice. We spent three days most delightfully with them. They took us on the twenty-third to see the Burning Springs at Bristol, about nine miles off, natural gas to which we set fire in several places. There is one town in this State lighted with natural gas. Canandaigua is as pretty a village as Geneva. They both resemble villages near London, detached villas surrounded with gardens.

The twenty-fourth being Sunday, Mrs. Cownie had an opportunity of hearing a good screed at the Presbyterian Church, the first sermon she says that she has understood since she came to the country. In the afternoon we heard a farewell sermon at the Episcopalian Church, the clergyman having, according to the law term, got notice to quit. There are no livings for life in this country as in England. The clergyman holds his situation at the pleasure of the congregation who have a right to turn him out when he does not please them. We parted with Mr. and Mrs. Greig yesterday after an early dinner. I think it not improbable that they may yet remove to Scotland to spend the latter part of their life.

As we are in the way of seeing sights, it is fortunate for us that part of the bank of the Canal had given way the day before, and it gave us an opportunity of seeing them at work repairing it. We made various other stops, one to see a great embankment on top of which the Canal runs, in short we did not arrive at Rochester until nine o'clock.

Rochester is the best place we have yet seen for giving strangers an idea of the newness of this country. In 1815 there was a population of three hundred persons, now it amounts to upwards of eight thousand, and this morning we have been to see various manufactures carried on, pails, window sashes, etc., besides saw-mills and flour mills, and everything, in short, bespeaking activity and industry. There are also two daily newspapers and three weekly ones printed. It is on the river Genesee, and the Falls, about half a mile from this hotel, are well worth seeing. We have had the advantage of the guidance of Mr. Grainger, a gentleman of Canandaigua, to show us the lions. Small houses and large and handsome ones are standing in the very midst of stumps of trees which do not appear to have been cut down above a year ago, on every side thick forest, but many acres of which are sold for houses, which are to form part of the town. In the course of our drive we came within a hundred yards of a wood where two men were chopping down trees. We went to them and they very good naturedly cut down two for our amusement. I never saw trees cut down at home, but I believe the dexterity here is far beyond anything of the kind in England. The two cut down one tree between fifty and sixty feet high and four feet in circumfer-ence, in three minutes, all but ten seconds. The more practised of the two then cut down one of hickory wood, much harder than the other and about the same size, but we did not time him. Whilst we were standing in the midst of a forest so thick that had I gone a few yards further I am sure that I should have lost myself, the men mentioned that all the lots of the ground were sold, and that we were then in the middle of a street! Were we to return here a twelve month after this, we should probably find a large tavern and innumerable stores where now there are only hickory and bass wood trees and only black squirrels for in-habitants.

It is impossible to describe the appearance of the outskirts of this town. To me it looks as if a box of houses had been sent from New York, the lid opened, and the houses tumbled down in the midst of the blackened stumps. There is one way of destroying the trees which gives them a very desolate appearance. They *girdle* them, which means cutting a ring into the bark near

From a drawing
by Capt. B. Hall. R. N.

THE VILLAGE OF ROCHESTER

Engraved by W. H. Lizars.

the base. This kills the trees and removes the foliage which would otherwise keep the sun off the crop of wheat or any other grain which in the mean time is sowed there, and when the tree is decayed it is more easily cut down, but a field full of those girdled trees has a very wretched appearance.

OAK ORCHARD, JUNE 27:—We left Rochester this morning at eleven o'clock, passed through Parma, and got to Clarkson, eighteen miles, to dinner. The country looks sufficiently new, but not so much so as that on the other side of Rochester. After dinner we came on the rest of our day's journey, twenty-two miles, and here the mosquitoes are buzzing about in such style that I expect to be all over bites before to-morrow morning.

LOCKPORT, JUNE 28:—"God sends meat and the Devil sends Cooks," is a saying which applies with full force to this country. There is food in abundance, but it is dressed after a manner that is enough to appall even a hungry stomach, and I often find myself skirmishing about amongst the dishes in a vain search after something a little more eatable than the rest. We have found the fare very bad indeed since we left Albany and large inns or small ones, it makes but little difference. Thick beef steaks, at least a quarter of a yard in diameter, swimming in grease, black joints of lamb, and forever and ever broiled ham. Breakfast, dinner, and tea, there is always broiled ham. On the whole the breakfast is the best meal of the day; it is the most plentiful, and if there are any little delicacies such as chickens, it is at breakfast they are produced. This phillipic against the cooking in America was begun just before I was summoned to dinner at Lockport where we now are. Our whole journey was only twenty-three miles, but we made so many stops to allow Basil to sketch, and met with some such very bad roads that we were six hours on the way. We always stop whenever we take the fancy, and little Eliza runs about amongst the trees and bushes, delighted with all she sees, whilst her Papa sketches and her Mama looks on. She is so admirable a traveller that we never have a feeling of wishing to get over the day's journey on her account. The scenery during this day has been similar to that of the two preceding ones, and this village is of still more recent date than Rochester, but not to be compared to it in importance. We met with one of the Superintendents of the Canal who told us that when he came here in 1821 it was impossible to come nearer than three miles to the village in any kind of carriage. The deepest cut in the Canal extends from this place seven miles west to Tonnewanta Creek; at Lockport there are five double locks to gain an elevation of sixty feet and to bring the Canal on a level with Lake Erie, the reason of the locks being double is to allow one set of boats to ascend whilst another descends.

I have omitted to mention that we have seen much finer trees since we left Albany than we had done previously, not so magnificent as what are to be seen in England, but very respectable trees indeed, tho' they fail to inspire the people here with any respect. They seem to look upon a tree as a natural enemy and chop down right and left and all around without the smallest mercy, and often where the tree instead of doing mischief might be spared and be a very great ornament and use, but taste is a word not yet understood on this side of the Atlantic, tho' they talk a great deal about it. The favorite word in America for expressing perfection of personal appearance is *genteel*. It is never out of their mouths. Handsome and elegant they are fond of too, but apply them to lakes and scenery.

NIAGARA FALLS, AMERICAN SIDE, JUNE 30:—How absurd it is in travellers to make an attempt to describe the scene where we now are, and as far as we have seen their attempts, the efforts of painters are about as fruitless. Ever since we set out upon this journey I have been endeavouring to bring down my expectations in regard to Niagara. The Falls are so spoken of and wondered at that I fully expected to be extremely disappointed, but on the contrary the first sight of them and every view we have

From a drawing
by Capt. B. Hall, R. N.

THE PORT OF BUFFALO ON LAKE ERIE

had since, have infinitely surpassed all that my imagination could have conceived, and yet we have not seen them from the best side, for even the Americans are obliged to confess that the view from the British side is infinitely superior to this. I cannot even describe what my feelings were on first coming in sight of the Falls. There was a mixture of awe, fear, and pleasure, which I have generally experienced on seeing or rather hearing a Fall, but never to such an extent as upon this occasion. Fortunately the evening was most lovely as we drove along the banks of the river for five miles. The first sight we got of it we saw down to where it empties itself into Lake Ontario. We had a distant view of that immense lake in the course of our afternoon's journey. It is in fact a small sea, and between us and it there was another noble sea of forest by far the finest we have seen. We did not reach this house till past seven o'clock and therefore had not light for more than a short walk, and we were so tired with our day's work that we had not strength for more. We hope to put our foot on British possessions before many hours are over.

Your ever affectionate,

MARGARET HALL.

At this point the travellers proceeded into Canada. They spent nine weeks under the Union Jack then returned to the United States. Mrs. Hall's letters from Canada have not been included in this volume. We take up her narrative at St. John's on Lake Champlain.

LETTER V

ST. JOHN'S TO ALBANY

A voyage down Lake Champlain to Larabee's Point, a drive past the ruins
of Fort Ticonderoga, and the exquisite scenery of Lake George are
described. The Halls find Saratoga Springs deserted of visitors.

CALDWELL, LAKE GEORGE, N. Y.,
September 8, 1827.

MY DEAREST JANE,

Once more we are in the busy, bustling States, a striking contrast to Lower Canada which we have just left, and where the
people look happy and contented and seem to possess quite sufficient
means to keep them comfortable and do not appear to have the
smallest wish to increase those means but are quite content to jog
on doing as their forefathers did before them—but here everyone
is elbowing his neighbour and never stops to enjoy what he has
but hurries on to grasp at what he has not. The American bustle,
in fact, began yesterday at St. John's. The landlord of the inn was
a native of this country and seemed to have imported with him the
fashion of allowing short time for meals, for with all the speed we
could muster we had barely time to cram our dinner down our
throats before there was an alarm that the steamboat was on the
point of starting. Off we hurried and just saved our distance.
The boat was without exception the noisiest steamer I have yet
been in, all night long I could have fancied that a couple of kettle
drums at least were close to my ear, and as to sleep I had none,
and such crowds of passengers and such heaps of bugs, altogether
it was vastly disagreeable.

When I got up this morning I found we had got really into

romantic scenery and had on every side what were not unworthy of being called mountains, altho' of a very wild character. We were on Lake Champlain. We had once more thought over our plans, and finding that we were still likely to meet some company at "the Springs," as the fashionable watering-places of Balston and Saratoga are called, we resolved upon getting them over whilst they lay so convenient for us, and it is a sort of thing we do more from duty than pleasure, for we do not anticipate a great deal of amusement from a visit to them, but it would never do to leave the country without having been there. We also wished to see Lake George, which is much celebrated for its beauty, and justly celebrated, too, for I never saw anything more beautiful. It is really quite exquisite and has all the character of a lake, which the enormous lakes in other parts of the country have not. There are very few houses on its banks, but, this after the immense population on the banks of every kind of water that we have been in the habit of seeing of late, was a pleasing variety, nor will there ever be much change in this respect, for almost all the mountains, most of them very rocky too, rise quite bluff out of the water. We landed from the Lake Champlain boat at a place called Larabee's Point in the State of Vermont and there crossed the ferry to the State of New York and in a stage drove around by Fort Ticonderoga to the village of the same name. The situation of the fort is very beautiful, but it is quite in ruins. We had only a drive of four miles to our dining place from whence we again started in time to reach the steam boat a mile off, and then away we paddled up beautiful Lake George, every turn of which called forth the strongest admiration. We got on remarkably well till within five hundred yards of Caldwell when something about the machinery gave way. This would have been very awkward further off, but so near our point it was of small consequence, and by the help of some small boats we were towed up to the wharf and landed by seven o'clock.

SARATOGA SPRINGS, SEPTEMBER 10:—It is singular enough that at this place where probably in the season there is a greater racket than anywhere in the States we should have an opportunity of enjoying the only quiet days we have been able to secure since we landed in America, and we are taking the advantage of the leisure to do many little odds and ends that we have not before had time to manage. We left Caldwell on Sunday at nine o'clock in the morning. It was our wish to have remained there for church, but had we let slip the jog trot course of getting on we could not have left Caldwell for three or four days, so we did as we were obliged by circumstances and made out a dusty, hot journey of twenty-seven miles by half past four o'clock, in the course of which we visited Glen's Falls and Baker's Falls, both on the river Hudson and very pretty in spite of the persons from whom they derive their respective names having done their utmost to spoil them by turning off the water to their ugly mills. If we live long enough I doubt not we shall see Niagara itself turned all into mill dams. We were told that the Congress Hall was the boarding house at which we had the best chance for seeing company at so late a season, so to it we drove and are here established. At tea that evening we sat down with fifteen persons, nine of whom took their departure next morning after breakfast, since when we have been a party of six, breakfasting, dining, and drinking tea, in a room eighty feet long and in a house capable of accommodating a hundred and fifty persons. We have a comfortable fire in our own room where we sit the greater part of the day writing, reading, arranging our accounts. Yesterday evening, as we were walking along we saw a bill pasted on a wall of a house intimating that in that house at seven oclock there was to be an exhibition by some Indians who were to dance the war dance, give the war whoop, go through the scalping manœuvres, and various other feats. As we had come abroad to see what is curious, this was of course too valuable an opportunity of gratifying curiosity to lose, and, accordingly, we swallowed our tea and set off forthwith to the appointed place. The exhibition was certainly sufficiently savage and strange to be quite natural, but for the scalping part of it I confess that my nerves were not strong enough to admit of looking even at the mere pretence of this barbarous practice. We were told by the handbill that part of the entertainment was to consist of playing on the violin by an Indian, and this proved certainly not the least curious part of the scene, for this Indian, dressed in a surtout coat between the acts of their barbarous dances and war whoops, filled up the intervals by playing Scotch reels, Strathspeys, Paddy O'Rafferty, and such like civilized tunes. Since beginning to write we have been to dinner and sat down a *partie quarée* in the room before mentioned. I rather think the couple who formed the quartet go to-morrow, and then we shall be left to the enjoyment of the eighty feet long room to ourselves.

ALBANY, SEPTEMBER 14:—It is just three months to-day since we left this place, and in that time we have travelled 2416 miles by land and water. We remained another quiet day, the twelveth, at Saratoga, and yesterday, the thirteenth, we set off at twelve o'clock meaning only to come half way to this place. However, we got on so well that we made out the whole journey, thirty-seven miles, by eight o'clock stopping at Balston, another watering-place, to dine. It is a much prettier place than Saratoga but not so much in fashion now-a-days, and like the other we found it deserted except by three gentlemen and a lady. Here again we find all in bustle. We are at Cruttenden's where we were formerly. At the door we met Commodore Hull, one of the most eminent officers in the United States Navy. Mrs. Hull was not visible, but her two sisters the Miss Harts I saw and have not before seen anything so dashing in America. They are very pretty girls and have just returned with their brother-in-law and sister from South America where the Commodore was employed. They were dressed Spanish fashion and have quite a Spanish air. I hope I shall meet them again.

Ever affectionately yours

MARGARET HALL.

LETTER VI

Being desirous of studying a State Legislature, Captain Hall arranged to spend twelve days in the capital of the State of New York. This gave Mrs. Hall a good opportunity for observing social manners and customs. An evening party and a dinner at Governor Clinton's are meticulously described as is the behaviour of legislators in the House of Assembly. It is clear from the narrative that Mrs. Hall had never been inside the House of Commons. Parties at the houses of General Solomon van Rennselaer, the Post Master General, and Mr. de Witt Bloodgood offered further material for criticism. The manners of Albany are found to be old fashioned; ladies are called "Madam" and are led to dinner by the fingers *à la* Sir Charles Grandison.

ALBANY, September 15, 1827.

My Dearest Jane,

I do not remember whether I have described to you at any time the extreme stiffness of an American party, at least as far as we had an opportunity of judging. We were last night at one at Mrs. Clinton's Mr. Clinton, you know, is Governor of this State of which this place is the capital. Consequently the specimen we had may be clearly reckoned a sample of quite the *haut ton* of this part of the Union. We were invited to tea and went at eight o'clock. On entering the first drawing room both Basil and I started back, for we saw none but gentlemen, not a single lady, and we thought there must be some mistake in asking us in there, but in a moment the Governor came forward and giving me his arm hurried me into the adjoining room at the top of which sat Mrs. Clinton who placed me on the seat next to herself. Round the room were placed as many chairs as could be crammed in and a lady upon each, a most formidable circle, and I had to go through the not less formidable ordeal of an introduction to at least a dozen of those who were nearest me. In the course of the evening the gentlemen did venture into the room and stood for a short time talking to one or other of the ladies, but there was seldom a chair vacant for any of the males to seat themselves upon, and altho' occasionally the ladies had courage to cross the room and change places with each other I never saw any lady standing during the whole evening, and the Mistress of the House alone seemed to enjoy the privilege of moving at her ease about the rooms. We had abundance of refreshments with several editions of tea and cake, then came two servants, one with a tray full of beautiful, china plates of which he gave each lady one, another man followed bearing a tray covered with dishes of peaches and grapes which were in like manner handed round, then followed another course of plates and in their rear a magnificent pyramid of ice, supported on each side by preserved pineapple and other sweetmeats. Then came wine, and again more plates and more ice. In short, Mrs. Clinton seemed to be of the opinion of a lady of whom I have been told by some of my friends at home, that the easiest way to entertain her guests was to keep them eating. I was introduced to many persons during the course of the evening, the Chancellor of the State of New York, and Mr. Van Buren, one of the most eminent men in this State.

This house, Cruttenden's, is pretty well filled at present owing to the Extraordinary Meeting of the Legislature. The Ordinary Meeting is in winter, but they are at present assembled to revise the laws of the State. Our friend Mr. Granger belongs to the House of Assembly and lodges here, and there are also several other pleasant persons, and altogether they appear to be more sociably disposed at meal times than we have usually found them. In general instead of being questioned and cross-questioned as to whither we are going and whence we have come, as we were led to expect, we have great reason to complain of the extreme taciturnity of those at the public tables in spite of Basil's efforts to draw them into conversation, and you would think, were you to see us upon these occasions, that the curiosity belongs entirely to the English part of the company. The Americans are in such prodigious haste to get away from the table at all their meals that they have no time for opening their mouths except for the purpose of eating. Occasionally in a steamboat I have been asked various particulars as to my plans and calling, but quite as frequently by an Irish emigrant as by an American.

SEPTEMBER 16:—I went yesterday morning first to the House of Assembly and then to the Senate. Perhaps you do not know that each State in the Union has its own Legislature independent of the general Congress or Government. The laws of each State are made by its Legislature but must not interfere with the general laws of the Constitution. The House of Assembly of this State consists of one hundred and twenty-eight members who are selected annually and chosen by universal suffrage, at least every male citizen of the age of twenty-one years and who has been an inhabitant in the State for a year preceding the election and six months a resident in the town or county where he wishes to offer his vote, has a right to do so. There are thirty-two members in the Senate. The State is divided into eight districts, each of which chooses four senators. In the House of Assembly I heard the continuation of a debate they had had the day before. I am not much qualified to judge of public speaking as I have rarely heard any, but I should imagine that what I heard yesterday was very bad. The speakers wandered strangely from their subjects, and less elegance either of language or action I cannot imagine. The favourite attitude of the principal speaker was his left hand in his breeches pocket whilst with his right he clutched a pencil and sawed the air in a like manner that showed him much in want of Hamlet's advice to the Players. Now and then he shifted his left hand from the favourite pocket back further than it would be quite delicate to particularise. In the Senate they occupied a complete hour in discussing whether or not there was a sufficient number present for the transaction of business, and then there was so long a paper read that we came away before they got through it. I believe that the members of the House of Commons in England are not very particular either as to their dress or manners, but I do not suppose they hoist their legs across the table nearest to them nor spit all over the floor, both of which inelegancies were practised by the Senators I saw yesterday. The spitting is really more abominable than I can find words to express. Some bad practices one gets, if not reconciled to, at least less annoyed by them with the habit of seeing them daily, but the spitting makes me more sick every time that I am condemned to see it.

We dined yesterday at Governor Clinton's. Mrs. Clinton invited us to a family dinner, and so it strictly was, for the party consisted entirely of members of the family, namely the Governor and Mrs. Clinton, her mother Mrs. Jones, the two Miss Clintons, daughters of the Governor by a former marriage, and Mrs. Clinton's niece, Miss Allen. Perhaps you would like to know what is considered a family dinner in the first style at Albany, which you know is the capital of the State and the seat of government, so I took a more particular survey of the table than I am apt to do, and on the other page you will find a bill of fare. I must first premise that we had beautiful china and cut glass an inch thick. [A sketch made by Captain Hall of Mrs. Clinton's dinner table is inserted in the letter].

Tarts, fruit, and cheese are always put on the table at the same time in this country, except at quite dress parties, when the fruit is a separate concern, but the ice is always along with the second course. The party was really very agreeable. Mr. Clinton is a very superior man, and Mrs. Clinton, tho' by no means elegant, is extremely good-natured and animated and amuses me very much by her strong aristocratic feelings, of which I believe she is quite unconscious. She has a little niece living with her, a child five months older than Eliza, who I was requested to take along with us yesterday. The little girl is a delicate little bit of a thing, by no means a match for my tomboy, which Miss Eliza soon found tiful china; and cut glass in inch thick.

First Course

Boiled mutton

Mrs Hall

Cauliflower   Mashed turnips

Roast ducks   a Ham

Potatoes   Beans

Miss Julia Clinton

Roast beef

Mr Governor

Mr Clinton

Mr Governor — who insisted ... in a style ... roast beef ...

Mrs Allan

Second Course

A pyramid of Ice, rivalling those of Egypt

Grapes   A huge dish of peaches

Array of various pieces of cheese   Peaches & Plums   Biscuits

Melon   Sweet meats   Melon

Bread pudding

Fruit and cheese, are always put on the table at the same time in this country, except at quite dress parties, when the fruit is a separate course. but the Ice is always along with the second course. The party was really very agreeable. Mr. Clinton is a very superior man, and Mrs Clinton is tho' by no means elegant, is a very

THE DINNER TABLE AT ALBANY

66

out, and when she discovers that any child is afraid of her, from that moment she tyrannises over her without mercy. So it was yesterday, and the poor little Livingstone was thoroughly frightened by Eliza's rough ways. We owe at least half our popularity in this country to Eliza; she is so perfectly at home with everyone, so ready to laugh and talk in her own fashion to those who will laugh and talk with her, that her good humour is quite irresistible, and altho' she is not what can strictly be called a pretty child there is something in her long, flowing hair, white skin, merry blue eyes, and broad shoulders that attracts the attention of all strangers.

We went from the Governor's to a party at General Solomon van Rennselaer's the Post Master. It was very much of the same kind as the night before, not so numerous, but the eatables were of the same quality and quantity. The attendance was not so good and was a very tolerable specimen of how ill that branch of polite society or at least of its accomplishment is understood. The first in the train was a black man in white trousers, next followed a lass in a black stuff dress and white apron with not a few holes, and last of all came a little girlie not more than ten or twelve years old. One of my correspondents remark that the ladies in America must be very stupid not to arrange their domestic concerns and their tables better, but it must be remembered that such a luxury as a good servant is not to be had, nothing but the very riff-raff of the Irish, and the ease of getting another place or doing for themselves in some way in case of dismissal, is so great that if you venture to find fault with your housemaid or butler they will tell you that you may suit yourself elsewhere. Exactly the same thing happens in Canada and from the same reasons so that the inconvenience need not be set down as the result of Republican principles, tho' they too may have their share. You may remember that the beauty of the ladies struck us very much in New York. I begin to suspect that this was in part occasioned by the length of time we had been without seeing ladies at all, for after we had left New York the beauty did not appear at all conspicuous, nor did we find it so on returning here. Philadelphia and Boston are both much famed for handsome women, and indeed for everything that is delightful, Boston too is reckoned quite the emporium of learning. We shall probably be there shortly and shall have an opportunity of judging for ourselves.

We went this afternoon to the English Church and heard a tolerable sermon from a young Irishman. We thought of paying some of our visits after Church, but upon questioning Mr. de Witt Bloodgood as to whether it was a proper time he advised us to wait till to-morrow, as here there is no visiting upon Sunday except amongst intimate friends.

SEPTEMBER 20:—I dare say many of our acquaintances here are extremely surprised to see us so long in one place, indeed the daily enquiries that are made of when we go and the numerous hopes expressed that we do not mean to go to-morrow and to-morrow are sufficiently indicative of their surprise at finding us so long stationary without the tie of business, which is the only thing that fixes Americans for any length of time in one place. Here, at this moment, many of the most intelligent men belonging to the State are so tied by their seat either in the House of Assembly or the Senate and the opportunity of making acquaintance with them is not to be lost, and as we are in no hurry we stay very quietly where we are, leaving our friends to wonder, whilst we wonder in our turn of the flying about which they choose to term travelling, for whether in the pursuit of wealth or pleasure, the rapidity of their movements is the same. The same quickness runs through their eating as I have already frequently mentioned, and how is it possible that in this way they are to become a polished nation? But there is a sort of inconsistency, too, along with all this rapidity of motion. One would imagine that such activity implied an equal liveliness of manner, but this is far from the case; they are the gravest people I ever associated with, and when seated in groups under the verandah of an inn they look so listless and idle that you would think they would never set to work. We are told by those who are in the habit of employing Americans and Europeans indiscriminately as labourers that, altho' an American will do a great deal occasionally for a spurt, they are not really equal in the daily routine of work. In the higher classes there is a great want of —I would call it romance, if I were not afraid that you would laugh at me, but even under that name I think you must understand what I mean; it is the charm of conversation and feeling which arises from more or less familiarity with the fine arts and acquaintance with the elegancies of life, mixed up certainly with tenderness of feeling. I really feel quite at a loss to explain myself, but I feel convinced that before you were six weeks in the country anyone of you would feel it and very likely give expressions more easily to the feeling. There is no want of talking, too, about sensibility and romantic scenery and being passionately fond of this thing and having a passion for that; a great deal more than would be considered either good sense or good taste in England, but it is all "words, words, words," and there is plainly a want of the sentiment, a want of enthusiasm, which is another of those bad things to talk of but admirable to have.

I have lately met here with an American painter, a Mr. Morse, who feels this want in his countrymen and women to the full and was delighted to get hold of someone to whom he might express it. He spent several years in England and feels the contrast of this plodding, money-making society to that which he there enjoyed very severely, and sighs for the companionship of thought which in his native country he cannot expect to find. In that address which he read before the Academy of Fine Arts in New York he alluded in very strong terms to the backwardness of America in this respect and confesses that, altho', for the sake of their country the young men who went to pursue their studies in those branches in Europe ought to return, for their own sakes they ought not, for so deeply would they feel the contrast on their return. I would not be condemned to live in this country for worlds, but for that matter I should consider Canada quite as cruel banishment as the States. Nevertheless, with all this I am exceedingly happy in the meantime, and if the Americans continue to treat us everywhere as kindly as they have done hitherto I shall feel grateful to them all my life. They really are so kind and so anxious to please us that I have a qualm of conscience every time I find fault with them. Their desire for our approbation exceeds anything I could have conceived, and to be sure they are not very discreet in their demands upon it; their whole minds seem to be bent in seeming quite English in their manners and customs, but a lurking suspicion that they are not quite what they ought to be makes them seek to have their opinion confirmed by those who they think qualified to judge. Our conscience and good manners are strangely set at variance sometimes. I think we have been every day to company except Sunday. On the seventeenth I determined to get through my task of visits, so after dinner, for we dine at the barbarous hour of half past two, we set off in a carriage and by perseverance got over them by the time we had to dress. We dined at Mr. de Witt Bloodgood's, a small party and a big dinner. He and his wife live with her mother and brother, and they, with the Governor and one other gentleman, made up the party, eight in all, but there was food enough for sixteen. The effort, which it plainly is to everyone, to give you a dinner makes it quite painful really, such a settling of dishes first placed in one corner and then shoved to another, such whisperings of the servants to each individual member of the family for fresh instructions. It is like a family living totally out of the world getting up a dinner for some fine friends once in six years. There is not so much pressing to eat as I should have expected from the other characteristics of the entertainments, but your plate is hardly removed before you are asked what you will eat next, and the master and mistress are absolutely labouring to do the honours throughout the whole dinner.

It is not the custom, in Albany at least, to spend the evening where you dine, indeed it would not answer at all, for the dinner hour is four o'clock even at their most dressed parties, and it would be a weary long time to stay. There are two little traits in their manners that bespeak very old-fashioned ways. In handing a lady to dinner the gentleman literally presents his hand, not his arm, and altho' he may transfer her hand to his arm I have frequently been led along by the fingers, much as Sir Charles Grandison might have done. Then the gentlemen always call a lady *Madam,* and anything so appalling to freedom and ease you cannot imagine, and they make use of it so perpetually too. We sat with our friends on Tuesday evening (the eighteenth) till eight o'clock and had a great deal of very agreeable conversation, chiefly on the difference between American and English society and the peculiarities we are struck with in this country, for altho' they are very sensitive to criticism they have too much sense to swallow unqualified praise. As for Mr. Bloodgood, he really presses me so hard to tell him what I consider their defects that I have more than once been tempted to give him a hint about the spitting, tho' I never saw him guilty of it.

Yesterday we dined at the Patroon's. The gentleman, whose name is van Rensselaer, is of a family originally Dutch and possesses the largest landed property and the greatest wealth, in this State at all events, and, I believe, in the Union. The Dutch call their landlords Patroon, and it is on this account that he has got the name, and it also serves to distinguish him from many others of the same name. His house is just out of the town and is a very handsome one, and his style is the best we have yet seen in America. Nothing, indeed, could be handsomer than the plate and china, and things were in better order than we are used to see them here, but still there wanted that nicety of arrangement that we are accustomed to in England. There was no head servant, no commanding-looking butler, but a parcel of mulatto lads, anyone and everyone of whom took off the dishes and put them on the table indiscriminately. We had an immense party and an equally huge dinner. Mr. and Mrs. John King were there. We knew them in London when he was Secretary of Legation the winter we were in town. We had also the Governor whom we are always happy to meet and Mrs. Clinton and various others of whom you know nothing. We went from the Patroon's again to Mrs. Bloodgood's, or rather to Mrs. van Schaick's, (pronounced *Squoik*), for it is her house, where we had one of the usual parties only the people moved a little more than usual and the fire was a point of attraction to the gentlemen.

SEPTEMBER 22:—It would indeed have been prodigious *coup manqué* had we left Chick in England. Independent of the privation to ourselves, we should have been deprived of one of the greatest auxiliaries to our popularity. She has won the hearts of all the Senators and members of the House of Assembly in this house. She is quite the child to please gentlemen, so lively, so intelligent, frank, and bold. She has not a fear of any kind. I have just had her downstairs with me after dinner, and they were all ready to devour her.

For the last three days we have had rain incessantly, and I have not been out since the evening of the nineteenth, nor have I seen many persons except those belonging to this house, but we have had time to become a little *au fait* of the politics of this State and in a smaller degree with those of the Union at large. In our present society we hear of nothing but politics, or rather electioneering, which seems to occupy them all the year round, mixed up with their other various occupations. It is not here as in England where one man is a soldier, another a lawyer, and so on, the same man may be both and many others at the same time. For instance, at dinner to-day I heard one man tell another that General So and So had come to Albany to plead in a certain cause which comes on two days hence. In fact their soldiers, of all people, would require to exercise some other profession, for the standing army they have consists only of ten thousand men, which out of such a population is nothing at all, and of course the greater number of those who were employed as soldiers during the war were thrown out of employment in that line when Peace came. In fact, the greater number of their colonels and Generals are militia men, and it appears to me that as they have no real titles, they are eager to snatch at any little distinction. This residence amongst a set of men who are in habits of great intimacy with one another has shown them to us in quite a new light. I have often spoken of their extreme gravity and the absence of all joking, but our friends here have really a good deal of fun amongst them. It is, to be sure, of a very broad, coarse kind, but nothing can be more good-humoured than the way in which they take this bantering. I have for several days been the only lady of the party, and even whilst there was one other here she bore so little part in the conversation that she did not seem to belong to it. I dare say many ladies would be quite horrified to do as I do, be the only female of the party and sit after breakfast and after dinner with the gentlemen and enter as far as I am competent into all their subjects of conversation, but I did not come to America to stand upon delicacies, and Basil says the gentlemen are quite pleased at my entering into their topics, but you must bear in mind that when I say their jesting is coarse I do not mean to insinuate that there is anything improper in it; I only mean that there is a total absence of the ease of elegance and wit, and a good deal of clumsiness. I am amused sometimes to be sure when I stop to consider the situation I am placed in, seated at table with gentlemen only and drinking wine with the landlord in the most friendly, familiar way possible, for Mr. Cruttenden is quite a privileged person and always takes the head of his own table. Many American ladies have spoken to me with extreme indignation of the drawback to the comfort of the house in being obliged to sit down at the same table with the landlord, but I am not so aristocratic and have not the smallest objection to Mr. Cruttenden making one of the company, and altho' he is a privileged person I must say he never presumes, and there are many little attentions he takes pains to show to Basil and me, amongst which not the least is seeing us provided at dinner with a silver fork apiece.

SEPTEMBER 24:—The steamboat last night brought an immense importation of lawyers from New York to plead in a cause which is to be brought forward to-day and which I mean to go to hear. In order to see something of the new comers and also because dinner at one and tea at five, as is the practice upon Sunday, made an additional meal very acceptable, I went downstairs to supper.

There were not above half a dozen persons present, but with them we had a very tough argument, chiefly upon the English language as spoken in England and America, and I wish you had heard the sturdy lawyers contending with the full aid of their nasal twang for the superiority of the language spoken on this side of the Atlantic and asking me through their noses whether I should have at all detected them as Americans. One man who has been a good deal in England insisted that there is no difference in tone, voice, or accent, between a well educated Englishman and an equally well educated American. What his ears can be made of I cannot pretend to say, but I gave him up as a hopeless subject on all points, for he appears not to have discovered much difference in any respect between the manners of the two countries, and yet he is one of the most gentlemanlike men I have seen. Our friend Mr. Granger tells us that generally speaking the men who go from this country to England and to other parts of Europe are of no use in forwarding the refinement of their countrymen on their return. They there acquire so great a taste for the superior elegancies of life, in manners, institutions, and every branch, that they either aim at too high a standard without keeping in mind the number of intermediate steps necessary to be gone through in order to fit their countrymen for the highest degree of perfection and so fail entirely. Others again feel so disgusted with the contrast on returning home that they think all improvement quite hopeless and sit still and say nothing so that the people say: "Well, this man has been to Europe, and what has he learnt? What does he know more than his neighbours?"

SEPTEMBER 26:—I have been amused since writing the aforegoing account of the dispute about language that we had with some of our friends here to learn that the gentleman who had been in England and could not there discover any difference in the quality of English spoken by the well educated men in either country and whom I consequently set down as a person totally devoid of ear, is Mr. Hackett, the American actor, who played in one of the

London theatres last spring and whose imitations, I am told, are excellent. This makes the obtuseness of his organ in this one respect only the more extraordinary.

The whole evening of the twenty-fourth we spent in the public room, which is not usual with us, but Basil got into animated discussions with several of the gentlemen on English liberty, systems of representation, and general education as compared with that in America. These were points to be battled with no small degree of earnestness, and I could not help putting in a word or two occasionally along with some of the less practised debaters. We sat till nearly eleven o'clock and till I had talked and listened myself into a headache. You cannot imagine what steady, sturdy champions we are for England, and how Basil battles the watch on every point where he is attacked. There is an extraordinary ignorance in this country upon most English matters, almost as great I think (except on some points) as our ignorance of America and surely much more extraordinary, as even they themselves can not deny the superior importance of England to them over America to us.

We went to a party last night at Mrs. van Rensselaer's, the Patroon's, one of the same kind as those we had been at before. In so far, however, it was better because the inner room, a library, contained several tables covered with books of prints and it was a relief to get leave to stretch one's limbs a little whilst looking over drawings of scenery at home, so much more beautiful than anything I have seen since I left it. The outer room was, as usual, bare of furniture except for the awful range of seats next to the walls, to me all the more formidable and dull because of the difficulty of any gentleman inserting himself in the room, and as the truth ought to be told I must confess that the ladies I have yet met are very dull companions, so exceedingly commonplace. I am afraid you will think that I affect to like no society except that of gentlemen. As far as this country is concerned I must plead guilty to the charge, but I deserve the reproach no further. I am extremely amused with the motley company we meet here, senators, lawyers, actors, editors of newspapers, one of them a Jew, all placed in-

75

descriminately at table and all joining equally in the conversation. There were one or two fresh arrivals last night, but except two ladies, wife and sister to one of our most constant companions, they were but birds of passage who set off by the next steamboat. We are going to Mrs. Clinton's to-night. We called on her one evening lately, when she put a little coral necklace round Eliza's neck. I had a very pretty, little piece of attention shown me this evening in the shape of a nosegay of hot-house flowers sent to me by Mrs. van Rensselaer. They will do to put in my hair to-night.

SEPTEMBER 27:—This letter may now be concluded, and with it finishes my visit for the present to Albany. Our last party in this capital was last night at Mrs. Clinton's, a more agreeable one, I think, than any we had before been at, because there was not so much starch in it, but the Albians have much to learn before they are masters of the secret of agreeable society. I cannot take leave of them, however, without expressing the gratitude we feel for all the kindness they have bestowed upon us, and we are not a little flattered by the regret expressed both by those in this house and our acquaintances without. We shall certainly come and take leave of them before we quit the country.

Ever affectionately yours

MARGARET HALL

LETTER VII

NEW ENGLAND

This letter opens at Stockbridge whither the Halls had returned for a second visit to Mr. Ashburner. They spend an evening with "the whole clan of Sedgwicks". The "circle" was formidable and "evidently got together to stare at and listen to Basil". A drive to Tyringham to see the Shakers and a cattle show were other experiences of this visit. After five days they left by "Exclusive-Extra" for Northampton, climbing Mt. Holyoke en route in order to make a bird's-eye sketch from the summit. They called on Governor Lincoln at Worcester and then hurried on to spend Sunday in Boston where they heard Unitarian Dr. Channing preach in the morning and Episcopalian Dr. Gardiner in the afternoon. Mrs. Hall expresses herself as "quite delighted with the town". They are entertained by the Daniel Websters, the Ticknors, Dr. Bigelow of Harvard, Judge Prescott, Mrs. Otis, and many more. They have a long talk with Gilbert Stuart and with Washington Allston, hear Justice Story address a Grand Jury, visit Charlestown Gaol, walk up Bunker Hill, and make an excursion to the cotton factories of Lowell.

STOCKBRIDGE, MASS., October 2, 1827.

MY DEAREST JANE,

For our journey from Albany to Boston we have a stage entirely to ourselves, or, as it is called, an "Extra Exclusive," which means that everyone is excluded from it except ourselves, and in this we go at any rate we choose for a certain sum. The distance is one hundred and sixty miles of which it is thirty-five to Stockbridge. We found Mr. Ashburner at the door to receive us, apparently in much better health than when we were here in June, tho' he has had occasional fits of asthma since then. On the evening of our arrival Miss Sedgwick, authoress of three novels (one of which *Hope Leslie* we bought the other day), accompanied her sister-in-law, Mrs. Theodore Sedgwick, to drink

77

tea in this house; another brother of the family, Mr. Henry Sedgwick, also came with his wife. The husband of Mrs. Theodore is absent at New York. Miss Sedgwick's novel *Hope Leslie,* which we had just been reading, had prepared us to think well of the writer of it, nor were we disappointed in spite of the extraordinary portion of drawl she has to contend with, but her countenance is pleasing and her conversation so infinitely superior to that of the ladies we generally have met in America, that it is, as Basil would say, "quite refreshing." The Sedgwick family is that of the greatest importance in this village, and both males and females are more cultivated than most families, but I do not think any of them particularly agreeable except Miss Sedgwick.

The twenty-ninth was Saturday, and at sunset the Sabbath began, finishing at the same hour upon Sunday evening. This is very common in many parts of New England. After sunset on Saturday evening no one walks or drives out, and they would not even drink tea in a quiet way with a neighbor. On Sunday evening, on the contrary, nothing is more common than a large party of friends assembling at some house, and they resume their usual occupations of work or anything else they may be employed about during the week.

We all spent Sunday evening by invitation at Mrs. Theodore Sedgwick's, and met the whole clan of Sedgwicks, no less than three gentlemen of the family with their respective wives, beside their sister the authoress, and various others of the society of Stockbridge. The circle was smaller but not less formidable than those at Albany, and the refreshments also were after the same pattern, somewhat different in kind, as they consisted of sweetmeats and cream, in the first place, then, apples and grapes, thirdly, almonds and raisins, and lastly, wine, and the double duty of distributing the plates and handling round the eatables devolved upon one female servant. The party was evidently got together to stare at and listen to Basil, and I was amused by watching the way in which the gentlemen changed guard upon him, only one at a time indulging in the gratification of such a treat.

Yesterday Mr. and Mrs. Ashburner and Ann took me for a drive about seven miles off to one of the establishments of Shaking Quakers, of which there are so many in the neighborhood. I expatiated a good deal on the beauty of the surrounding scenery last time I was at Stockbridge. This second visit has not diminished my admiration of it, and all the way to Tyringham, where I was last night, is most particularly picturesque. Ann Ashburner and I both remarked that the Shakers seemed to select the situations for their establishments on account of their beauty, and we asked one of the Sisters who was with us if such were not the case, but her answers clearly proved that she, at least, bore no part in such an arrangement, if the fact were as we supposed. She said, when we remarked on the beauty of Lebanon and Tyringham, that for her part she thought Hancock much more beautiful because it is so *level;* that she guessed there was no great beauty at Tyringham before "them buildings" (great, staring, red and white, manufacturing-looking things) were erected, for that there was not an acre of land cultivated till the Quakers came there. I said that still it must have been very beautiful owing to the trees and the hills. Yes, she said, she liked the hills very well because they kept off the North West wind. But as for the excellence of picturesque beauty on its own account, that seemed to be a thing she had no place in her head for, or rather perhaps I ought to say in her heart.

NORTHAMPTON, MASS., OCTOBER 3:—Our journey to Northampton was forty-three miles through the most beautiful highland scenery, wooded hills, rocks, narrow valleys, and a lonely, mountain stream running through the whole. The road wound very much, and at every bridge we crossed, at least twenty in number, we had a fresh and more beautiful view. The autumnal tints are considered particularly brilliant in America, they are very lovely, certainly, but not more so than those at home. I think that the variety of them added much to the richness of the landscape today. The road was on the whole not so rough as many we have travelled but very hilly. After travelling twenty-seven miles, in the course of which we changed horses once, we came to Chester where we dined, and by a little after five we had accomplished our journey. This is a very pretty little village, and there is a large public school for boys, but unfortunately the vacation is at present and the Masters are both absent. I hear Mrs. Cownie trying to persuade Eliza to say, or rather listen to, the prayers said for her, but little Miss does not appear to be at all in a mood for devotional exercises and is singing in a voice as little pious as anything ever heard. She slept nine miles of the forty-three to-day and during the wakeful thirty-four was as good as possible.

IN THE HOUSE AT THE TOP OF MT. HOLYOKE, MASSACHU- SETTS, OCTOBER 4:—If inspiration came through the medicine of fine scenery I ought to write charmingly now, for I am looking down upon one of the most beautiful prospects I ever saw, part of the valley of the Connecticut. This mountain is only three miles distant from Northampton; it is about eight hundred feet high. The greater part of it a carriage brought us up, but about a quarter of a mile we had to walk up as rough a road as ever I saw, and as we were not aware of the difficulty we had brought Eliza and Mrs. Cownie with us. However, we all arrived safely at the top and hope to get down equally well, and in the mean-time we are enjoying this lovely day to the utmost. The country at our feet is very rich and has the appearance of having been much longer settled than any part of the State of New York that we have seen. In the Northampton plains, or meadows I believe they call them, there are no ugly, wooden fences dividing the fields, and very picturesque trees are scattered over them, at the same time that there is not a stump nor a girdled tree to be seen. On every side there are hills at a little distance, and the Connecticut winds in every direction like a serpent. Over the level ground beautiful, white villages are spread, and altogether I cannot imagine a more cheerful looking landscape. We meant to have set out an hour earlier, but just as the carriage came to the door a lady

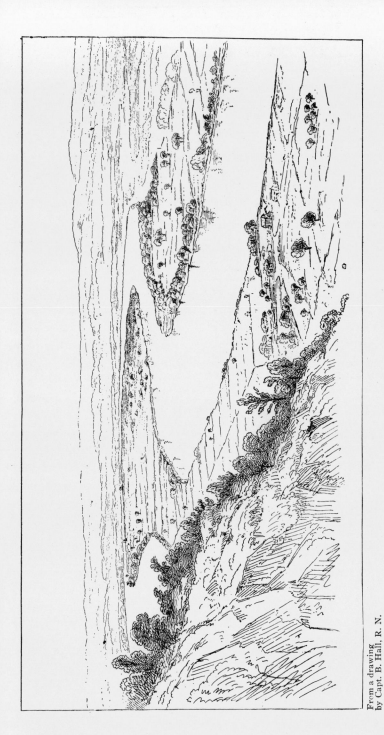

From a drawing
by Capt. B. Hall, R. N.

VIEW FROM MOUNT HOLYOKE IN MASSACHUSETTS

who was in the room happened to mention that there was to be a wedding in the house in half an hour, one of the daughters of the innkeeper. We have often wished to see a marriage in this country but none ever before came so opportunely in the way. Basil got hold of the Master of the House, and a little civility and speechifying about our being strangers travelling through the country and anxious to see everything relating to the manners and customs of it, promised us admittance to witness the ceremony. The company were seated according to the American fashion as if they were pinned to the wall, and the gentlemen divided from the ladies, whether by design or accident I do not know. The Bride and Bridegroom were placed at the bottom of the room, also upon chairs, the Bridesmaid next the Bride and the Best Man next the Bridegroom. The Clergyman was a merry looking little mannie in a pair of top boots. When the ceremony was to be performed he placed himself about the centre of the room with a chair before him, on the back of which he leant. It was by the Presbyterian form they were married, which I never witnessed before. All the company rose up whilst he repeated a prayer in commendation of the Institution of Marriage. He then made the couple join hands whilst he asked them nearly in the words of the Episcopalian form whether they would "love, cherish, etc," and then followed another prayer, after which we all resumed our seats and a most funereal silence prevailed, not a soul going near the Bride to wish her joy. In a few minutes the solemnity of the scene was in some measure relieved by the entrance of a boy bearing a tray covered with plates and two beautiful wedding cakes, of which each guest helped him or herself to a large piece, even the newly married pair seemed to have retained their appetite for plum cake, and the gentleman had still his senses sufficiently about him to take proper care of his wedding suit and followed the examples of the other males of the party in spreading his pocket handkerchief over his knees to protect his trousers from the grease of the cake. We next had wine handed round, and I thought that now surely we should hear a few congratulations, but, except the Best Man and Basil, not a soul drank their health. The ladies for the most part wore white, thick, muslin gowns without any sort of pretence at finery, some of them were in black, and the father of the Bride himself wore a black coat. This was a great relief to me as I am travelling in black, and I was afraid that my dingy dress might give offence, but they have no such superstition in this country. As soon as we could decently get away we left the quiet party and set off on this expedition. We return to Northampton in a little while and shall not proceed towards Boston till to-morrow morning.

BOSTON, OCTOBER 6:—We are now in the Capital of this State and a city whose fame is much spoken of in this country. We have been told too, when at a distance from it, that we should find ourselves quite at home here, because everything remains so much more like England than in any other part of the Union. Of this we shall now have an opportunity of judging. Hitherto we have seen nothing but a very handsome street just as we entered, for it was sunset when we arrived. We are lodged at Mrs. le Hain's boarding house in Pearl Street and have had tea with the other lodgers at present six in number, all males. We have a handsome, well-furnished parlour and altogether things promise well. We have been greatly struck by the improvement in point of Inns since we entered this State, the rooms are better furnished, particularly the bedrooms, and both yesterday and to-day, instead of being all crammed into one room for dinner like so many pigs in a sty, we had a separate, neat, small dinner for ourselves. This was the more remarkable as there happened to be several other parties dining at the same time that we were, and each party had a parlour and a dinner for themselves. The whole appearance of the country, too, is different from what we had before seen, no stumps, no newly cleaned land, and great abundance of old and picturesque trees. Very little corn or grain of any kind, indeed the land is so bad—covered with stones—that it would be very unprofitable work to cultivate it except as pasture, but altho' not possessing beauty in the eye of an agriculturist there is an abundance of picturesque beauty in the landscape the whole way from Stockbridge to Boston, particularly the first part of the journey, and the New England villages may really vie with those of Old England, of which they have retained, or rather borrowed, many of the names.

Yesterday morning we left Northampton at eight o'clock. The place we meant to sleep at, Worcester, was fifty-six miles distant, and we increased the day's journey a few miles by going to Mount Pleasant School at Amherst. It has been established within the last six months, but it is in a flourishing state, so far that they find it already necessary to enlarge their accommodation for a greater number of pupils, tho' I believe they do not mean to take beyond a hundred boys. Basil merely wished to call to make a few enquiries, but the Masters had no idea of letting us off so cheaply, and we had first Rhetoric and then Mathematics (very edifying to me!) to attend to, and our many efforts to escape were quite unavailing until we had undergone a tolerable dose of each. The School is delightfully situated and the boys looked well-dressed and clean. At Amherst there is also a College and a Grammar School, indeed these New England States are quite nurseries of learning for the whole Union. Having bid adieu to Mount Pleasant we drove on our way, changed horses at Belchertown, and dined at Ware, a neat manufacturing village. They are all manufacturers in this State, but as yet we have not stopped to see any of their works. From Ware we drove on to Brookfield and from thence to Worcester, where we slept.

On looking at our notes this morning we found that Professor Silliman of Yale College at Newhaven mentioned Worcester as the residence of Mr. Lincoln, the Governor of the State of Massachusetts. It was raining hard, but we ordered a hack and proceeded to call on His Excellency, whom we found a very agreeable, conversible person. In due time and after various ringing of bells and sending of messages, Mrs. Lincoln made her appearance in a clean, white, muslin dress and magnificent, blue turban.

I believe I have remarked before that when we go to pay a visit we never find the ladies ready to receive us; they are never sitting at work or employed in any way, but we are shown into a room of most undisturbed neatness, where after ten minutes or a quarter of an hour's delay the lady appears, draped for the occasion. I think this may in part arise from the want of good servants, which makes it necessary for the ladies to assist in many menial offices, particularly in cooking. We were invited to spend the day with Governor and Mrs. Lincoln, but to-morrow being Sunday we felt anxious to reach Boston this evening and therefore declined what otherwise we should have been very happy to do. We got away from Worcester by half past ten, by which time the rain had ceased, and by and by the Sun broke out to cheer us up. We dined at Farmingham, nineteen miles from our starting point, and made out the remaining twenty-one to Boston by half past five, and, having established us here, I shall bid you goodbye till I see what turns up.

BOSTON, OCTOBER 7:—I think I have before mentioned that Unitarianism has made great progress in this State. Boston is the headquarters of this faith, and Dr. Channing its great apostle. He had been absent on account of bad health for many months, but on ascertaining this morning that he was to preach for the first time since his return we resolved to go to hear him. I was till of late so ignorant of the peculiar doctrines of the Unitarians that I think it possible you may be as much in the dark on the subject as myself, and therefore I may as well mention that they deny the supreme Divinity of Christ. In fact, as Basil says, they are neither more nor less than Mahometans, for they allow that our Saviour was a Prophet, and that in order to be saved we must follow his example and do as he told us, but it is not through the merits of Christ alone, as Christianity inculcates, that we are to look for salvation. I never heard so good a Preacher in my life as Dr. Channing, so eloquent and yet so perfectly quiet and free from the appearance of wishing to produce an effect, and, however mistaken we may consider him in his doctrines, I am sure that he is perfectly sincere, and my predominant feeling when listening to him was the deepest regret that such talents should be perverted into a wrong channel. His sermon was entirely on the occasion of his return to his parishioners after a pretty long absence, and the manner in which he alluded to the changes by death which had occurred in the interval was quite beautiful, as well as the way in which he touched upon the uncertainty of his own life. His description of the effect produced upon his mind by contemplating the works of God was poetic in the highest degree, and had the doctrine been but sound I should have been thoroughly delighted and pleased (for the morality was excellent), but, as it was, I only felt melancholy. We have a letter for him from Mr. Rathbone, and I hope we shall make his acquaintance.

In the afternoon we went to the Episcopalian Church where we heard a most orthodox sermon from Dr. Gardiner. It was called forth, I dare say, by the return of the great Unitarian preacher, but feeling that we had been wandering from the right faith in the morning (and my conscience occasionally pricked me for going astray) I felt as if the discourse were particularly addressed to us. Dr. Gardiner spoke of Unitarianism as "that Paganised Christianity," an expression which quite upset my gravity. After our second church we went to call on Mrs. Boott, an old Scotch lady, and mother to Dr. Boott, a physician in London who gave us many letters for his family and friends in Boston. We have walked about a good deal this afternoon, and we are quite charmed with this beautiful town. The Americans are so much in the habit of praising and overpraising everything that, when they said to me, "You will be delighted with Boston," I paid no attention, and only fancied that it was part of their usual laudatory system.

OCTOBER 9:—This climate is to the full as uncertain as that of England, and this circumstance throws us sadly out in all our arrangements, which in spite of experience are all made without any allowance for such contingencies. This day was appointed for a visit to the Naval Establishment at Charlestown, a mile from hence across the River Charles, but it rains as if it would never cease, so it is out of the question, but we mean to make use of it to return the numerous visits that have been paid to us in consequence of having sent round our letters. Our visitors began on Sunday evening, and yesterday we had a constant succession of them from before ten o'clock. The person we have seen most is Mr. Daniel Webster, a very eminent lawyer and one of the Members to Congress from the State of Massachusetts. He is a very celebrated man in this country and well known by reputation to many persons in England. He is by much the most generally informed and cleverest man that we have seen in America. We dine with him and Mrs. Webster to-day.

Professor and Mrs. Ticknor were with us a long time. They, too, are very agreeable persons; Mr. Ticknor was in Edinburgh in the beginning of 1819 and was then acquainted with Sir James and Lady Helen Hall. He is Professor of Belles Lettres in the College of Harvard at Cambridge, three miles from Boston. The short hour that intervened between the cessation of our visitors and the hour of dinner (half past two) we spent with the Ticknors at the Athenaeum where there is the best collection of books that we have seen in the country. We had not long finished dinner when Dr. Jackson, the first physician in Boston, and for whom we had a letter from Dr. Boott, called and sat with us till nearly tea-time. Mrs. Le Hain is quite lost with astonishment at the length of time our visitors sit with us. Our companions in the boarding-house, with whom we have hitherto breakfasted, dined, and drank tea, are a very gentleman-like set of men, infinitely superior in manners and appearance to those we were in the habit of associating with in the State of New York, indeed our observations yet lead us to form a much higher opinion both of the ladies and gentlemen in this State. The gentlemen are much better dressed and the ladies much *less* dressed than those of New

York, and there is a much greater degree of politeness amongst them without so much formality.

SAME DAY, EVENING:— Well, my good opinions of Boston and the Bostonians gain strength by seeing more of both. I am quite delighted with the town, which even in this wet, nasty day looked cleaner than any town I was ever in. The outward appearance of the houses is so handsome that I feel a wish to go into each one as I pass, and those that I have been in do not fall short of what they promise on the outside. We got over all our visits, but on returning home found that we have a fresh batch to begin. I also found a fine basket of grapes that had been sent to me from Colonel Perkins, and yesterday I had an equally handsome and excellent one sent to me by Mr. Pratt, an English gentleman who has a garden opposite. The dinner arrangements at Mr. Webster's were much better, according to our notions, than what we have before seen in this country. The party consisted of twelve, Professor and Mrs. Ticknor, Mr. Charles Adams (a son of the President), and some others. The table was not so much loaded and the servants on the whole understood their duty better, altho' still this branch of good style is far from perfect. After the first course there were two dishes of game alone, and then followed a course of sweet things, but the Ice was put down along with the dessert, which was very prettily set out on handsome china, which, by the by, they generally have, and one thing that the Americans manage very well is the lighting of their rooms. I have not yet been in a dark room. But what was still more essential to the comfort and cheerfulness of the party was the informal manner in which we seated ourselves in the dining-room. There was a table in the middle of the room covered with books and prints, and it was the centre of attraction, but both gentlemen and ladies moved about like free agents, and did not appear to be glued to their chairs. I have no experience yet of an evening party, so perhaps it may have as much stiffness here as elsewhere that we have been, but I will hope better things, and to-morrow we are to have a sample of one at

Dr. Bigelow's, also one of the Professors of Harvard College. But I must go to bed. I am quite tired out at night with the excitement of each day.

OCTOBER 11:—At length we have a day of bright sun, and we mean to take advantage of it and go to the top of the State House, the view from whence is said to be very fine. We have an engagement to go there along with Miss Cochrane, a Halifax lady with whom Basil was acquainted three and twenty years ago when a Midshipman on that station. She was then a reigning beauty at Halifax, and I have heard much of Belle Cochrane from him, as well as from others, and even the number of years that have since passed over her head have not deprived her of her good looks, for she was certainly by much the handsomest woman that I saw last night at a large party where we met her. Without, however, wishing to take from her claims as a beauty, I must observe that I was sadly disappointed in the appearance of the Boston ladies last night, indeed since we came here I have seen but one lady tolerably handsome, and that is Miss Marshall, a very celebrated person in Boston. But everything else here surpasses my expectations. The style of society and the people are much more English than we have before met, and there is not that appearance of effort, which is painful to the entertained as well as to the entertainer. Yesterday we dined at Professor Ticknor's, and but for one whisper from the lady of the house as to the placing of a sauce boat there was nothing amiss; all was well-ordered and the style particularly handsome. The party consisted of eleven persons; Mrs. Webster was the only lady besides Mrs. Ticknor and myself—her husband was too busy to dine out. Of gentlemen there were Professor Farrar of Harvard College, Dr. Channing, brother to the clergyman, Mr. Bancroft of Northampton School, Mr. Higginson, and Colonel Baldwin, a civil engineer. Most of those gentlemen had travelled much in England and on the Continent of Europe, and the conversation around the table was really worthy of a London dinner party. I have not yet seen any plate at the tables of those we have dined with, but they have most beautiful china. At Mr. Ticknor's there was the most beautiful set of Sevres dessert china that I ever saw with ice pails to match, for here, as the day before, we had the ice, in what *we* consider the proper place, along with the fruit instead of side by side with the puddings and pies. One part of the arrangement of the desserts in Boston is, I think, well worthy of being copied in England. Instead of putting the grapes in one dish, the peaches in another, and so on, they group the various kinds together in each dish, which not only has a prettier effect, but prevents the necessity of pulling about the dishes over the table. Every part of Mr. Ticknor's house is well furnished; the stair carpeted from top to bottom, and altho' a few more sofas and ottomans might be a good addition the want of them is not very apparent. I ought to have mentioned that in the morning we had been at Harvard College in Cambridge, three miles from Boston, but the rain was so violent that Mrs. Ticknor and I could not even go from one building to another, as in getting out and in to the carriage we were like to be drowned, so after seeing the Library, the Museum, and the Natural Philosophy class room all under one roof, we were glad to return home. We went from Mrs. Ticknor's bodily to a rout at Dr. Bigelow's, really a rout, and a very pleasant one, no formality nor dullness of any kind and everyone moved to or fro as their inclination prompted them. There were refreshments of various kinds handed round, and the Ice instead of being in one great pillar was in glasses, as is the fashion in England. At Albany I was told that this is considered very *ungenteel,* their favourite phrase, for in America everything is genteel or ungenteel. Champagne is a never failing sequel to the refreshments at a party, and at their dinners they have it likewise, only instead of being placed on the table and drank with their neighbours it is handed round between the first and second course. There is a very little claret and less port. No claret is ever put down after dinner, occasionally there may be a bottle during dinner along with the Sauterne or Vin de Grave, but that is all. Madeira is their wine, and they pique themselves particularly upon it. Fortunately for us, as we are so much engaged, the hours of the parties are early, they begin soon after eight, and we are always at home before half past ten. The company dinner hour is four o'clock, and that, I believe, is considered very early. We find it rather a bore to have to dine so early, it shortens our day so much, but we must of course conform to the fashion of the country.

OCTOBER 13:—I have been in such a whirl since the eleventh that I have had no time to write a word. The eleventh continued sufficiently clear to make a climb to the top of the State House worth the trouble, and, accordingly, at the appointed hour we called on Miss Cochrane. She is living at Mr. Sears' at a very handsome house indeed and well ornamented within as well as without. There is a great taste for ornament in Boston, clocks, vases filled with artificial flowers, and many such things. There are a few, good paintings too by an American of the name of Allston, one of his, "Miriam", is at Mr. Sears'. The view from the State House is quite a bird's eye one, of which I am not particularly fond, but it is well to see Boston from a point where it is possible to discover the junction of the town with the mainland, for it is placed upon what is all but an island; indeed, the little neck which makes a peninsula of it is, I believe, almost entirely artificial. We were engaged to dine seven miles out of the town at three o'clock, so we had to dress and be off before two, accompanied by Eliza who was invited to spend the day with the children of our host, Captain Wormeley, a brother officer of Basil's, who found us out the morning we arrived. He married a Boston lady. The Ticknors were there and as many others as made up a party of thirteen or fourteen.

It is very much the fashion for the people of Boston to go to the country during the summer, and there are many beautiful villages all round it where they live. The labours and pleasures of the day concluded with a very small party at Mrs. Otis's. Here the Albany sin of a circle prevailed a little, but not nearly to so great a degree as there, and the small numbers offered some sort of apology for this dereliction from the ease of good manners. We made our retreat as soon as we could, but not until we had gone through the ceremonies of the blancmange, ice, and red champagne, at least not until *I* had, for Basil has thoroughly established himself as an abstemious man, and though they wonder that he neither eats nor drinks they let him do exactly as he pleases without any sort of trouble or pressing.

Yesterday we were up betimes and off at nine o'clock to the great manufacturing establishment at Lowell, which has grown up in the last five years. The journey was twenty-five miles, and we made it out by one o'clock. We went at once to the house of Mr. Kirke Boott under whose immediate superintendence the works are. We rather expected that we should have had time to visit the manufacturies before dinner, which by the way was somewhat *young* in us, considering the experience we have had of American hours, but we were not prepared to find (altho' we arrived at one) we had kept the family waiting beyond their usual dining hour. In ten minutes we were seated at table, and such is the capability of one's appetite to accommodate itself to any hour, that, dining at one or at six, I always feel equally hungry. We swallowed our dinner with somewhat of American speed, as the days are short now and we had a great deal to see before dark. Five years ago Mr. and Mrs. Kirke Boott took up their residence at Lowell where there was then no building except one or two little hovels, but last night we went over very extensive cotton manufacturies that have sprung up since that time, and on every side fresh ones are starting into life. This State is so very bad for agricultural purposes that they are driven to manufactures to gain a livelihood, but as yet they have neither skill nor capital to attempt anything fine or expensive, and the finest cottons they make at Lowell (printed ones I mean) are not beyond the value of fifteen pence a yard I should think. But with time and their desire to improve they will soon advance the quality. Mr. Boott's father and mother were both English or Scotch and he himself educated in England. He was for some years in the English army, but after the battle of Waterloo, seeing that the trade of war was over, he very wisely turned his sword not into a plough but a spinning wheel. His wife was a Derby lady, and they have a large family of young children, as all the world has in this most marrying country. We breakfasted this morning before eight and were off before nine to Salem, a drive of twenty-five miles more. Salem is a place whence in former years there was a very extensive trade carried on to India and China. It contains not more than thirteen thousand inhabitants, but I have been told that some years ago there was more business with India done there than in Boston and New York put together. Latterly the trade has fallen off owing to the competition that has arisen in other places. We were engaged to dine there at half past two with Judge Story, one of the judges of the Supreme Court and a remarkably agreeable man and very talkative withal. We found Mr. and Mrs. Webster and Mr. and Mrs. Ticknor, besides half a dozen Salem gentlemen assembled to meet us, and had really as pleasant a dinner as could be met with anywhere. The conversation here has generally quite a different character from what it has elsewhere that we have been in America. It is much more general instead of being confined to the praise of their own men and things, their wonderful country, and all their various perfections. The people of Boston seem to have travelled more in Europe and not merely for the purposes of gain like our friends in New York. There is a museum at Salem belonging to the merchants there; we went to see it after dinner, but the light almost failed us and we saw only enough of a handsome, well arranged collection to make us wish to return. After this we had still fourteen miles drive before we reached Boston, where we arrived between eight and nine.

October 14:—We had two invitations for this evening, but we thought that Sunday, at least, might be a day of rest, and, therefore, declined them both. I remained at home with Eliza this morning whilst Mrs. Cownie went to Church. The dinner hour on Sunday is one o'clock, but between the *coming out* of the morning church (which *goes in* at ten) and that hour, we had quite a host of visitors. In the afternoon we went under the escort of a certain Mr. Isaac N. Davis to the Episcopalian Unitarian Church. How the hair of the Bench of Bishops would stand up on end were they to hear of such an abominable heresy! At this church they have preserved the liturgy of the Church of England, carefully expunging every expression relating to the doctrine of the Trinity. They deviate a little in form, and seem to stand up or sit down according as the fancy seizes them. When the psalms or hymns were sung the greater part of the congregation sat still, when the prayers were said most of them stood, and very few knelt at any time. The sermon was upon charity and from a very commonplace preacher indeed, who kept all doctrine out of sight and might as well have been addressing a parcel of heathens as of Christians. A gentleman whom we saw in the morning said that it was a pity we had not gone to hear Dr. Channing, who preached a sermon even more indicative of his peculiar doctrines than the one we had heard.

After Church this afternoon we went, still under the auspices of Mr. Davis, to call upon Mr. Stuart, the painter, an American by birth, but who spends many years of his life in England. His professional education was under West, who, you know, was also an American. Mr. Stuart has done likenesses of many English naval officers who flourished some forty or fifty years ago. With Lord St. Vincent he was on terms of very great intimacy. His conversation is extremely interesting from his acquaintance with so many eminent men. In his painting room there is an original painting he did of Washington, merely a head, the figure and drapery left unfinished. He amused us exceedingly by the account he gave us of the embarrassment at first as to how he was to get on with it, he found it such hard work to make General Washington speak on light subjects; however, he resolved to try at all hazards to make him laugh, accordingly he told him the old Joe Miller story of King James II's journey to gain popularity, in the course of which he arrived somewhere that the Mayor of the place was Baker and no speech-maker and had to be prompted, so that when his friend jogged his elbow and said, "Hold up your head and look like a man", the blundering Mayor repeated the admonition to the King. This stupid story had the desired effect, "and from that time," said Mr. Stuart, "I had him on a pivot and could manage him nicely." I was still more interested with his description of David Hume and Voltaire whom he remembers sitting together in the Stoop of Mr. Hume's house at the end of the North Bridge in Edinburgh. Mr. Stewart was then a little boy following his education in Edinburgh, and Mr. Hume used to call him in and converse with him as he came home from school. Mr. Stuart was the first person to set Sir Thomas Lawrence agoing when he arrived in London from Bath, quite a young man, now upwards of forty years ago. Till then Sir Thomas had occupied himself merely with little drawings in crayon, but Mr. Stuart saw at once that he was a man of genius, and overlooking the rudeness of the speech asked him abruptly what made him waste his time doing such *damned* things as these? The poor young man's abashed air reminded Mr. Stuart what a breach of politeness he had been guilty of, but the complimentary apology amply compensated for the pain occasioned by the first speech. The Church we were in to-day still goes by the name of the King's Chapel. It is a very handsome one. The fine October the Americans promised us has not yet arrived, and altho' we have had no rain for the last three days it has been surly and cold. I am amused by the apologies made to me on all hands for the disappointment, but after all the Americans have such a habit of talking of everything in their country as belonging to themselves that it is not surprising that they should feel answerable for the imperfections of climate. They talk of, *"Our* weather", *"Our* climate", *"Our* October", all as exclusively belonging to themselves. In like manner I hear, *"Our* great men", *"Our* laws", in short, it is endless to particularize, for the same form of speech runs through everything.

OCTOBER 17:—On Monday, the fifteenth, Colonel Perkins had made an appointment with us to go to the Rail Road at Quincy, a few miles out of town, but by breakfast time a note from him came to say that the rain must put an end to our arrangement. Our time is too precious to be left without some specific employment for each morning and so we considered for a little what objects we should turn it to as our first plan had misgiven. We soon learned that Judge Story was to open the Circuit Court of the United States at eleven o'clock and was to charge the Grand Jury. We therefore set off in the interval of the showers, which by this time were abating in frequency and violence, and for the first time I saw the Grand Jury empanelled and heard them addressed. Judge Story speaks so rapidly, so very rapidly when compared with the slow speech of his countrymen, that I listened with great interest and without weariness to his address. I did not know till after I had been there that I am the first lady who has ever been in that court. The jury are chosen by the names of a large number of individuals being put in a box from where they are ballotted for. I don't think I ever saw such an ugly set of individuals collected together as the "Gentlemen of the Grand Jury." They are chosen from the yeomanry of the country. I was amused when their names were called over by what has struck me throughout every-where, the universal prevalence of Scriptural names, Elijah, Ezra, Amos, indeed every one of the Prophets and their contemporaries have their namesakes. I fancied that there were still to be found in those New England States names similar to those which char-acterized the Commonwealth of England, but I have not heard of any such except one, and that was of a man in New York within the last few weeks,—"Through much tribulation we enter into the Kingdom of God." As soon as we had heard all that Judge Story had to say we left him for the Type and Stereotype Foundry, a thing which I might have seen at home any day in the year by walking a mile, but it is very true that one must go abroad to learn what is done at home, and at the same time I saw the Marine Railway, which was invented by Mr. Morton at Leith though I never saw it there. When we had got through all those sights it was time to go home and dress for a large dinner party at Mr. Prescott's, or Judge Prescott's as he is called, tho' he was not on the Bench more than a couple of years. It is by no means uncommon here, a man going back to the Bar from the Bench, and in New York it is very frequent indeed, as in that State no man can continue to be a Judge after sixty, and altho' many a man is in his full vigor at that age I think that we have had more than one instance of late years in Edinburgh that would have justified the regulation had it existed there.

I had the pleasure of sitting next Judge Story at dinner, and it really is a pleasure, for he is a remarkably agreeable man. The party was of the usual size, sixteen, Captain and Mrs. Wormeley, Mr. and Mrs. Franklin Dexter, daughter and son-in-law to our hosts, and several others. It was to the son, Mr. W. H. Prescott, that we brought a letter of introduction, but in that family as in many others we are acquainted with the young people live with the father or mother of one or the other party.

Yesterday, the sixteenth, we left home at nine o'clock and calling first for the Revd. Mr. Dwight, who was good enough to accompany us we proceeded to visit the jails. We went first to one in Boston, where we saw a good many females under the superintendence of a Matron who has done a great deal to reform them since her establishment two years ago, but finding her endeavours very much frustrated by the want of regulations for solitary confinement at night. We afterwards went to Charlestown, a mile off, where the State Prison is, and where a new one is building on the plan of the one now erecting at Sing Sing, and it is to be hoped that the same discipline of strict silence and solitary confinement at night will be followed. At present things are on the old plan and nothing can be worse. I do not know any subject with which I am so little acquainted that interests me so much as Prison Discipline. My attention was never called to it at all at home, but in travelling I make it a rule to go and see everything, as I think that amidst the multitude of objects that pass before me it will be very extraordinary if I do not find some that I shall understand and profit by, besides Basil has become so used to companionship that he cannot bear to go anywhere without me. It is melancholy to become acquainted with the extent of abuse which has till late existed in prisons. Much still remains uncorrected, but the great efforts now making we may hope in time may eradicate the evil. It is curious to trace prisons from their origins when they were considered mere places for stowing away the wicked and obnoxious from the reach of the well ordered part of the community down to the more enlightened time when they are looked upon as places for reform as well as for punishment. Mr. Dwight appears to have the amelioration of this large part of the community most thoroughly at heart, and like a sensible man goes to work slowly and surely. I am sure he is a truly excellent man and he seemed to be amazingly delighted to find strangers enter with so much interest into his schemes. Since I have read and heard this matter I have remembered with astonishment the opinions I have heard expressed in England "that prisons ought to be let alone." I am persuaded that those who say so have never attended to the subject. I am sure nothing more is required to make the fallacy of this opinion be felt than to read one of the Annual Reports of the Prison Discipline Society at Boston. Another argument used by those lovers of old fashions is the danger of making prison too agreeable or too comfortable, as they call it, but I am very sure that those who are subjected to the discipline of Auburn or Sing Sing will have small wish to return, and indeed the very limited number of recommitments compared with those in the prisons on the old plan are sufficient proof of the efficacy of the punishment.

Bunker Hill, where the second battle during the Revolutionary War was fought, is in Charlestown. It is a small eminence but a good site for a monument to commemorate those events, and accordingly they are now raising an obelisk of granite, which is to be two hundred and twenty feet high. We stopped there on our way from the prison to Commodore Morris's house, where we called for him to take us to see the ships now on the stocks at Charlestown. There is one calculated for one hundred and two guns, which I went over, and two smaller ones. They are now building a dry dock at Charlestown and we went with Colonel Baldwin, the Engineer, to see the sheet piles of the copper dam driven, which had its interest too as I had never seen the like before. From Charlestown we drove back to Boston to Dr. Channing's to see a picture in his possession done by Allston, a very admirable painter here. The subject is *Jeremiah in Prison, dictating to Balak his prophecy of the destruction of Jerusalem.* I am no judge of pictures, but it is impossible to look at any of those of Allston and not to feel that they are fine. In colouring he particularly excels, and this picture of Jeremiah is perfect in this respect. I was glad too of this opportunity of having a new view of Dr. Channing, who altho' small in all his proportions is nevertheless a very striking person, and the combing of his hair over his left eyebrow lends considerable addition to the expression of his countenance. It is always interesting to know what a great man is occupied with, and when, therefore, Dr. Channing took from the mantelpiece a book which he said interested him much and was by a Scotch author I was curious to discover what moralist or divine he was bestowing his leisure hours upon, but to my no small amusement I found, on looking at the title page to which he pointed, that *Clan Albin, a Novel* was what claimed his praise.

After all this hard work I had still a large dinner party at Commodore Morris's where we met the Ticknors and no less than four men in uniform, a most extraordinary number in this peaceful country. Our labours did not end there, but we summed up all with a large party at Mrs. Minot's, the sister of Mrs. Henry Sedgwick whom we met at Stockbridge. There we saw the beauty, Miss Marshall, and heard Miss Davis sing—two remarkable persons in their own way. Miss Marshall is handsome, certainly, but I have not seen any very striking face since I have been here. Miss Davis sings better than any of the few young ladies I have heard in America, but there is a good deal of broken glass in her voice. She has the great merit of making the words be heard, and as the song she sung was Lord Byron's, *My Native Land Good-Night,* this excellence was the more valuable.

NEW ENGLAND

OCTOBER 19:—At last the Bostonians are relieved from the disgrace of bad weather under which they have been labouring ever since we came amongst them, for I believe I told you that each individual seemed to feel him or herself answerable for the rain and wind with which we have been annoyed since our arrival. It was only yesterday that the change took place, and now they all cackle as if they had the merit of the improvement.

At half past eight on the seventeenth we went to a ball at Mrs. Ticknor's, where I danced eight quadrilles. The music was good and the room well lighted, two grand points towards a good ball. But in spite of those favourable circumstances I was not struck with much female beauty, I am quite disappointed in Boston faces. I was led to expect that the ladies were particularly handsome, but the same want is felt here as in New York, that style and air which is requisite to make a good appearance in a drawing room. They have one very dancing-school-like practice before beginning each quadrille, the ladies and gentlemen bow and curtsey to each other and to the person standing next to them on the other side, not a mere inclination of the head but the profoundest reverence. The lady of the house generally (for it did not happen at Mrs. Ticknor's) appoints one of her friends as sort of Master of the Ceremonies whose business it is to call out, "Gentlemen please to take your partners for a cotillion." One great difference between the society here and in England is that in England in good society there is so little effort and such a want of bustle that a stranger looking on would find it difficult to discover which were the Master and Mistress of the House. But here there is a constant labour to do the honours on the part of the individuals who give the entertainment. This, however, applies less to Mr. and Mrs. Ticknor than to anyone else whose house I have been in. They are both of them animated and intelligent persons, and he never says *Madam;* he might indeed pass current for a well-informed, well-bred Englishman. I think they are on the whole our most intimate friends here. In one of the little rooms there was a table laid out with refreshments of all kinds, and by eleven o'clock the whole thing was over.

Yesterday morning Basil went off to the Rail Road at Quincy with a certain Mr. Isaac Davis, the most useful man in Boston. I did not go as I wished to save myself some fatigue, so I, took Eliza for company whilst I got rid of some of my visiting debt, and then had to dress and be at Colonel Perkins's six miles off by three o'clock dinner. There we met two interesting persons in very different ways, the one was Mr. Washington Allston, the painter, of whom I can tell you nothing as he sat at the opposite side of the table and spoke so low that no word fell upon my ear. Perhaps by strict watching I might have caught something, but my time was so agreeably taken up by the other most remarkable person of the party that I had neither leisure nor inclination to watch Mr. Allston. Mr. Everett was my neighbour. He was formerly a clergyman and a most eloquent preacher, but his heart was not in his profession, and altho' he liked the notoriety of being a great preacher he had no fancy for the more quiet duties of the parish. In short, ambition is his ruling passion, and as in the Church in this country there is no means of indulging such a passion he asked leave to visit Europe, and having obtained it he never again returned to his parishioners, and he is now one of the Representatives to Congress from this State. His manner and appearance do not indicate any of that spirit which led him to abandon his first calling. To me there seems to be a great degree of melancholy in his countenance, and he has all the slowness of speech which characterises the Americans so much, but I am told that he is very gay. His countenance is interesting, and even in common conversation he blushed like a timid girl. His conduct has exposed him to much censure, and he is not generally popular, altho' I believe all are willing to acknowledge his talents. There were many other persons at Colonel Perkins's, but none of them worthy of note. We concluded the evening with a ball at Mrs. Boott's. There we had the usual refreshments of ice, etc., and then hot oysters and dressed lobster, but the gentlemen had a table of their own laid out in one of the rooms and covered with beef, ham, and various other things, which they washed down with Champagne and Porter, taking care that the ladies should not come in for a share of their peculiar privileges.

Adieu, ever affectionately yours,

MARGARET HALL.

LETTER VIII

Disengaging themselves with difficulty from hospitable Boston the Halls
set out on October the 23rd for Providence and thence posted to Hartford
where they investigated Weathersfield Prison and Deaf and Dumb Asylum.
Mr. Pilsbury of the Prison and Mr. Gallaudet and Dr. Tod of the
Asylum were found to be remarkable and enthusiastic men with souls
wrapped up in their work. On the road from Hartford to New Haven Captain Hall inspected Colonel Partridge's Military Academy. As it was the
dinner hour they saw the young men bolting lumps of meat and spitting
right and left during the meal. At New Haven Professor Silliman showed
them a graveyard, pointing out his children's tombstones with what Mrs.
Hall thought was unbecoming indifference, then he took them over the
college and drove them up to the Crags and "the Regicides' Cave." They
take ship for New York.

BOSTON, *October 22, 1927.*

MY DEAREST JANE,

This is the day that we had appointed for leaving Boston, and
after making all our arrangements to that effect and refusing every
invitation we thought our best plan was to take one quiet day for
finishing up any unseen sights, paying accounts, packing, and all
the various items necessary to be done after a fortnight's halt and
before starting on a new journey. I finished my last letter to you
on the nineteenth, but I do not think I gave any account of what
we did that day. At eleven o'clock the Mayor called for us, and
with him we went to South Boston to see the House of Industry
and the House of Refuge. The House of Industry is apparently
very well managed, but Mr. Mayor is one of those uncomfortable
chaperons who insists upon hounding you over every establishment
and is jealous of your looking at everything except after his own

particular fashion. He certainly deserves credit for his arrangements where he carried us, but I would more willingly give it to him did he not assume so much. In one of the wards in the Alms House we found an old woman knitting very busily, whilst placed on the bed before which she sat was a book which appeared completely to fix her attention. I looked over her shoulder and found this to be *Peveril of the Peak!* I afterwards learned that she is Scotch and a great reader and has no doubt feasted on all the works of the same author, and even in her dependent and indigent situation I dare say she has felt a glow of pride in the consciousness of belonging to the same country with Sir Walter Scott. The House of Refuge is only lately established and is at present in a building meant for the House of Correction and quite improper for the purpose it is now applied to, at least three times larger than necessary. It made me melancholy to see the little creatures that were there; children not more than five years old, but the very circumstance of their extreme youth proved the excellence of having such an establishment, as but for that they would either have been shut up along with those more practised in vice and quite willing to initiate their young companions in it, or from an unwillingness to condemn such mere children to prison they would again have been turned adrift upon society only to be greater pests and learn more wickedness. In the House of Refuge they are well educated and learn some trade by which they can earn a livelihood when they return into the world.

We dined at Professor Ticknor's on the nineteenth with Judge Story, Dr. Jackson, Mr. Guild, Mr. Sullivan, and Mr. Greenwood, the Unitarian Episcopalian Clergyman. We returned home from Mr. Ticknor's dinner at eight o'clock, and in half an hour Mr. Allston the painter walked in. His habits are very different from those of his countrymen, generally speaking; he lies long in bed in the morning and goes to bed late, and towards midnight he gets more agreeable and conversible till one or two o'clock in the morning. Basil had taken care to provide himself with a case of very choice segars, knowing that they are quite essential towards the comfort of the evening, and soon after he came to us Basil handed them to him. He at first slightly resisted the temptation thinking it not proper to smoke in my company, but I assured him that I had a genuine love of tobacco, and presently he was quite at his ease and by twelve o'clock had finished half a dozen exquisite Havannahs, the best he said he had seen in Boston. I do not know whether he would have left us then had not Eliza, whose bed stands behind a large screen in our parlour, fairly wakened up at last after many a faint grunt called forth by the more animated parts of our conversation. He made himself very agreeable during the whole of his visit. He is at present employed upon a very large picture, the subject of which is *Belshazzar's Feast*. He has been employed upon it for many years, but even his most intimate friends are not allowed to see it. He has been engaged to be married for the last seven years, and I believe his marriage is to take place as soon as this picture is finished. I do not think that the dilatoriness about the picture argues any great haste to be married.

On the twentieth at nine in the morning the Mayor again called for us to go and see some schools. We visited three, one for girls, the other two for boys, all public schools. The number of the public schools in Boston is, according to the report of the School Committees for 1826, seventy-four, and the private ones added to that make two hundred and fourteen. The education in this State is supported by a tax, a poll tax I believe it is called, but at all events each man pays according to his property, so that the man who pays but one dollar a year has the right to send his children to the same schools as he who pays fifty dollars. To Basil there appears to be a certain degree of dependence in this system, and he has many tough arguments with the upholders of it who are with very few exceptions every member of the community. The rich in many cases send their children to private schools where they have high prices, besides their share in the tax for the maintenance of public schools. Certainly education cannot possibly be more diffused than in this country, and a more sober, sedate steady set of people cannot be found, too much so indeed for mirth, and the few holidays that they had are gradually falling into disuse. I believe that the fact is that they do not choose to lose so much time in play that might be spent in making money.

After we had been to the schools Basil went to the hospital to witness what the surgeons call "a great operation." I, in the meantime, drove over to Charlestown taking Eliza with me that I might compare her with Commodore Morris's little boy, just ten days younger than herself, but he was so unwell that he could not hold up his head. I should tell you of a little adventure that Miss Eliza chalked out for herself that morning. Mrs. Cownie was packing in my bedroom and Eliza amusing herself by running about and keeping up an animated conversation with her companion as usual, when all at once her little voice ceased and Mrs. Cownie looking up found that she had vanished. Mrs. Cownie went into our sitting room, she was not there; into the public room, but neither was there any trace of her there; into the butler's pantry, no one had seen or heard of her; so then Mrs. Cownie proceeded downstairs, and seated on the second step outside the door she found the little lady talking with much earnestness to a boy who stood opposite her at a respectful distance. Only think what a thing it would have been if someone had stolen her!

Yesterday the Ticknors invited us to sup with them. The fashion here is the same that it was in Edinburgh some forty years ago, when the Sunday suppers that you and I have heard so much of from Mama were so common. I believe there at that time as here now people dined between services at one o'clock. Many families here have a party regularly every Sunday evening, the Ticknors always have. Last night there happened to be only two gentlemen besides ourselves.

This morning I went with Basil to the Lunatic Asylum. I had great repugnance to the thoughts of going and it required a considerable struggle to make up my mind to it, but I thought it was foolish to give way to the feeling and I am very glad I overcame it. It is at Charlestown in an airy situation and so comfortable and nice in every respect that it was quite gratifying to see it. My dislike to visit such an establishment has quite vanished, which it never would have done had I continued to give way to my former feelings. So ends our first visit to Boston. We have met with a great deal of kindness here, but that indeed we find everywhere, it would be difficult to say where most.

PROVIDENCE, R. I., OCTOBER 23:—We left Boston this morning at eight o'clock. The weather for two days had been very surly and cold, and all last night the rain fell in such torrents that we almost doubted the practicability of setting out to-day should the same bad weather continue. This morning, however, the sun broke out most cheeringly, and we had a mild tho' a very blustering day for our journey of forty-two miles, which we made out by three o'clock, tho' we stopped at Pawtucket to look over the bridge at a very respectable fall of the river of that name and we also walked thro' one of the numerous cotton manufactures established at that place. The country which we passed through to-day is of the same character as the rest of the New England States that we have seen, "hard land," as some people call it, I suppose in ridicule, as it is neither more nor less than good, honest rocks and stones. As one method of clearing their fields of the stones they make stone fences between them instead of wooden ones, just Scotch dykes, but it must be a sad prospect for a farmer to look upon such land. The rain has sadly spoilt the beauty of the autumnal foliage, which instead of the bright hues it had a few weeks since is now mostly of a brown tinge. Many of the trees are entirely stripped, and there is altogether an appearance of winter much greater than we are accustomed to at so early a season. The journey from here to Hartford, our next stopping place, is seventy-two miles. We wished to get an "Extra" to carry us on there and to go part of the way after dinner to-day, but there were so many difficulties in the way of both these wishes that we have been obliged to give up not the wish, but the practice. First of all, the Stage Proprietor had the want of conscience to ask thirty-six dollars for an "Extra." Then, even if we had been willing to give this exorbitant sum there was no possibility of our proceeding further to-night owing to the want of horses, and when we did go even by "Extra," there was no way of going except the whole distance in one day. This was as bad as going by the public stage, by which we could be transported for twelve dollars (four apiece). So after abusing the people for throwing so many difficulties in our way and wishing to overreach strangers, which perhaps after all they did not, we finally determined upon the economical plan and for once taking our chance of a long day of discomfort in a crowded stage. We are to start at five o'clock, and in preparation for this Miss Eliza is going to bed with half her clothes on, as she is to be lifted from her bed into the Stage. What inclined us to suppose that people were cheating us about the Stage was that we had met with treatment of the kind in the boarding house at Boston, when the bill was sent in on very different terms from the agreement we had made when we arrived, and this put us out of humour with the people in general. I have no doubt that many shop keepers in England cheat abundantly, but I do not think there is the same amount of imposition practised by respectable persons in their own calling as is to be met with here.

HARTFORD, OCTOBER 24:—Now that we are seated beside a comfortable fire in a blazing parlour it is all very well to have saved four and twenty dollars, but a more uncomfortable day I have rarely passed. We were roused this morning before four o'clock, for, as usual, the Stage was ready to start considerably before the time named, and at a quarter before five we were off. It was still quite dark, but by the light of the candle which was held for us to find our way into the Stage by, we discovered a lady seated in the corner of one seat, and there followed us a gentleman. I ought to have mentioned that Eliza had been awoke some time previous to our getting up by the noise of various stages coming in and going out. This being the case she was dressed before starting, and I was rather disconcerted at seeing her awake so early. However, in five minutes she was sound asleep again, and her repose continued until we reached Scituate, fifteen miles. Here we breakfasted. We had but a poor meal and no time to eat it for it was not ready till twenty minutes after we arrived, and in half an hour the driver was all impatience to be off. At Scituate we picked up an additional passenger, a labouring man, who discoursed on the sobriety of the people in this country, at the same time emitting fumes of whisky and gin that contradicted his assertions at least in one instance, but I suspect him to be one of that class of persons who are never sober. He kept talking too constantly, and each time that Eliza shut her eyes she was disturbed by some new remark from our talkative companion. At length at the end of a fourteen mile stage, Brooklyn, we were relieved of his company which we exchanged for that of a very quiet mulatto girl, and with this party we jogged on another fourteen miles to Wyndham where we found dinner. When we again set forth we found to our dismay that we had the full complement of passengers, nine inside, that is to say three on each seat. This is crowded to a degree that you can form no conception of, and had not one of the ladies left us after about ten miles, I know not what poor Eliza would have done, but the vacancy allowed her a little elbow and toe room, and a more delighted child I never saw than when she was relieved from the thraldom of a confinement little short of the Black Hole of Calcutta. Not that the climate partook of that, for it was bitter cold the whole day. We again changed horses at Coventry, and about eight o'clock, that is to say about fifteen hours from starting, we actually accomplished the seventy-two miles I told you of. You must bear in mind that it is in the Mail we have travelled to-day so that one would think that if celerity of moving is to be met with anywhere in this country it must be by this conveyance. We had several letter bags to deliver, and the driver bestowed ten or fifteen minutes upon what might have been done in as many seconds. They made many other stops besides, and the whole journey was not unlike some of Sir Walter Scott's descriptions of a stage coach in Scotland some fifty or sixty years ago, the "High Flyer" in the *Antiquary* for instance, and quite as many disasters occur to the harness and traces. Eliza's patience was fast taking wing before we reached Hartford, and had she not fallen asleep I do not know what we should have done, for the poor thing in spite of having more room than the other passengers was sadly squeezed as we had shifted into a fresh coach infinitely narrower than some of the others we had travelled in, in the course of the day, for we were in no fewer than three coaches.

HARTFORD, OCTOBER 25:—We have seen a great deal that is very interesting to-day, three establishments differing very much in their nature but each as nearly perfect of its kind I should think as possible. We determined to give the whole of this day to Hartford, and so we did not hurry ourselves in the morning, and after breakfasting at a reasonable hour and writing for some time we set off at eleven o'clock to the State Prison at Weathersfield. It is not yet completed, but there are about fifty convicts in it, and the arrangement and management are admirable. The discipline is on the same plan as that at Auburn and Sing Sing, and Mr. Pilsbury, the warden, seems to have his heart as completely in the business as Captain Lynd at Sing Sing. We got to Weathersfield just before the prisoners went to dinner and had an opportunity of seeing the perfect order attendant upon each manoeuvre. When the prison is complete it is not intended that visitors shall at any time have access where the convicts can see them, but they are to be taken to a passage behind the workshop where through slits in the wall strangers will be able to see without being seen. The intention of those slits is that superintendents should be able to have constant watch over those employed in the shops. The prisoners know this, and as they cannot possibly form a guess as to when they are or are not overlooked they are obliged to be constantly diligent. There is also an overseer constantly in each shop. Round the prison there is a high wall which also encloses a court, and in the court a man with a loaded gun is stationed. They have each a separate cell at night, and in their cells they also take their food. The next place we went to was of a very different character, the Asylum for the Deaf and Dumb. The head teacher, **Mr.** Gallaudet, went both to London and Edinburgh, where he met with but little cordiality. There seemed to be a jealousy of letting a foreigner into their secret, so he went next to Paris, and there he was taken at once into the Abbé Sicard's school, got all the information and instruction he wished, and brought out with him a young man who had been educated there to be one of the teachers at this institution. Four of the teachers are deaf and dumb, the other five have all their faculties. This happened to be the last day of vacation, so that the schools were not in operation, but most of the pupils had returned, and a more cheerful or more intelligent looking group I never saw. Mr. Gallaudet brought three of the girls and two boys into the school room to give us a specimen of their advancement. One of the young men, nineteen years old, is now a teacher. He is uncommonly intelligent and has read a great deal. There was no trick, nothing got up in the exhibition. We wrote down questions on the slate and they answered them, sometimes off hand, at other times they required a little reflection. We then wrote a word, an adjective, or adverb, or any part of speech we chose which they brought in in a sentence and always so as to show that they understood the meaning perfectly. There was generally a great deal of imagination in the form of their replies. The system of signs is very quick. They use the alphabet very little and entirely with one hand. One poor girl we saw who is deaf, dumb, and blind, of course she cannot be taught much, but I saw her knit and thread a needle. They do not teach their pupils to speak, in which I think they show their sense, for nothing can be more unearthly than the sound made by those who have lost the organ of hearing by which to modulate their voices. At first when they go to the Institution the children are in the habit of making disagreeable sounds, but the masters check them immediately, and except for one boy who had been there a very short time I did not hear a single sound except a hearty laugh, which had nothing strange in it. Mr. Gallaudet married one of his own pupils and Mr. Clerc, the teacher who came from France, also married a deaf and dumb person. He was extremely anxious to ascertain after the birth of his eldest child whether it heard, and it was sometime before they could persuade him that it did. He has since had two more equally gifted. Having gone through his own hobby Mr. Gallaudet next asked us if we would not go to the Retreat, the asylum for the insane, which is also particularly well conducted. We went there, accordingly, and were fortunate in finding the physician, Dr. Tod, who by the by is almost insane upon the subject, at home. His treatment of his patients is very different from that generally followed. Unless the person is in a state not to listen to anything, he tells him why he is sent there, that he is mad, and sent to be cured. He treats them all with the most perfect frankness, never resorts to confinement so long as the patient can be at large with safety to himself and others, provides amusement and occupation for them, and to those whom he thinks it will benefit carries strangers to visit them in their sitting room, where they have the companionship of those in an equal state of convalescence with themselves. The result of this system has been hitherto the cure of ninety-five persons out of a hundred. This appears a great many, but it is to be hoped that there will be no relapses, for as yet the establishment has only existed three years. It was delightful to see the three men at the head of those three institutions, each equally enthusiastic in his own department. Mr. Pilsbury at Weathersfield seemed to have no thought but for the improvement of prison discipline and reformation of prisoners; Mr. Gallaudet's whole soul is wrapped up in the sharpening of the remaining faculties of his interesting charges; whilst Dr. Tod when speaking of the happy effects produced on the insane by gentle treatment, lashes up and kindles into a degree of enthusiasm which might lead one to think he may one day be a fit subject for his own experiments, especially when we are told that his father and only sister have both been mad and many other relations more or less deranged. Imagination carries one a great way while visiting such places. At the prison I saw crime in every countenance though the prisoners proved often to be very trustworthy keepers. At the

Deaf and Dumb I started when I heard anyone speak, and at the Retreat (having the first impression of the prison still on my mind) I wondered to see the women allowed to sit together and talk, forgetting that solitary confinement was not necessary there as a punishment.

NEW HAVEN, OCTOBER 26:—I have not much to say of this day's operations altho' we visited two sights, if I may call them so, in the course of our journey of thirty-nine miles. We left Hartford at a quarter past nine and after a drive of fifteen miles reached Middletown. Here there is a military college on the same plan as West Point but a private institution not patronized by the government as the one at West Point is. Near Middletown also there is a manufactory of arms where there is a new method of turning gun stocks. It was to see this that we went, but we had not calculated very well and reached Mr. North's factory at twelve o'clock, just when the men had ceased to work and gone to dinner. Basil saw the machine and said he understood it perfectly even altho' it was not at work, but I cannot say I did as much, so you are saved a description from me at least. We then returned back by the way of Captain Partridge's Military School. He was from home but we saw one of the instructors and here also, as the young men were just going to dinner, we saw them march to their meal. They may be admirably instructed in Classics, Philosophy, and all the "Ometries" that were or were not heard of, for of some mentioned in the prospectus I certainly never before heard, but in those branches I am not qualified to judge. But I can judge of their manners and appearance and I must say that those are sadly backward. They all walk with a slouch and with their hands in their breeches' pockets. The carvers instead of preparing the meat neatly actually tear it in lumps as if it were for dogs not men, but indeed as far as I have yet seen no American, male or female, has the smallest idea of how to carve. They helped themselves to butter, stewed onions, salt, or potatoes, all with their own nasty knives, with which the moment before they had been eating, and spit to the right and left during their meal. They are a nasty people, the Americans, at table; there is no denying that fact. But altho' they have yet much to learn in the science of good manners there is a great deal to admire and praise in their country, and they have many admirable institutions which would do honour to any country. We dined at Middletown and by six o'clock reached New Haven. At the first inn where we stopped we could not gain admittance, but we are likely to be very comfortable here by the help of blazing fires, for it is bitterly cold. Most persons in travelling from Boston to New York take steamboat at Providence, some at Hartford, but few come on to New Haven. We, however, on many accounts have no great fancy for steam or for water conveyance of any kind, and we are still undecided whether we shall proceed from hence by land or steam. By steam, it is but an affair of ten hours, so I dare say we shall go that way.

OCTOBER 27 :—The greater part of our occupations to-day have been of a very different nature from what they were at Hartford but equally interesting in their own way. I do not know whether I mentioned to you our having seen Professor Silliman when he passed through Albany. He is one of the professors of Yale College in New Haven, and his Scientific Journal is well known in England. Basil sent this morning to let him know that we were here, but as he was longer of coming than we expected we supposed there was some mistake and set off to his house about three-quarters of a mile distant. As usually happens when people act impatiently we missed our man, he having set out by a different route to go to us. However, as it was a bitterly cold morning we sat with Mrs. Silliman and her daughters for more than half an hour, taking in a good supply of heat to fortify us against the cutting wind, and just as we were again losing patience the master of the house returned. The first thing he took us to see was the grave yard, as they call their burying grounds in America. They cannot in fact call them Church yards, for I do not in fact ever remember to have seen such a place attached to the Church. This grave yard is the neatest and most cheerful looking I have seen, at the same time quite free from ornament that would be out of place with the purpose to which it is appointed. It covers twenty acres of ground and is divided into streets along which the relations attending a funeral may drive. The lot belonging to each family is staked out with little poles, and there were many very neat little monuments. Talking of grave yards leads me to mention what I have observed of the careless way in which people in this country speak of their dead relatives. Now to-day, for instance, Mr. Silliman said in passing one part where four little stones were ranged alongside of each other, "There are some of my family. I had the misfortune to bury four of them." The sight of the little graves was sufficiently affecting to me, even altho' those who occupied them were nothing to me, but the father gave the information as if he had been pointing out beds of cabbages or cauliflowers, and I mention this as the more extraordinary because he is a man of taste, and good feeling generally accompanies good taste I think. In like manner you hear gentlemen talk carelessly of their dead wives, first or second, and widowers constantly joke about their being candidates for matrimony. I know innumerable instances of this. Now I do know that people marry for a second time in England and are not ashamed of doing so, of course, but I don't think one hears gentlemen in society talking of their first wife as if she were in the next room, whilst she is snug in her grave. From the graveyard we went to Yale College. The afternoon, that is to say from twelve o'clock, is a holiday, so there was nothing doing in the way of lecturing except by the Professor of Theology, who we found discoursing to his pupils on the doctrine of the Trinity, a very fit subject for me who have been lately going astray amongst the Unitarians. We saw all the class rooms and every part of the building, but there was nothing of peculiar interest in them. By this time the very Gothic dinner hour of one had arrived. We should not have minded skipping it, but as our *cicerone* had to go home to his dinner we returned to ours, which was gobbled after the usual American fashion so that by two when Mr.

Silliman came in his carriage for us we had finished. We went directly to the Cabinet of Mineralogy. We might have spent a great deal of time there but as daylight is now short we were obliged to be economical of it and in half an hour proceeded to a very beautiful crag—I am told geologically like Salisbury Crags[1]—and certainly resembling them to an unscientific, as much as possible both in shape and colour. We clambered up amongst the rocks, and from the top had a beautiful view on one side of Long Island Sound and on the other of the very prettily diversified country of hill and dale.

Our next visit was to a place of considerable interest, "the Regicide's Cave", so called, because it was a place of concealment for many years to those who sat in judgement and condemned King Charles I. They were afterwards in Cromwell's army and made their escape on the restoration of King Charles II. Their names were Goffe, Whally, and Dickswell. This place, New Haven, being originally settled by a party of very democratic London merchants, they readily lent their aid towards the concealment of those men. Only a few persons knew that the regicides were amongst them. Mr. Davenport, the clergyman, was one of those, and sometimes by his texts gave warning to the friends of the fugitives that the enemy were at hand, for several times the King's messengers came in pursuit of them, but they always managed to elude their search either by returning to the cave I mentioned, or if still more hotly pursued, they made their escape to the mountain which we had previously been to. On one occasion when the clergyman knew that the messengers were at hand he chose for his text: "Betray not the fugitive, betray not him that trusteth in thee," which was quite sufficient notice of the danger. There is a story current that at Hadley, a village between Northampton and Amherst and through which we passed, the inhabitants were upon one occasion attacked by the Indians and almost overwhelmed by them when suddenly there appeared amongst them a venerable looking man who led them on, and they in their turn completely defeated the Indians. Their

[1] Edinburgh.

leader was one of the regicides, whose knowledge of military matters enabled him to be of so much use, but as soon as the end was attained he disappeared. All the three died peaceably in this country. The grave of one of them is in the Green within two hundred yards of the house from whence I now write. The cave scarcely deserves to be so called; it is merely a place where the rock overhangs very much, and it is said that in front there was a stone wall, but at all events a thick forest surrounded it, and there was not then as there is now, a nice path leading to it, so that it was quite sufficiently secluded. Professor Silliman was quite as indefatigable in leading as we were in following, so we drove on from the cave to another crag similar to the one we had first visited. This we did not mount but walked along the foot of it by the side of a pretty little stream to a manufactory of gun stocks and arms. But by this time it was six o'clock, the sun had set, and, altho' the moon shone bright, her light was not sufficient to illuminate the darkness of a manufacturing establishment, and we could just discern the large wheels made of iron instead of wood as is generally the case, and which looked so light that it seemed almost fit for a toy. We summed up our evening's excursion with drinking tea with Mrs. Silliman, and by eight o'clock we were glad to get home to scribble as usual.

ON BOARD THE STEAMBOAT *United States* IN LONG ISLAND SOUND, OCTOBER 29:—I am going to try whether writing will make me forget the disagreeable little kicks the steamboat has in spite of smooth water and no wind. Indeed, we could not possibly have had a more favourable day for our voyage, but still the sea is the sea whatever name it may go by, and this sound is a large arm of it. Yesterday was so calm and warm compared with the weather we have had of late that we determined to go to New York by water instead of land, which would have been the choice between great discomfort and night travelling by the public stage, or an exorbitant overcharge for an extra, and having no wind and the tide in our favour we hope to reach New York before dark.

NEW YORK, OCTOBER 31 :—We accomplished our voyage by
seven o'clock on the evening of the twenty-ninth. We passed
through Hell Gate at slack tide so that there was none of that com-
motion which so terrified the Dutchmen mentioned in *Knickerbocker's History of New York*. We had written to Mr. Dixon,
one of our companions on the *Florida,* to take lodgings for us in
a boarding house which we named. He could not get them there
so secured them for us on the opposite side of the way. Here we
spent the night of the twenty-ninth but discovered in that time
that we had quite mistaken the style of the house we named, which
turned out to be a large, crowded place, and morning found us
resolved to shift our quarters and go to Mrs. Wilkinson's, an English woman, who does not take more than ten or twelve. Accordingly, the moment we had swallowed breakfast yesterday we set
out to Mrs. Wilkinson's, and in half an hour had all arranged, and
right glad we are to find ourselves in a quiet place with only English
people. We feel as if we had returned home in coming to New
York, and all the strange dreamy feeling that we had so strongly
during our first visit has given way to the most perfect familiarity
with all the objects that surround us. There is so great an uncertainty over our plans at present that I will not attempt to tell what
we will do next, in fact we do not know.

Believe me ever affectionately yours

MARGARET HALL.

LETTER IX

NEW YORK

The novelty of New York had passed off, and the second visit was sedate enough, though they arrived on the eve of the Election at which Jackson was chosen President. Colonel Aaron Burr calls on Mrs. Hall to renew an acquaintance made in Scotland. She sees "a magnificent fire," meets Judge Benson, the only man in America to wear mourning for George III, hears Emmett speak in Court, gets to know Chancellor Kent, visits the Lunatic Asylum at Bloomingdale and the Navy Yard at Brooklyn. A great deal of dining out and tea drinking punctuate this month spent in studying New York and its ways.

NEW YORK, November 3, 1827.

MY DEAREST JANE,

Yesterday morning the servant came to tell me there was a gentleman in the drawing room who wished to see either Captain Hall or myself. I went down accordingly and the moment I saw him recognised Colonel Aaron Burr, altho' it is nineteen years since I saw him. I do not know whether you recollect him. He dined one day at my grandmother's, but I was not aware then of the conspicuous part he had played, a few years previous to his visit to Scotland, in this country. I think he was at one time Vice-President, at all events he was within an ace of being President. Upon one election for President none of the candidates for that office had the majority of votes of the electors. It was, therefore, referred to the House of Assembly who balloted for Burr and Jefferson. Thirty-seven times the ballot was equal for each, but at length it was carried by one in favour of Mr. Jefferson. He was afterwards suspected of treasonable purposes and of a wish to subvert the government, and finally he destroyed the little reputation he had

118

left by killing General Alexander Hamilton in a duel. It was after that he went to Europe. From being a man of considerable consequence he has sunk into the utmost insignificance, and as the insignificance arises from contempt felt for his character and conduct I should not think his feelings at all enviable. Basil, however, who has no notion of being withheld from making the acquaintance of a remarkable man merely because he is a blackguard got introduced to him and told him that I had a perfect recollection of having seen him, and he came to call accordingly. I dare say it is many a day since he has had his acquaintance sought.

NOVEMBER 8:—I have laid aside my journal for many more days than is my habit of late, and this is all the worse because of the want of incident to mark the different days.

We had a visit from Mr. Seth Hunt, a gentleman who has salt mines in the State of Alabama and who has travelled much in those southern countries, and he has given us the information about travelling there that we have long been in search of, for those States are wonderfully little known in this Northern part of the country, and we have in vain sought for a man competent to give us the advice we wanted.

I had a note from Mrs. David Colden saying that as the day was so fine they wished much to carry us to Mr. Wilkes's little cottage in the country. Accordingly, at one o'clock she and Mr. Wilkes came in the open carriage which the warmth of the day made very agreeable, for the climate here is more changeable than that of England, and a summer day often follows one like the depth of winter. Woodlawn is the name of Mr. Wilkes's place; it is at Bloomingdale, four miles from New York and close to the Hudson, on the banks of which they have seats placed where they can have views of that magnificent river both up and down. It must be a lovely, little place in summer, for even the dead, dirty look which November gives to everything could not do away the beauty of it. We took Eliza with us and she either slept on the sofa or toddled about on the lawn whilst Basil made a *camera lucida* sketch of the house. We drank tea at Mr. Colden's that evening, as we so often do either there or at Mr. Wilkes's, working and talking, sometimes there are a few people there and at other times no one but ourselves, but it is always pleasant, they are themselves so agreeable and so kind.

On Sunday, we went to Grace Church and were amused to find how much we have become habituated to the varieties inserted in the Litany according to the will and taste of the officiating clergyman at each different church. When we first arrived in New York we were quite teased by the choppings and changings introduced into the services, but during the last six months we have heard so many more mangled services that this one at New York seemed quite like an old friend when compared with them. We set off in the evening between seven and eight to go to the African Methodist Chapel, but unfortunately we were too late. The sermon was over and they were proceeding to Church business. However, perhaps there was no great misfortune in the case, for the heat was intolerable, and if a crowd of whites is disagreeable, a crowd of blacks is some hundred degrees worse. On Monday, as Basil was walking along the street, he met our old friend Captain King of the Grenville Canal and with him Mr. Pooley of the Engineers who is employed at the Rideau Canal. We walked a little along Broadway with them, but Captain King did not seem at all at ease in his old jacket and hat beside me in my beautiful Polish cloak, and I rather think was glad to cut the connection. Sam Hay has been here some weeks. He talks of going home in May but is to come out again I believe. The sixth we were at our old task of paying visits, tho' we have done but little of this duty since we came to New York for we have only called on those few who have found us out, and there is no sort of gaiety going on at present. People are thinking of nothing but elections, but they all finished yesterday. We drank tea at Mrs. Colden's and met there Mr. and Mrs. Cary and Miss Perkins, daughter of Colonel Perkins at Boston. Yesterday it rained cats and dogs, as the saying is, without one moment's intermission. I wrote letters till dinner time for the day's packet. Basil dined with Chancellor Kent, as he is still called, altho' he is no longer on the bench, having reached the proscribed age of sixty beyond which no man can remain on the bench of the State of New York. I was not invited. Indeed I suspect ladies are seldom included in dinner invitations in this ungallant place. Mr. Proctor, a lodger here, told me that many of the ladies of the first families in New York have never dined out. I cannot say I have any such want of attention to complain of, but I fancy I owe that to being a stranger, and that were I to become less of one I should be allowed to remain at home, where I suspect Basil would remain too, for he has no great fancy for this plan of separating.

NOVEMBER 9:—We dined yesterday at Mrs. Murray's, at least it is her house, but the old lady does not make her appearance, and the honours are done by her two daughters, elderly maiden ladies approaching to fifty, her son, and his wife, for they all live together as is so common in America. The Miss Murrays are the first ladies of their age whom I have seen unmarried in this country; it is very rare indeed to see an unmarried woman above five and twenty. There was nothing very characteristic about the dinner except one little trait which Basil remarked. Miss Murray, who sat at the head of the table, sent some pudding to a gentleman who she thought asked for it, but he said no, he did not wish for pudding, it was custard he had sent for, so without more ado, Miss Murray tumbled the pudding back into the dish and put the custard on the same plate. Handing your own plate across the table is quite common, indeed how can it be otherwise where as yesterday there were but two servants to wait on sixteen persons?

NOVEMBER 11:—At length I have seen a fire, and a most magnificent one it was. Last night between nine and ten o'clock the Church bells began to ring as they always do when a fire breaks out. Basil and I were seated snugly in our own room beside a comfortable fire, rendered all the more agreeable by the intense frost that made its way into the house and was to be felt the moment one got into the passage. Such being the case I think we should have been inclined to let the bells ring on and have taken no heed had not Mrs. Cownie whose room is very near the front of the house run up to tell us that she thought the fire was very near us, as many of the engines were running past the house. This induced us to go down to the door, and there we saw the light shining most brilliantly upon the houses in Broadway. I ran for my bonnet and cloak, and off we set in pursuit of the fire, which altho' no great distance proved to be much further than we imagined from the bright light that spread around. When we got in sight of it I was astonished by the magnificence, indeed I am told by those who are accustomed to see fires in this inflammable city that I was in very great luck in the spectacle I witnessed. There were four houses destroyed. They burnt as if they had been made of paper, and the water of the numerous engines played upon it without having the smallest effect. Basil stood groaning because they had not the triangle now used in Edinburgh to throw water from the top with which, he says, he would have undertaken to have saved all except the first house. We staid till eleven o'clock and then left the flames raging.

On the evening of the ninth we had a visit from Judge Benson, an old man of fourscore and upwards, whose faculties are still as entire as they could have been at sixty, and he does not at all approve of the law of the State which puts a man off the bench at so early an age. He told us that he believes he is the only man now alive in this State who wore mourning for George III, his father having been a steady loyalist. We had been in the morning with the elder Mrs. Colden to the Lunatic Asylum at Bloomingdale, six miles from town, and were much gratified by the arrangements there. The treatment is the same as at the Retreat at Hartford in Connecticut. There are defects in the house which cost upwards of four hundred thousand dollars, a great part of which was expended on ornament. It was built by the Quakers, whom Mr. Colden says he has invariably observed spend a great deal on ornamenting whatever they undertake, being interdicted from the use of it on their own persons, they are anxious to bestow it on buildings or books or any other matter they take in hand. The principal defects in the Retreat at Bloomingdale are that if one patient is noisy he is heard by all the others, and there is no private accommodation for the sick, so that if a patient dies the next who occupies the room is frightened by the stories told him by the others of the recent death which has taken place there. The matron who takes charge of the females, an elderly Quakeress, seems to be admirably adapted for her situation.

NOVEMBER 12:—An Englishman might hang himself in New York to-day with quite as much reason as in England. It is as gloomy and foggy as in London. No, not quite, for I begin to feel what I used to laugh at Basil for expressing, that I shall dearly love a London fog, because it is so true an indication of being in London. We begin to feel it is time to be off to the South as we wish to escape the frost and snow of this Northern climate. There has been snow at Albany, which is only one hundred and forty-five miles distant, and to judge by the temperature our turn is not far off.

After tea hearing that some Iroquois Indians were to exhibit we went to see them but were grievously disappointed, and had no hesitation in pronouncing that they were imposters and not Indians at all so we soon left them, and it was after our return from this exhibition that the alarm of fire again roused us out of our comfortable room.

Yesterday we went over to the Navy Yard in Brooklyn on Long Island to call upon Commodore Chaunsey; he had called upon us some days before, but there was no Mrs. Chaunsey's card. However, we took it for granted that there must be a Mrs. Chaunsey, as every American is married, so we went boldly on, asked for the Commodore and being shown into the room found him surrounded by Naval Officers and two ladies whom he introduced to us as his wife and daughter. The flag lieutenant, as in duty bound, was deep in flirtation with the young lady, as Eliza will be some twenty years hence I doubt not, when Basil is the gouty old admiral we have so often talked of.

NOVEMBER 14:—Yesterday we promised the elder Mrs. Colden to attend an exhibition of the Deaf and Dumb on purpose to collect money for that institution, in which she takes great interest. We went at seven in the evening, accordingly, to the City Hotel where the meeting was to be held, but on entering the large room found all dark and soon learnt that in consequence of the bad weather the meeting was postponed for a week. As we were equipped for going out at any rate we resolved not to have all our trouble for nothing, so we turned round and walked off to Mr. Wilkes's where we found as usual a cheerful party assembled round the work table, and there we sat till past ten o'clock. We are living so very quietly at present that I feel as if I had nothing to say. The novelty of New York has entirely passed off with us, and we sit at home as sedate as if we had been here all our lives. We shall be on the move again in the course of next week, and then I shall have something to tell you, as we shall once more be in the midst of new scenes and with quite a different style of persons, we are led to expect, from those in New York.

NOVEMBER 18:—A great sensation has been caused today by the sudden and alarming illness of Mr. Emmett, whose name was familiar to most people, at least his brother's unfortunate fate was. After the failure of their enterprise and some years of imprisonment, this one was let off and came to the United States in 1804, and here he has remained ever since in great practise and high repute at the bar. He was much esteemed too in private life, and much anxiety was felt and expressed on hearing of his seizure in court on the fourteenth with apoplexy. At eleven o'clock the same night he died. We consider ourselves fortunate in having heard him speak in court only five days previous to his death, not on any very interesting subject, but still it is something to have heard him.

The fifteenth we dined at Mr. Wilkes's to meet Chancellor Kent, also Mr. de Rham, a great friend of their's, and Mr. and Mrs. Hamilton Wilkes, the youngest son, and wife, and we went to drink tea at Mrs. Henry Wilkes's with a large family party. Mr. Henry Wilkes is nephew to Mr. Wilkes of Hudson Square and brother to young Charles Wilkes of the U. S. Navy. Mr. and Mrs. David Colden and Mr. and Miss Wilkes were also there, and we had a very merry work table, meeting in this way in the evening which is very common with the Wilkes's and all their set. I believe it is so with others also, but we are not so intimate anywhere else. Their tea tables and work tables are quite after the fashion of those at home, indeed that style of society prevails much more than with us, owing to the earlier hours. They are very pleasing young women, those who compose the little circle that we frequent, not particularly cultivated, but lively and chatty, taking very little part and seemingly not much interest in the settlement discussions which take place between Basil and the gentlemen on American politics and manners. There is at all times a great separation between the ladies and the gentlemen in society here, less I think with our particular friends in New York than elsewhere, but still it always exists more or less. To-day, the eighteenth, after hearing Bishop Hobart preach at Trinity Church, we went to call at Colonel Barclay's and at last succeeded in seeing him and Mrs. Barclay, who remembered very well the little Basil they were kind to some three or four and twenty years ago, tho' I cannot suppose that they recognise in the grey-haired, bald-headed man, the boy who used to be so much at their house.

NOVEMBER 21 :—I took Eliza on the nineteenth to see Colonel and Mrs. Barclay. The old lady made much of her and was delighted to see her. Her daughter, Mrs. Parsons, (who has not seen Basil for three and twenty years) said that Eliza reminded her very much of him, which I can understand, as the picture I have seen of him done when he was a midshipman has the same chubby broad face that she has now. Mrs. Barclay says that she remembers thinking it such a pity that such a nice, little fellow should be on board a ship, exposed to all the privations and discomforts to be there met with. He was the least of all the boys that used to visit them from his ship, and "little Hall" was a great pet with them, but I don't know that he was the youngest, for I believe he was uncommonly short for his age. His daughter certainly is not so. She is growing very fast, as is to be seen from her petticoats. She is improving in her understanding too, for she has a most perfect idea of what being naughty and being punished is, for the other day she took her wooden dog and put him in the corner, where, having left him for a minute, she returned to him saying, "good doddie? doddie good?" and relieved him from his disgrace. Talking of disgrace, do you know we have somehow or other deeply offended the good people of Boston, tho' how, why, or wherefore we are at a loss to discover, further than that Basil got very angry with and most heartily scolded the woman of the boarding house for trying to impose upon us by making out a bill nearly twice as high as that we had bargained for. It is always wrong to get angry even where there is cause. There is no denying that fact, and I don't pretend to justify it nor does Basil, but I call you and all those to whom I wrote from Boston to witness whether I did not write more favourably of the place, people, manners, customs, and so on, than of any other place or persons that we have visited since we came to this country. But there is no mistake in the impression in England that the Americans are the most inordinately vain people. Their capacity for swallowing praise far exceeds anything I could have imagined, and they are so much in the habit of lauding themselves and really thinking themselves faultless that they do not know how to bear censure. We have heard of the offence we gave at Boston from more than one source. Our wish to return to Boston which was whilst we were there very great has much diminished since we have learnt how little satisfaction we gave there.

We talk of going from here on the twenty-sixth but it will be some days before we reach Philadelphia as we mean to pay at least one visit on the way. That one is to Joseph Bonaparte, formerly King of Spain, who has for some years resided in this country under the name of the Count de Survilliers. His daughter married her cousin Charles, the son of Lucien Bonaparte, and they also live in America, calling themselves the Prince and Princess de Musignano. This is absurd enough, but they may all be sufficiently worth seeing in spite of the folly and weakness which prompts them to retain shadows of that rank to which they were never entitled. We are told that Joseph's household still accosts him as royal. We shall see.

NOVEMBER 22:—We had quite a fête at old Colonel Barclay's last night, I believe they have not had so gay a party since before they lost their son, poor people. We were invited to tea at the very primitive hour of six and found a large circle, altho' there were none present except Miss de Lancy and ourselves who did not stand in the relation of son or daughter, either by blood or law, or else of grandchild. There were three sons with their wives, a daughter with her husband, two granddaughters, and a grandson. The entertainment was a succession of trays, ice and coffee, then, creams and jellies, thirdly, preserves of various sorts, fourthly, hot whisky punch, next, pickled oysters and collared port, and to conclude, porter. How stingy the Americans must think the refreshments provided at parties in England.

NOVEMBER 23:—Eliza and I dined yesterday at Mr. Wilkes's while Basil made one of a male party at General Gaines's, a gentleman on whom he went to call because he understood that he was one of those most likely to give us information relative to things in the South. He has been very obliging indeed in doing so.

Believe me, ever affectionately yours,

MARGARET HALL.

LETTER X

A tasteful dinner with Mr. and Mrs. William Astor concluded the Halls' social activities in New York. They take steamboat for New Brunswick, sleep there, and drive to Bordentown to call on the ex-King of Spain, Joseph Bonaparte, who was living at Point Breeze under the name of the Comte de Survilliers. Prince de Musignano, son of Lucien Bonaparte, greeted them; he had married his cousin, the daughter of Joseph Bonaparte and had a boy of three years old, who took a great fancy to Eliza and gave her a doll. Mrs. Hall having lived in Spain when Joseph was King, was intensely interested in him and surprised to find that "acting a conspicuous part on the stage of Royalty" had not given him perfect ease of manner. They sat with the family for an hour, went back to their hotel to dress, and returned to eat a perfect French dinner with the exiles. Next day they moved to Miss Boyd's boarding-house on Chestnut Street, Philadelphia.

NEW YORK, November 26, 1827.

MY DEAREST JANE,

We paid a visit to-day which has made me quite melancholy, although perhaps the person for whom my commiseration is excited does not consider herself an object of pity as I do. Mrs. Clement Moore is the lady whose situation has called forth my pity. She is an Englishwoman by birth, and I pity an Englishwoman married to an American much more than if she had made choice of any other country whatever for her home. The continent of Europe is so much nearer home that the separation does not seem so entire as where this great Atlantic flows between the two countries, and in America there is just that sort of resemblance to England which is sufficient to remind one constantly of the inferiority. You must have seen by now that our admiration or approbation of America has not increased upon acquaintance, far from it, and of late it has gone down very fast. Not one of you who sit at home in your easy chairs know one half of the value of the country you belong to. Our friends here, the Coldens and the Wilkes's, are quite aware that our good opinion of their country has not increased. They regret it, and I dare say think us wrong, but it is much better they should be aware of the true state of the case than that they should have reason to say by and by that here we expressed ourselves one way and when we returned home another.

NEW BRUNSWICK, NEW JERSEY, NOVEMBER 28:—Here we are once more at our old trade of travelling, but before I start you off again I may finish with New York. The twenty-sixth was the anniversary of the evacuation of the city of New York by the British in the Revolutionary War. There was a grand turn out of militia upon the occasion, and Eliza at least was enchanted by the sight and delighted with the music, though neither had great attractions for older persons. At the Park Theatre in the evening there was an entertainment after the same fashion, and we talked of going to see it but our theatricals generally rest in talk and we stayed very comfortably and quietly at home.

Yesterday, the twenty-seventh, we dressed for a dinner at the very fashionable hour of five at the house of Mr. and Mrs. William Astor. The father of this gentleman, John Jacob Astor, is a man of considerable consequence in New York from his very great wealth. He began the world with nothing, but his own industry and acquired all this large fortune. He came out to this country upwards of forty years ago, a steerage passenger, in the same vessel in which came Mr. Wilkes on his first visit as a cabin passenger. It is in the fur trade that he made his fortune. He is a good, honest, plain sort of a man himself, totally free of the affectation of pretending to be a gentleman, but who has had sense enough to do his utmost in order to make his son so, and as far as I can judge upon a short acquaintance, he has succeeded, for he is in appearance and first manner very gentleman-like. His wife is a very pretty, nice-looking young woman, and the whole style of their house is good.

We had a dinner in much better taste than any I have before seen in New York, no load, good attendance, and no mixing up of columns of ice along with pies and puddings. We had an immense proportion of gentlemen, which is the unfailing drawback of an American dinner, and the few ladies that there are generally contrive to get together, which is absurd enough. A daughter of Mr. Astor's married a short time since a foreigner, Baron de Romph, and as her father told me spends her winters in Paris and her summers in Switzerland. What an exquisite change from New York and Saratoga! She is now upon a visit to her friends in this country and is at present at Washington.

You must now once more have recourse to the map as you follow us in our wanderings and opening that of New Jersey proceed between Staten Island and the State of New Jersey to the entrance of the Rariton River and so up that river to New Brunswick where we are settled for the night. We left New York to-day in the steamboat at eight o'clock and arrived here, forty-five miles, at four. We dined on board and had a very comfortable stove in the cabin, so that Eliza enjoyed herself as much as possible, but although there was as much frost as there had been for the last three weeks there was so little wind that the cold made itself much less sensibly felt. The River is so full of ice that the navigation of it will be very soon stopped. This is an unusually early winter here and promises to be very severe.

The first person we recognised on the boat was Colonel Aaron Burr, so we congratulated ourselves that Mr. Wilkes had not accompanied us to the boat as he intended, for once before they unluckily met whilst visiting us, and I know Mr. Wilkes would as soon see I won't say who! There is no great beauty in the Rariton River, its banks are low and sedgy and look as if they must be often overflowed. It is particularly crooked but the bends are not graceful.

Philadelphia, December 1 :—We left New Brunswick on the twenty-eighth at nine in the morning. The rain began then and continued to increase rapidly as we drove along. When within a few miles of Bordentown, we learnt that we should pass Point Breeze, the house of Joseph Bonaparte, before reaching the village. Accordingly, we desired the driver to take us there before going to the Inn and overcame his scruples about carrying us there "without a permit," as he called it, by assuring him that we came by invitation of the Count. The approach to the house has nothing very striking to recommend it, and the weather was such as would have disfigured the most beautiful out-of-door objects. We were ushered by the servant through a suite of handsome rooms into a large drawing room, the only thing like a fine house that we have seen since we came into the country. The walls of all the rooms were covered with pictures and the furniture of a very different quality from anything we have before seen on this side of the Atlantic. The first member of the family who came to us was the Prince of Musignano, Charles Lucien—son of Lucien Bonaparte and married to Joseph's daughter. He was accompanied by his son, a boy of three years and a half, between whom and Eliza there immediately sprang up an intimacy beyond anything I ever saw in the course of even her coquettish life! He brought a half worn out doll for her which he insisted she should carry away with her. Missie took it accordingly, and although conscience whispered to me that this little piece of property ought to have been restored to its rightful owner, the sister of the little boy in question, I saw that such a bit of overstrained honesty would have quite broken Mrs. Cownie's heart, who was delighted that Miss Eliza should have such an addition to her stock of curiosities as a doll presented to her by the grand-nephew of Bonaparte. I suspect, however, that she had some twinges of the same kind, for next day Eliza's new doll was sent to little Joseph who received it with much delight and named it Eliza, whilst the one he gave has been christened Miss Bonaparte and is to be locked up forthwith that she may go down as an heirloom to Eliza's descendants.

The Prince of Musignano was soon followed by his wife, an enormously fat young woman, but with a pretty face. Her father was not long of making his appearance, a hale-looking man, wonderfully young looking for his age which I am told approaches to seventy. There can be no comparison instituted between the interest of seeing Napoleon and that of seeing his brother, but still any relation of so wonderful a man cannot be looked upon without considerable curiosity, and Joseph has himself acted rather a conspicuous part on the stage of royalty, but even having been a King does not give him perfect ease of manner, and there is a very marked degree of awkwardness and diffidence in his first address. None of the party, indeed, have much to say for themselves just at first, though when they become intimate they have a great deal of conversation. We sat with them about an hour and then went off to Bordentown, which is not a quarter of a mile distant, to dress and returned to dinner at six o'clock. We then found the party augmented by the secretary, Mr. Sari, and his wife and an American gentleman, Mr. Hopkinson. We had a dinner such as I have not seen since I was abroad. When we sat down there was nothing on the table except raw oysters in the shell, and lemon was handed round to squeeze upon them, but as I could never in my life swallow an undressed oyster I had to wait till the soup came round. Then followed the usual routine of an excellent French dinner. Basil says the Count de Survilliers is extremely like Napoleon. Of this I am no judge, but what did strike me very forcibly was the strong resemblance between Charles Bonaparte and the pictures of Napoleon.

We returned to Bordentown to sleep, and yesterday morning Basil went to breakfast with them. It rained so hard that I stayed at home, which I regretted afterwards as he had a great deal of interesting conversation with the Count and had leisure to look at the pictures.

At half-past one we went on board the steamboat which was to carry us down the Delaware to Philadelphia, in hopes that we should start immediately, but the roads from New Brunswick were so cut up that the stage for which the boat always waits did not get in for an hour and a half after the usual period, and it was three before we got off. Mr. Sari was one of the passengers. He is the man who conducted Napoleon from the Island of Elba to Fréjus. It was impossible not to feel a deep interest in all those unfortunate remnants of royalty whilst he was speaking of them, more especially as he did it without any expression of bitterness towards those who occasioned the change in their fortunes. Murat's two sons are in the country and have become citizens of the Union. Alas! what a fall from Prince Royal of Naples, surrounded by all the luxuries of art and climate, to be a citizen of the United States married to a Virginian wife and chopping wood in Florida! Such is the fate of the eldest, the other has some land and a house near the Count de Survilliers. He is at this moment in Philadelphia and I hope we shall see him. Their mother is still alive and lives at Florence.

Three hours found us at the wharf in Philadelphia, where we found a hack to bring us to Miss Boyd's in Chestnut Street, the best boarding house and the best situation in the place. In the room into which we were ushered we found Commodore Hull, whom we had met before at Albany and at Boston. There was another young man sitting with him whose dress bespoke him a lieutenant in the American Navy. After a little while he came to me and said that he would take the liberty of enquiring if I was not an acquaintance of Mrs. General Pye and Miss Douglas. I said I was, and he then introduced himself as their cousin, Mr. Ramsay. He added that he and all his family had heard from those ladies of our being in the country and would be delighted to show us every attention in their power at Washington where they reside. The party in the house consists of from fifteen to twenty, of whom two besides myself are ladies. We have got two excellent rooms close together. To-day we got all our things comfortably arranged before we stirred out or let anyone know that we were come, and then we set forth, going first in search of a certain Mr. John Vaughan, an Englishman by birth but a resident of, I believe, fifty years in this country. He was not at home, but since he has called twice, the second time of which we saw him, and he is to arrange all the business of sightseeing for us, and to-night Basil goes with him to the Wistar Party, a club of gentlemen which meets once a week alternately at the houses of the gentlemen who compose it. Our next visit was to Mrs. Cornwall, and whilst we were with her came in three ladies, one decidedly old, the others not so young. They seemed to know us by a sort of instinct, at least I did not hear Mrs. Cornwall name us, but presently the two elder ones began asking for Lady Helen, and the old lady mentioned that her husband, Major Lenox, has an estate near St. Mary's Isle, whilst the other asked if it were not true that Lady Helen Hall composed the air, *Ye banks and braes of bonny Doon,* and on Basil disclaiming this merit for his Mother begged that at least he would not contradict her story in Philadelphia, as she has spread Lady Helen's fame as a musical composer throughout the city! This lady is Miss Keene, who must have been in Scotland as well as Mrs. Lenox, for she talked with much delight of having heard Lady Helen play when she herself was quite a little girl. When we left Mrs. Cornwall we proceeded to leave some of our letters of introduction without having any intention of going in anywhere, but just as we got up to the house of Mr. Gilbert Robertson, the English Consul, Basil recognised him standing at his own door, although he has not seen him since he dined with him in New York in 1804. He introduced himself to him, and he asked us to walk in. We had not time to go much further, as the dinner hour is three; breakfast at half past eight or nine and tea at six; supper between nine and ten. We have sent out all our letters of introduction and now must await the result. The very first sound we heard last night upon our arrival in this quietest of Quaker towns was the cry of fire, with an uproar as great as I ever heard on the same occasion in New York. I thought I heard it again just now, but on opening my door find it is only someone screeching on a flute.

DECEMBER 3 :—The huge pile of cards I found awaiting me today when I returned home before dinner shewed me the necessity of writing while I have any leisure left, and as this evening we are without engagements I shall tell you what we have been doing for the last two days, having brought up my letter to the first of December. Yesterday, the second, being Sunday we went to St. Stephen's Church, where we were not particularly edified. We had a clergyman who meant to be very impressive, and in my impression totally failed in his object through the very effort that he made. We had many visitors during the course of the evening, for here it is very much the fashion to visit in the evenings, a very good practice in summer, but one not at all congenial, I should think, to the cold climate of the winters in this country.

This morning we began our course of sight-seeing under the chaperonage of Mr. Clement Biddle who for this day was our escort. The High School was the first place visited. It is an admirable establishment in all its branches, as far as I can judge, although I am of course not qualified to form any opinion as to the proficiency attained in learning, but where the plan is good I should think the result must be also favourable. There is not, however, the same immense manufactury of education going on here as at Boston. Mr. Biddle estimates the number of schools at about two hundred in a population of seventy thousand, whereas at Boston where the population is about forty-three thousand the number of schools is two hundred and fourteen. We spent nearly two hours at the High School and then walked on a mile further to the Institute for the Deaf and Dumb where we were highly initiated as usual. Mr. Weld, the head-master, was a teacher at Hartford, the Institution there being the parent of all the others of the same kind in the United States. I think a few more visits to them would make me very familiar with their signs, which are beautifully graceful, and there is something quite affecting in the expressive intelligence of countenances which a few years ago had little to distinguish them from brutes, than whom they had little more mental knowledge. There is a happy look about them, too, which is very delightful to see. We saw them at dinner, a very excellent dinner of beef and potatoes and apple dumplings, and we also inspected their nice, clean bedrooms. We did not devote any more of our time to seeing sights, as we find the best plan is not to try to overtake too much in one day, so we filled up what remained before dinner in returning some of the visits that had been made to us.

Philadelphia is the most regular town that ever was built, far more so than Edinburgh, for it is in a plain. Those streets which run from east to west are named after trees—Chestnut, Spruce, Walnut, Mulberry, Pine, and some others which I do not know. One street running from east to west from the Delaware almost to the Schuylkill is called Market Street, being where the market is held. Streets running from north to south are numbered 1st, 2nd, 3rd, and so on. There never was a town where the faculties of finding one's way were so great. We are in the heart of everything that is fashionable as to situation, and the house is by far the best in every respect that we have been in since we came to America.

DECEMBER 5 :—Yesterday morning, the fourth, we were under an engagement to go to the new Penitentiary with Mr. Robert Vaux at ten oclock. The Penitentiary is not half built and so part of it is not yet occupied. There is a controversy going on at present as to the system to be pursued, and upon this decision depends the method of finishing the building. Mr. Vaux, the principal person concerned, condemns the system pursued at Auburn, Sing Sing, and similar establishments, and is all for solitary confinement by day as well as by night unaccompanied by any occupation except a bible in each cell. I cannot enter into his views in this particular and think that the good old copy line, "Idleness is the parent of mischief," may hold good in a prison as well as out of it, and although the culprits may be shut out from the power of doing evil with their hands their minds must run to still greater waste than before. Of course they would be allowed the instruction of a clergyman and occasionally might be visited by the directors for the same purpose, but still the greater part of their time would be passed in utter solitude and idleness. A very serious objection to the plan of building this Penitentiary is the enormous expense, three hundred and fifty thousand dollars have already been laid out upon not one half of what there is to be. The rain unluckily came on as we were at the

Penitentiary, and as we were two miles from town we had to send for a carriage, and this loss of time combined with the rain obliged us to relinquish any more seeing of sights for the day. Basil went at seven o'clock with Mr. Reuben Haines, a Quaker, to the Philosophical Society and returned before nine to accompany me to a party, a ball at Mrs. Hewson's, the wife of Dr. Hewson, by much the shortest man I ever saw, but his wife is by no means of a size in proportion being as tall as me and at least twice as broad. This party, I was told by Sam Hay, did not consist of the *haut ton* of Philadelphia. There were not half a dozen members of that most select set present. There were certainly not many pretty women, and their clothes were ill put on though very good in quality. There were two remarkably pretty girls, however, who would have done credit to any drawing room; their name is Barry. The style of entertainment was much the same as in other towns in the Union that we have visited. Frequent trays of a variety of refreshments; rooms lighted entirely with candles and very well done. They were not in lustres, but in the middle of each room there was a circular frame in which were placed three or four dozen candles and at the sides of the rooms were semi-circular frames fitted with candles in the same way. Each of the frames was entirely concealed by a wreath of artificial flowers. The doors were taken off and green baize curtains substituted in their place. A large party went from this place. Most of them did not come home till one o'clock, but Basil and I with our usual sobriety at eleven, after I had danced five quadrilles and Basil none.

This morning we have been to the jail in Walnut Street, one on the old plan with little to recommend it and a great deal to condemn. This new Penitentiary is meant to take the place of the Walnut Street Jail. Basil and I have got laid up with colds. One of my cheeks is swelled twice the size of the other; I am not fit to be seen. It was at the Penitentiary that we caught cold. We were to have gone last night to Mr. Vaux's to tea, but sent an apology. To-night, too, we are asked to a party but shall have to decline it also, and I am much afraid that even to-morrow we shall have to excuse ourselves from going to Mrs. Palmer's, which I shall be more sorry for as I am told that she has the best society at her house.

I must mention, as I told you of the disgrace we supposed we had got into at Boston owing to what we heard from some quarters, that the other day a lady here talking of our visit to that place said, "I am sure that Captain Hall and yourself must have been pleased with your visit there. You gave such very great satisfaction and pleasure, as I heard by letters from my friends there."

Yours ever affectionately,

MARGARET HALL.

LETTER XI

PHILADELPHIA

Twenty days were spent in Philadelphia visiting Schools. Asylums, Gaols, Academy of Fine Arts, Mint, and Navy Yard. The city was found to be more cosmopolitan than New York, since many diplomats lived there while Congress was not sitting. Mrs. Hall, therefore, was able to valse and flirt to her heart's content. She describes the company at the Boarding House, the parties to which she is invited, and her feelings about "our Canvas Bag (!) ducks".

PHILADELPHIA, Dec. 8, 1827.

MY DEAREST JANE,

I finished my last letter by informing you that we were both laid up with colds, so I may begin this one with the information that we are both mending fast, as you will believe by the fact of Basil's voice having sufficiently increased and my cheek decreased to admit of our going to a ball last night. The ball was at Mrs. Palmer's, a lady in the first society here, and certainly the whole thing was infinitely superior to any other of its kind that I have seen in America. The Philadelphians claim being the first in rank in society of any town in the States, and the specimen of last night makes good the pretension so far as we are competent to judge. The ladies were infinitely handsomer, more stylish, and better dressed than any I have before seen here, and there was a considerable mixture of foreigners, Spaniards, French, South Americans and Dutch, which was a great improvement particularly on the male part of the population. I was introduced to the Spaniards and had plenty of talk and dancing with them. All these persons belong to the *Corps Diplomatique* at Washington and will soon adjourn there, but until Congress is fairly in action there is little business for them, and Philadelphia is a much more agreeable place of residence. There was a very pretty little supper up stairs, which we remained to and came away immediately after it, I having danced six quadrilles and Basil three, and both of us having had a good spell of valsing. It was really a charming party. I don't think I have enjoyed any ball so much since I was married. The ladies in Philadelphia are, generally speaking, much taller than most American women, and I think the men have the same preeminence in size, but it is more remarkable in the women. There is much less formality in the society, none of the bowing and curtseying that appalled me in the quadrille at Boston, nor are the ladies dragged in the same merciless way from their husbands by the master of the house without their inclination being consulted. In short, things are left more to follow their own inclination, and so the company also is of course left more at liberty.

This morning broke more wet and gloomy than even its four predecessors, but we could not afford to waste any more time, and as our unpaid visits weighed rather heavily on our consciences we resolved manfully to brave the rain in a hackney coach and at once to free ourselves of this very disagreeable burden. Accordingly, we set out at twelve, and by three we had paid no less than sixteen calls, at one half of which, at least, we gained admittance, besides a great deal of time wasted in seeking for persons who had left no address and others who left a confused one such as "corner of Spruce and Fourth." Now Fourth Street intersects Spruce and consequently each of these two streets has four corner houses each answering to this description, so that one day Basil sought the same gentleman in eight different houses!

I have not yet seen anything in Philadelphia, I mean as to the town, at all to compare with the beauty of Boston, either in the outward appearance of the houses or the situation and surrounding country, but to be sure nothing can be more unfavourable than the weather in which we have hitherto seen the place, foggy, smoky, damp, unbecoming weather, the very kind to make people and things look ugly, but certainly the inanimate part of creation has suffered more for it than the animate, and my little pet flourishes in it as charmingly as though the sun shone brightly, and she has been out only once since we arrived here.

DECEMBER 12:—I have to begin my history at Sunday, the ninth, when a little gleam of sunshine made us flatter ourselves that we were to have no more rain. We went to St. James's Church with Mr. and Mrs. Nicklin, and there heard old Bishop White preach. He is the first Bishop they ever had in the State of Pennsylvania. He is rather old now, poor man, to be edifying, more particularly to those whose pews are at a distance from the pulpit, who can have heard but little of his discourse. We went after Church, by appointment, to call upon Mr. Walsh, who Lady Helen may remember some eighteen years ago in Edinburgh. He talks of Edinburgh with the greatest rapture but abuses all Englishmen (which includes Scotchmen) in the *American Quarterly Review,* of which he is the editor. This, I believe, is done to make his review sell, for to abuse England is one very sure road to popularity. They are queer people, these Americans, very queer indeed, utterly indescribable in many little points of character which put all together go to make up the whole. There has been, as they say, an unusually rainy autumn this year, which has vexed them all, man, woman, and child, to the very heart, because they are particularly desirous of making their best appearance to us, and instead of allowing their responsibility of climate to rest with providence they seem to feel that they are answerable for every drop of rain and ounce of mud that we have to wade through, and, fret and fume as they will, they find that they have not the smallest control over it, in the bitterness of their spirit they are constantly casting up to us how like this is to English weather! I never try to defend my own country from the numerous and implied attacks made upon it by these most sensitive of all persons to blame imputed to themselves. I let it pass, feeling how well England can afford to be abused, whether with or without desert, in consideration of her high standing amongst nations, and according to the same rule we ought to make great allowance for the Americans, who tho' very high in their own estimation are well aware that other countries are not prepared to rate them by the standard that they would choose. But to go back to Mr. Walsh. He is a man of talents, I believe, and of lively conversation certainly, tho' as deaf as a post, tho' all that I have heard of him does not contribute to give me a good opinion of his principles. He is now confined to his room with a hurt on his knee, so I went to visit him, as he was disabled from coming to see me. We went to drink tea with Mr. and Mrs. Vaux, Quakers whom I have before mentioned to you. Being Sunday night of course we had nothing like a party, only Mr. and Mrs. Neiderstatter, the Prussian *Chargé d'Affaires* who married a few months ago the Dutch Minister's daughter, and one or two American gentlemen.

The little sunshine on the ninth was succeeded on the tenth by more violent rain than ever, but we felt that it was in vain to wait for good weather and, accordingly, at ten o'clock we set out on a sight-seeing tour in which Mr. and Mrs. Vaux accompanied us. Our first object was the Bridewell, a disagreeable one as all prisons are, more especially when they are ill managed as this is without classification of any kind, except in some cases, when for comparatively small offences they are put into solitary confinement, Mr. Vaux's favourite system in which he and Basil totally disagree. Our next visit was of a much more agreeable nature, the Orphan Asylum, an admirable institution, where upwards of sixty children are well taken care of and educated until they are twelve years old, when they are bound into different trades, the boys at least, and the girls go into service. Close to the Orphan Asylum is another excellent institution totally unconnected with it, an Asylum for Poor Widows, where for thirty dollars of entrance money, a sum easily procured amongst friends if the individual possesses it not, any widow of reduced circumstances and too infirm to better them, can gain admittance to a comfortable home for the rest of her life. There are forty-three now in the establishment, and really the old ladies look most comfortable, fifteen of them are unable to leave their rooms, at all events not able to go downstairs, but on each story there is a gallery round the centre of the building where they can take exercise without having the fatigue of climbing the stair. Some have a room entirely to themselves, in other rooms there are two persons, but all of them look neat and clean and comfortable. It would be an excellent establishment in England for old housekeepers and such like.

We finished our day's work by going to the Academy of Fine Arts and the Museum. At the Academy there are some fine paintings by the ancient masters, most of which I believe belong to the Count de Survilliers. There is one fine picture too of Allston's, *The dead man restored to life by touching the bones of the prophet Elisha,* but the best I have yet seen of his is that of Jeremiah in the possession of Dr. Channing. At the Museum the thing most worthy of notice is the skeleton of the mammoth which was found near Newborough in the State of New York upwards of twenty years ago. Close to it is placed the skeleton of an elephant of the largest size, and very liliputian indeed it looks by comparison. We have got a general ticket for admittance to the Museum from the proprietor, Mr. Peale, and have given it to Mrs. Cownie and Eliza, for it is nearly opposite to this house, and they can amuse themselves there for an hour or two very nicely.

Yesterday we commenced our rounds with the Mint, a very contemptible sight, I suppose, for those who have seen the same establishment in London, but as I had never seen money coined before it had some interest for me. We then went to the Navy Yard and saw the immense ship called the *Pennsylvania,* which is building there and beside her a first rate frigate. They looked like the mammoth and elephant at the Museum. The Navy Yard is on the Delaware. We drove from thence the whole length of the town to the Water Works on the Schuylkill, whence the whole city of Philadelphia is supplied with water, and coming back crossed the two bridges over the Schuylkill. This was sufficient work, we thought, for one day, especially as we were engaged out to dine and spend the evening at Mr. Lenox's. Mr. and Mrs. Lenox have a niece, Miss Keene, who lives with them.

Miss Keene is still very handsome altho' not so young as she may have been, but her beauty has not gained her universal popularity, as the foolish trick that was played on them yesterday is a proof of, for everyone was convinced that it was done to spite her. When we went into the room I was struck with something odd in the reception, and many particular enquiries were made about my health and many hopes that I was better. I assured my enquirers that I was in the most perfect health and had been so ever since getting the better of my swelled face last week, so then the ladies told us that they had received a note of apology from us only half an hour before. They brought the note to me and there I read that: "Captain and Mrs. B. Hall regretted that her increased indisposition would prevent them from having the honour of waiting upon Mr. and Mrs. Lenox," that day. I said it must mean Mrs. Hull, who is also lodging in this house, and as the two names write so much alike this satisfied them. Miss Keene then told me that she was sorry the Cornewalls could not come on account of some domestic affliction they had heard of. I was very sorry for this but still more surprised when two minutes after, in walked Mr. and Mrs. Cornewall, she with a white satin dress trimmed with the gayest of flowers. I thought that at least she might have had the grace to put on a black gown for her deceased relation. Nothing was said at the time, but after some going out and into the room we were at length summoned to dinner. After dinner we talked it all over and Mrs. Cornewall's excuse was produced. All this had, of course, made the people of the house anxious to fill up their table, which they in part did, besides reducing the size of it, so that we were pretty closely jammed, when those who ought and those who ought not to have been there were collected. Certainly, a poorer piece of wit never was thought of nor a more malicious. There was an evening party also with an abundance of dancing on the carpet with not a little valsing, of which I have seen more in this Quaker city than anywhere else I have been in this country. So many foreigners are here, besides a good many young ladies lately returned from the Continent of Europe, that they make it fashionable. The Spaniards were there, and we had really a pleasant party and got home by eleven, which is one of the great pleasures of society here.

There is no rest for the wicked, you know, and of that number we most especially are, to judge by the constant motion we are in. We were off at our usual hour of ten to-day on our peregrinations, and having picked up Dr. Richard Harlan proceeded to the Alms House, one of the ill-regulated institutions of the place, but there are so many good ones that the Philadelphians can afford to have the bad ones seen. The bad part of the Alms House is the want of classification between patients and paupers and many other evils. It is an immense building in which in winter there are from twelve to fifteen hundred persons, and it is an immense expense to keep it up, but it is to be put under better management shortly. From the Alms House we went to the Pennsylvania Hospital, which owed its birth chiefly to the exertions of William Penn. In front of the Hospital stands a full length statue of this worthy old gentleman. It was found by an American at the door of a plumber's shop in London where it had been sent by the nobleman whose property it was, to be melted down, the possessor having no value for such a statue. This gentleman told John Penn of his having seen it and advised him to send it as a present to Philadelphia, which he did accordingly. Nothing can be more unpicturesque than the dress in which the honest old Quaker is represented. Nevertheless, there is a great deal of spirit in the figure, and the artist deserves great credit for having rendered so uncouth a costume so pleasing without having altered one iota of its formality. The hospital is an admirable institution in all its parts. West, the painter, who was a native of Philadelphia, made a present to the Institution of his picture of *Christ Healing the Sick,* a very appropriate subject for the situation, but all West's pictures are to me disagreeable daubs.

On we went from the hospital to Franklin's grave, which few Americans, nay not even many Philadelphians, know, honours their city. We must go abroad to learn what we have at home. Not long ago an American on the coast of Manila was asked with much eagerness and interest by an Englishman where the grave of Franklin was. The American was shocked to be obliged to answer that he did not know. I have found many persons in the same state of ignorance. Certainly no grave can be more inconspicuous, a plain, marble slab covers it, bearing no other inscription than this: "Benjamin and Deborah Franklin, 1790." Some persons say that there is more of coxcombry in this simple statement than there would have been in the most elaborate epitaph. It may be so, but it pleased me. In fact, what can you say of a great man after death that will not appear to some like flattery where it least ought to be, and to others inadequate of his merits? I think the greatest compliment that can be paid to him is that there is a little path trodden in the grass to the quiet corner where he lies.

Let me see; where did we go to after this sentimental visit? Oh . . . I took Eliza to visit Mrs. Cornewall's boy, exactly ten months younger than herself. We went from Mrs. Cornewall's to the Athenæum to meet Mr. Vaughan of this place. He took us to the town library where there is a collection of twenty-six thousand volumes and where everyone may go to read. This was enough of work for one day, and most fortunately we had no engagement for the evening.

DECEMBER 13:—This has been another regular sight-seeing day. We commenced this morning by going out of town about two miles to see the Marine Asylum, now building. It is not yet very far advanced but when finished is meant to contain accommodation for about three hundred and fifty sailors and forty officers, with the plan so arranged to enable them to add as much more building if required. It is near the Schuylkill, very prettily situated with nice garden ground about it. When we reached our own door we found Mr. Vaux come to escort us to some more Lions. The Bank of the United States came first in order. It is a fine building with handsome Grecian columns in front but little of interest inside. The fact is that in "doing up all the Lions" in a town one goes to see many things that have no interest in themselves, but in the course of seeing everything one gathers information somehow or other that in the end comes to be useful. We went with Mr. Vaux also to the school founded by William Penn. There were no boys in it but Basil saw their astronomical instruments, and he and a gentleman who works with them soon got deep in a conversation about occultations and moon culminating stars and all the other branches of that, apparently, most bewitching of all studies. We closed our career with the old State House and the room where the Declaration of Independence was signed, which they have been gothic enough to pull to pieces with a view to modernising it, instead of allowing it to remain without a chair or a table moved. It is melancholy to see how little judgment or good taste people sometimes have. Here we stopped and employed the rest of the time before dressing for dinner in paying off the rest of our visits.

We dined at Mr. Harrison's. He is said to live in the best style of anyone in Philadelphia, and most assuredly we had a grand dinner, such heaps of plate, silver and gold, such beautiful French china, and such heaps of dinner, well-dressed however. I have rarely seen the attendance too, far better than anything I had hoped to see in America but still many, many degrees below good English service, and it is this which invariably marks the difference between an American and an English party, and it gives an appearance of effort throughout and an air of anxiety to the mistress of the house totally against the spirit of good entertaining. It is extremely disagreeable to sit near the head of the table, as you are then sure to have the advantage of all the admonitions and scolds and hints bestowed upon the servants. Many of the persons who lodge in this house were of the dinner party. By the by, I have never said anything of them altho' they are on the whole the pleasantest set we have met with. There is Commodore Hull with his very pretty wife, and two sisters, the Miss Harts, but the elder of the two is confined to her room by sickness and I have never seen her. The Commodore is a good-natured, excellent man, an excellent sailor but as deaf as a post. The ladies are not generally popular, I don't know why, but I believe they are considered as giving themselves airs and appearing to think themselves above their associates, which as they are *nobody* won't do in this aristocratic country. They are very civil to me, of course. Our most prominent female character is Mrs. Scott, wife of General Scott of the United States Army, now commanding in the Southern and Western districts, but the lady likes gaiety and has no idea of immuring herself in the wilderness, so she lets him take care of himself in the woods whilst she dances in Philadelphia. She is a pretty woman still, albeit I should think not very much on this side of forty, somewhat light-headed I should say for her years. She has three girls, two at school here and one of two and a half who lives in this house with her. In single gentlemen we are strong. There is Colonel Coles, a tall handsome gentleman-like Virginian of large property; Mr. Ramsay, a lieutenant in the United States Navy, I mentioned to you before. He returned to Washington some days ago. Mr. Middleton is a young man whose father is Minister from the United States at Petersburgh. His mother is an Englishwoman and he himself has travelled a good deal in England and Scotland. He belongs to Charleston in South Carolina. Mr. Shortt is an elderly gentleman who has travelled much on the Continent of Europe and is more of anything than an American, a bachelor who loves his ease but hates the early dinner hour he is obliged to conform to at the boarding house, flirts with young ladies, either married or single, wears a brown wig, is nice and tidy in his person, and, in short, could be told to be an old bachelor all the world over. There is a young Scotchman, a Mr. Gordon, son to the Consul, an intelligent young man. Then we have a couple of judges, Mr. Gibson, Chief Justice of this State, as bigoted an American as ever breathed, and Judge Rogers, who, I believe, in truth is no less so, but he has won me by his extreme partiality for Eliza. Mr. Farran, once a bookseller, is our only other single man, except a young Mr. Buchanan, from I know not where. I do not know what it is about American nationality which is so extremely disgusting. It is a failing which with persons of other countries we very willingly excuse, but it is impossible not to be provoked by Americans when this is their theme, which it is so often. There is a selfishness about their love of their country very different from the generous sentiment that is with those of other nations. But I have omitted to mention one other couple who make up the sum total of our company, a Mr. and Mrs. Olney from Portland in Massachusetts, whether or not she is very sensible I shall leave you to judge for yourselves. This morning she sent the black chambermaid to Mrs. Cownie to enquire whether or not I had gone out, and having ascertained the fact she came herself to the room with a request to Mrs. Cownie to show her my blue topazes which I had had on some evenings previous, but she had not seen them and heard so much of their beauty that she longed for a sight. Mrs. Cownie accordingly exhibited them for her amusement and told me that the foolish woman almost shed tears over them. "To think of the good fortune of some people. She had no such things, had scarcely ever seen them. She could not say but what she was happy, but she has married a man with nothing and all the money they had to keep them was what her father gave them." This is not the first time that my trinkets have been brought out for the amusement of boarding house lodgers. My dress, too, has often been requested as pattern from Mrs. Cownie and many attempts made to see it. Mrs. Cownie gets prodigious credit by the dressing of my hair, and this same Mrs. Olney was back to her in the evening to get her to arrange her crape and flowers in her head!

DECEMBER 16:—In talking of the dinners we have been at here, I forgot to mention one peculiarity in the arrangement. After the first course, which invariably includes all the meat, game also, that is to say, there is no meat of any kind along with the sweets, altho' the game sometimes forms a separate course by itself, but after all the meat, comes the cheese, salad, celery, and sometimes cold pickled oysters. That part, in short, which in England comes immediately before the dessert. Then follow the pies and puddings with all their accompaniments and then, of course, the dessert. This is the season of Canvas Bag (!) Ducks, a most uninviting name, but an excellent bird, really, in spite of the constant wearisome praise bestowed upon it by the Americans, and which disposes me to find fault with what is belaboured. They are very abundant and are brought on the table in what in England we should consider most vulgar quantity, at a dinner of ten persons yesterday there were no less than a couple at top and another couple at bottom. They are invariably talked of as *"our* Canvas Bag ducks," as if they belonged exclusively to the people of the United States. Now it strikes me that no Scotch person or persons would think of talking of "our grouse". It might be done once in a way, but not perpetually and forever as if to remind unhappy strangers that it is only by the generosity and magnanimity of the Americans that they are allowed the high privilege of eating so delicate a dish. I believe they do belong exclusively to this portion of the United States, Maryland, Pennsylvania, and Virginia, that is to say, they are not fit to eat elsewhere, altho' they make their nests and breed on the shores of Lake Erie from whence they emigrate to the South at the commencement of winter and after fattening for a fortnight or three weeks on a certain plant of which they are very fond, they are good for the table.

We were to have gone on the fourteenth to the "Friends' Retreat for the Insane," an asylum exclusively appropriated by the Quakers to their own sect. You know they denominate themselves "Friends". A foggy, damp morning, however, made me feel warranted in indulging in the laziness which the hard work of the week had brought on, and Basil was quite enchanted when I suggested the possibility of staying at home for one morning, and completely cutting one sight. In this it is I think that we show our superior sense over other travellers, that when we are tired we do not make it a point of duty to go on seeing more. You see, I have not failed to profit by the example of boasting which I see so universally practised. But altho' we gave up the Retreat, we kept our appointment with Mr. and Mrs. Vaux to go to the Infant School. I had all along been resolved to carry Eliza there. I was sure she would be so much amused by seeing so many little children, and she was so pleased that we had difficulty in persuading her to come away. The school is only lately set agoing and is not yet organised. They have not hitherto taken any under the age of two years, and as yet the system is not brought to that state of perfection I have heard of in the English schools of the same nature. We also went to see one of the Common Schools, for the lower orders, on the Lancastrian plan. The chief interest in this particular school consisted in its being held in the room in which Lancaster himself actually taught. We drank tea the same evening at Mr. Harlan's, the father of Dr. Richard Harlan, with whom we have made acquaintance here. The family are Quakers, and the old couple adhere rigidly to the plain dress and the plain language as they call what the French term "tutoyer" implies. The younger part of the family, excepting our friend the Doctor, I presume also belong to the Friends' Society, but they have laid aside the close cap and untrimmed gown for plainly dressed hair and gowns like other ladies, only of a more sober colour and make. Every member of the party, with the exception of a very few gentlemen, were Quakers and a very merry, cheerful, conversible set they were, and many of the ladies talked to me most good-humouredly of the peculiarities of the practice of their sect. One in particular condemned the amusements of their children in their youth which has the effect of making them run wild in pursuit of pleasure when they get to be their own masters. It is considered improper even to teach them music, and the sister of the lady who spoke to me had been restrained from learning, altho' she has the greatest genius and liking for it. The Quakers eat and drink like the rest of the world, and we had the same quantity of tea, cakes, and ice handed round by little black boys and great tall Meg Merrilies's of women as at other places of not the first fashion. The servants in Philadelphia are universally black or "yellow," as they call those who have some mixture of white blood in them.

DECEMBER 17:—We were to have left Philadelphia to-morrow, but on making enquiry we find that our best plan is to go straight through to Baltimore without stopping by the way as we had intended to do, so we do not go till the nineteenth. Mr. and Mrs.

Cornewall also go that day and our fellow lodger, Mr. Gordon. We went yesterday morning to St. Andrew's Church to hear Mr. Biddle, who is one of the most celebrated preachers here. He is certainly the best in Philadelphia, but except Dr. Channing I have heard no very good preacher in America. We went afterwards to see some drawings by a young artist of the name of Doughty, nothing in the least surprising but better than the daubs usually denominated drawings in this country. Basil dined with a single gentleman of the name of Craig, a man without a profession and consequently much adrift, as there are few others in the same predicament here, so that he finds no sympathy and little companionship. We both drank tea at Mr. Vaux's, our Quaker friend, who has a very pleasing lively wife. Mr. and Mrs. Neiderstatter, whom I have before mentioned, were there. She is a pretty, pleasing young woman. They are soon going to Washington, where I suppose we shall find all the diplomatists assembled. This was packing day, as we did not know that we should change our plan till late in the day, so I had Eliza's company exclusively to myself, for Basil was out and Mrs. Cownie busy. I took her to pay some visits for which I had in vain waited for fine weather but none such occurring, except two days last week when she had a little cold, she and I braved the rain together in a carriage and paid our visits. By the by, I ought to mention, as I fear I may have done her injustice in this respect, that the other day it was remarked by some one of the party that an old gentleman belonging to the house had taken her in his arms, altho' they had never before seen him touch any child, upon which one of the young men said that he was not surprised because she was always kept so clean and nice and was at all times so touchable.

DECEMBER 19:—We are just setting out for Baltimore so that I must finish. We drank tea last night at Dr. Mease's, quite a quiet party. The weather is clearing up a little for us, which is so far comfortable.

Ever affectionately yours,

MARGARET HALL.

LETTER XII

Travelling by boat from Philadelphia to French Town the Halls crossed the
neck of land from Delaware River to Chesapeake Bay by road, and then
completed their journey by water to Baltimore where they saw Mr. Hackett
play in "The Comedy of Errors", climbed the Washington Monument and
the Exchange, inspected the rather "imperfect" jail and Penitentiary, and
visited the Almshouse at Calverton. The great sight of the city, however,
was Mr. Carroll, aged 82, the only survivor of those who signed the Declaration of Independence. He kept a handsome establishment and three servants
in livery. Eliza was presented to him and "behaved beautifully as always".
On Christmas Day the Halls were taken by Mr. Carroll's daughter, Mrs.
Caton, to the Catholic Cathedral. Three hours of it was "too much of
such mummery" for Mrs. Hall who sweepingly condemned the ceremonies
she had attended.

BALTIMORE, December 20, 1827.

MY DEAREST JANE,

We started from Philadelphia at eleven o'clock and found the
boat well filled with passengers many of whom had been waiting
for a tolerable day and others hurrying on to the end of their journey in case of being stopped by the freezing of the rivers which
will soon follow the commencement of frost. We dined on board
the boat and at three o'clock landed at French Town, a distance of
forty miles which we accomplished in four hours. Here was a very
curious scene. No less than eleven Stages drawn out in a double
row before the doors of the inn. These were to convey the passengers across the neck of land from the Delaware River to Chesapeake Bay, and during those sixteen miles we were in the State
of Delaware, the only portion of the State that we are likely to see.
Nor did we see much of it, for one half of the time it was quite

dark. We had taken care to secure an "Extra" and moved fifth in the procession, which when the lamps were lighted had a very curious appearance, as each carriage went floundering along trying to pick out the dryest and least rough part of the road, which altho' not so bad as we had been told, was yet sufficiently so to detain us three and a half hours to the sixteen miles. If the first boat was full, the second one had at least twice the number of passengers. I never saw such a squeeze, not even in the Lake Ontario boat, with the additional *désagrément* of the iron stoves which the cold renders absolutely necessary, at the same time the oppressive, choky sort of heat is extremely unpleasant. Eliza had slept during the greater part of the land journey so that she was as brisk as a bee and ate her supper with great relish and then trotted about among the passengers, male and female, whoever chose to take her, and she has the gratification of finding her advances always favourably received. After we had all ate and drank our fill the tables were removed and preparations were made for night accommodation. The passengers were so unusually numerous that it was out of the question that each should have a berth. The ladies were pretty well provided for by cribbing eight berths from the gentlemen, who drew in a lottery for those that remained, and Basil was fortunate enough to draw a prize. Sleep, however, does not dwell much in steamboats. Soon after one this morning we reached Baltimore, and about one half of the passengers went on shore, which made noise enough to awake the other half, but after a little time this ceased and there was quietness till daylight set them amoving. We remained till near eight o'clock, and then Basil came up to the City Hotel and secured accommodation for us before we took Eliza out of her bed. I cannot tell you anything of Baltimore yet, there is such a fog this morning, at least there was when I came from the boat that I saw nothing. We have got a nice parlour with a bedroom leading off from each side, which makes a very nice suite. Eliza is amusing herself looking out of the window, perfectly unconscious, I suppose, that she is not at Philadelphia. I am amused when I hear people talking of not liking to take their children a few miles off, because all the things they are accustomed to at home cannot be taken with them, and they are put out of their way. It would be a puzzle to anyone to tell what Eliza's way is.

DECEMBER 21:—Yesterday Eliza went out to walk, and in a few minutes she and Mrs. Cownie returned to tell us that they had seen a number of ladies and children come out of a house where there seemed to be a sort of a fair going on, as they had toys of various kinds in their hands, but no admittance was to be had without money so Mrs. Cownie brought her little charge back for some. They were provided accordingly, and off they set once more. When we went out some time after we bent our steps in that direction, and in the Assembly Room found a Ladies' sale going on, similar to those there were last year in Edinburgh. We found that it was for the benefit of the Orphan Asylum, but by the time we got there most of the company had gone home to dinner, the dinner hour being two o'clock. Several of the tables, of which altogether there seemed to be from twelve to fifteen, were covered with eatables, and even at those tables which contained other articles there was a huge plum cake covered with sugar. We afterwards walked through many of the streets and were struck with a foreign air about them, different from any town we have before seen in this country. The toys in the different shops resembled more those I have seen in Spain than what are made in this country. I don't in the least know why this is, or whether it may not be a mere fancy on my part. There are certainly many more blacks, and we have now got into the land of slavery. I like the appearance of this town much better than Philadelphia. There is more variety in the plan, and it is not so flat. There are some handsome houses too, whereas in Philadelphia there were none that had that appearance outwardly, tho' many were very good inside. The formality and flatness of Philadelphia are very tiresome, but perhaps I may think more favourably of the town if we return there at a better season, altho' Mr. Beckett (who tho' a resident there is an Englishman) told us that it is by no means a good climate. Indeed, whoever heard of any part of America commended for its climate? How can it be when people are obliged to fly from one part to another at particular seasons to escape certain death, and in the very best parts of it, the thermometer frequently falls twenty or thirty degrees in twelve hours. In summer, too, they are occasionally roasted and in winter frequently frozen; in short, the Americans have no sort of right to talk of their climate as good, but they are so fond of arrogating all that is best to themselves that they do not stop even when they have reason on their side.

As we walked along yesterday we saw by the playbills on the walls that Mr. Hackett was to perform in the *Comedy of Errors,* in which there is good scope for his powers of imitation. We are so apt to stick going to the play, either because we make engagements elsewhere or if we are not engaged we are glad to spend a quite evening at home, that we resolved to go now whilst we were still free from an engagement of any sort, so we walked to the Theatre soon after six o'clock and got very good places. The play is, to be sure, the most absurd that it ever entered into the head of mortal to write, nevertheless, it acts better than many a better play, and we were very much amused. The actor who represented Dromio of Syracuse was very good in his way, and Hackett as Dromio of Ephesus imitated him perfectly. He afterwards in the character of Sylvester Daggerwood gave imitations of Keane and Macready very well indeed and also of Barnes (the other Dromio) and some American actor with whom we are not acquainted. The house was very full. We were in the second row of a box, and next to Basil was a gentleman who leant forward and said to his wife, "Captain Hall the British tourist is in town. He brought me a letter from Mr. Walsh." I felt it would be so awkward for the poor man to allow him to go on talking of a man who was seated next to him that I begged Basil to make himself known to him, which he did accordingly. It was a Mr. Skinner. I have met with so many interruptions in the course of writing this morning from visitors that I forget in the middle of a sentence what I am saying. All those to whom we brought letters have called and some others also. It

is very difficult to judge, perhaps, but we have been struck with
a great difference in the tone of conversations of those persons
and that held by the society in other towns of the Union, more
particularly in Philadelphia. No one here has spouted to us of
their Institutions and their buildings and their liberty and fifty
other things of which the Philadelphians boasted morning, noon,
and night. We are also spared the repetition of the "wonderful improvement" of Baltimore, in fact, fortunately for us, Baltimore is
either standing still or retrograding in the march of improvement!
You may think this a very unchristianlike remark, I dare say, but
had you been exposed for as many months as we have been to the
never ending history of the rapid advancement, "wonderful improvement", "extraordinary increase of population", "marvellous
extension of towns", you would congratulate yourself as we do
that for once you have come to a place where this cackle-cackling
is not sounding in your ears.

DECEMBER 22:—I opened my eyes at streets covered with snow
this morning, pretty deep snow, too. Eliza was much astonished.
It is the first that she has seen, for of course, she has no recollection of what she saw before leaving Edinburgh. After all
our visitors left us yesterday we set out for a walk. We soon
came in sight of the Washington Monument, situated on the highest spot in the town. The sun broke out just then, and as we knew
that the best view of the city was to be had from the top of the
monument we determined to climb up. We were told that the
spiral stair was very dark and that it was necessary to have a lan-
tern; however, we set off very valiantly calling to the boy to follow
us, but no sooner had we got out of reach of the benefit of the
light of the only window than we were obliged to come to a complete standstill, for such utter darkness neither of us had ever
been in before. It is a stupid contrivance not to have left slits in
the wall. There are two hundred and twenty-eight steps in the
stair. From the top we had an admirable view of the town, with
the appearance of which we continued to be much pleased. There
is a great variety of hill and dale in the streets, which is an unspeak-

able relief to the eye after the flatness and the sameness of Philadelphia.

Mr. and Mrs. Caton, father and mother of the Marchioness of Wellesley, and their daughter, Mrs. MacTavish, with her husband had been among our morning visitors. They all live with Mr. Carroll, the father of Mrs. Caton, and the only survivor of those who signed the Declaration of Independence. Mrs. Caton told us that he had not been so well as usual for some days, but that she knew he would be glad to see us if we would go there to tea at six o'clock. Our experience of the genius of exaggeration that possesses the Americans had prepared us to find Mr. Carroll by no means the extraordinary person they talked of, but herein we had done them great injustice, and we found that they had not represented him at all so extraordinary a person as he really is. He met us with as light and active a step as the youngest person in the room, and I cannot say that I discovered one single mark of old age either in his manner, appearance, or faculties, altho' he is now in the ninety-second year of his age, he is not more deaf than I am, has not the smallest hesitation in his speech, has not so many wrinkles as many a one half his age, and in his sentiments and conversation there is not a trace of old age. We said to him that we were very desirous of bringing Eliza to see him, as we wished that she should have it to say when she is old enough to appreciate the value of such an interview, that she had seen Mr. Carroll. He said he would be delighted to see her, and it was agreed that we should take her there this evening. All the family stay at home every evening to play a rubber of whist with Mr. Carroll. They have a delightful house and a very handsome establishment, no less than three servants in livery, which I dare say you will laugh to hear me mention as a thing worthy of remark, but except at Mr. Harrison's and Mr. Lenox's at Philadelphia, I have not seen a servant in livery in the country, and you cannot think how *grand* it appears to me. We met there Colonel and Mrs. Keene. He is an American who has been in the Spanish service for twenty years and she is a Spaniard, neither speaking nor understanding a word of English, and as Mrs. Caton and Mrs. MacTavish do not speak a word either of French or Spanish, the conversation carried on between them before we arrived was not of the most animated description. All parties were enchanted when they got hold of interpreters. She is a beautiful woman with brilliant black eyes and black hair and a most beautiful complexion. She is living in this house, and I must go and see her by and by.

DECEMBER 24:—We carried Eliza to Mr. Carroll's on the evening of the twenty-second. The interview appeared to give mutual satisfaction, if we are to judge from the fixed attention with which she gazed upon the old man who, in his turn, was delighted at having attracted her notice to such a degree. She would scarcely look at Mrs. MacTavish's baby, in spite of all the blandishments the little creature put forth to attract her, but her great-grandpapa interested Eliza too much to admit of her bestowing much notice upon the third generation below him. Mrs. Harper (another daughter of Mr. Carroll's) and her daughter were the only persons there. Eliza behaved beautifully as she always does. She is a child that never gives the least uneasiness as to how she is to conduct herself in company.

We went in the morning to St. Paul's Church where we were much gratified both by the reading and the preaching of Dr. Wyatt, the clergyman who we met at Saratoga, though we had no idea then who he was, or even of his name. He is infinitely the best reader and the best preacher that we have heard in this country. Basil went back in the afternoon to hear his address to the teachers of the Sunday schools. I was obliged to remain at home with Eliza, as Mrs. Cownie went to Church. We drank tea *en famille* with Mr. and Mrs. David Hoffman, for whom we had a letter from Mr. Denison, but as we were engaged both the nights they asked us to dinner they begged us to go last night. We met only some of the members of their own family, four or five Mr. Hoffmans and one Miss Hoffman. We took Eliza to-day to the Museum, a place which always delights her much, and she went about from one room to another exclaiming, "Oh dear! Oh dear!", so much was she pleased. We had as many visitors to-day as we had the first day we were known to be here, and had we been at home all the day should have had quite a *levée,* as the Americans call it, but we also had visits to pay and went besides to see the Exchange, which really is as poor an apology for a sight as can well be imagined, altho' it is a fine building, but we trailed up to the highest part of it from whence after all there was nothing to be seen on account of the haze, and were most carefully ushered into the apartments of the Common Council, and had all the pictures pointed out to us of persons of whom we never saw nor heard anything, and whose fame probably never reached beyond the walls of the Exchange, but such is the fate of sightseeing travellers who must submit to seeing a great deal that is quite unworthy of notice along with what there is actually an interest in.

DECEMBER 25:—I wish you all a merry Xmas. We went this morning with Mrs. Caton to the Catholic Cathedral. We wished to see service in a Catholic Church for once in the States, and as this town is, I rather think, the headquarters of Catholicism in this country, we thought we had now a good deal of opportunity for gratifying our curiosity. The Church is a large and handsome one, but the service was very long and the sermon the most bombastic stuff I ever heard, delivered by a young man whose manner was worthy only of the stage. The preacher was formerly a Protestant and became a Catholic Priest some years ago. When I first heard this story I thought that however mistaken we might consider the young man, he must be a conscientious person, as the Roman Catholic Church does not in this country as it does on the Continent of Europe hold out the temptations of wealth and ambition to the avaricious and aspiring, and nothing I thought, short of the strongest conviction of doing what was right could induce a man to change his faith to another in which there was neither profit nor honour, but his sermon and his manner thoroughly put to flight all my notions of tenderness of conscience having a part in this change, and I am quite adrift as to his motives, nor do I care much, I must say, for I never saw anyone whose heart seems to be less in his business. On the Continent the magnificence of the Churches, the beauty of the music, and a variety of assistant circumstances contribute to render a visit to a Catholic Church very impressive, especially if one does not remain long enough to allow the delusion to wear off. But three hours of it, as we had yesterday, is too much of such mummery, and I never before was so struck with the mockery of their ceremonies.

The State of Maryland, of which Baltimore is the chief city, altho' Annapolis is the capital in so far as the legislature meets there, was originally settled by Catholics and was remarkable even in early times for being the most tolerant State in the Union, very different from the Puritans in the Eastern States, who tho' they fled for the sake of enjoying religious liberty persecuted every other sect with the same relentless zeal from which they themselves had suffered at home. We dined at Mr. Bosley's with a family party at three o'clock, a most inconvenient hour to dine out; it shortens the day so sadly. In the evening we went to Mr. Caton's where we had also been invited to dine. Mr. Carroll was, as usual, the most cheerful-looking member of the group.

DECEMBER 27:—Yesterday we went with Dr. Wyatt to visit the jail and penitentiary, both of which are very imperfect in their arrangement, but Dr. Wyatt has done much good in both by his personal trouble. However, it is very discouraging even to the best disposed persons to find their labours counteracted by the mischief arising from free communication and many other evils, and, as there is a constant change of prisoners, of course there is as continual an importation of fresh wickedness. From the jail we walked to the hospital by a road so muddy that I could scarcely keep my shoes on, but I never experienced more fully the excellence of india-rubber shoes, for in spite of the mud and water I walked through, I came home at the end of three hours with my feet as dry as when I set out. We saw some beautiful views of the town from different points in our walk. It is really a pretty place, Baltimore, notwithstanding the unfavourable season at which we have visited it, but yesterday was beautiful overhead, mild and bright. We dined at Mr. Wilson's, the correspondent of Mr. Rathbone at Liverpool. We had a huge party. Ten gentlemen I think, to five ladies, but this is not an unusual proportion of the sexes at an American dinner. Yesterday there were no females except those belonging to the family. The dinner hour was half past three, which is really the saddest waste of time that can be imagined. It is of less consequence in summer when one can walk after dinner, but in winter that is impossible, and we can never get one half done that we wish, because we must come home in the middle of the day to dress for dinner. This morning Mr. Caton called upon us at half past ten and with him a Mr. Thomas, a Quaker and one of the directors of the Alms House, to take us to that establishment at Calverton about two and a half miles from Baltimore. It is a Workhouse as well as an Alms House and is capable of containing between seven and eight hundred persons. It is under excellent management. But the greatest pleasure we derived from the morning's expedition arose from Mr. Thomas's conversation, which was of a very different stamp from that of most persons in this country, whose views are generally by no means the most enlarged, indeed you cannot imagine anything more limited than not only their topics but the way in which they treat them. Except Mr. Thomas, I really do not think I have met one man who as far as his practice went seemed capable of generalising on any subject whatsoever. When I go into a house I know as well what is to be talked of and how as if it were all written up before me.

DECEMBER 28:—This letter is of a much smaller size than I am in the habit of sending, but I think it is best to begin afresh at Washington, so I shall send this from hence, small as it is. We dined yesterday at Mr. Caton's with a large party and everything in grand style and well arranged. There was a party in the evening, likewise, and Mr. and Mrs. Keene were there, the American gentleman with the Spanish wife whom I have before mentioned. He and I as usual got upon Madrid, and at last he asked me when I had been there, which led me to mention that my father was Consul General there. "Sir John Hunter!" he exclaimed, "I had been puzzling myself to remember where it was that I had seen you before," and then he went on describing so many things so minutely that I saw he remembered us perfectly. "But you had a sister," he remarked. I said yes, and that you had now five children. He was not acquainted with us but used to see us every evening of the summer of 1814 walking in the Prado where he frequently was with persons of our acquaintance. I was surprised to meet with anyone who should recognise me after such a lapse of time, but this man's manner left no room to doubt that he at least had done so. This morning we went to the University and the Infirmary, which is taken charge of by the Sisters of Charity and is the nicest and cleanest establishment that I have seen. Such a changeable climate to be sure this is. Yesterday it rained without ceasing and the rain froze into icicles as it fell. To-day it is like summer. To-morrow I trust it will be the same, as we have to travel to Washington.

10:30 P.M. :—We are all packed and ready to start at nine o'clock at latest to-morrow morning. I dined to-day at Mr. Caton's, *en famille,* and carried Eliza with me to bid farewell. Basil dined at a bachelor party at Mr. Oliver's. Mrs. Caton and I went to the play to see Miss Kelly in *The School for Scandal.* She is by no means a good actress, but I was well amused with the play, altho' not much edified. I have just come home from it and must now go to bed.

Ever affectionately yours,

MARGARET HALL

LETTER XIII

WASHINGTON

Captain and Mrs. Hall settle down for a month in the Capital. The British
Minister welcomes them and introduces them to the President and Mrs.
Adams at the *levee* on New Year's Day. After the presentation Mrs. Hall
wanders about in search of "oddities" and finds the smell of gin very strong
in the refreshment rooms. They go to balls at the houses of the Commander-in-Chief, General Brown, and the Secretary of the War Department, Mr. Barbour, and also to parties at Mrs. Decatur's and at various
foreign legations. Mrs. Hall finds much to grumble at in the shabby, ill-
lighted receptions where there is so little room for dancing that, to her, they
resemble a ticket ball in a tavern. The Halls take to giving themselves
"a daily dose" of debates in the House of Representatives.

WASHINGTON, December 29, 1827.

My Dearest Jane,

We left Baltimore this morning soon after nine o'clock and
found the road much better than we expected, at least as far as the
weather had any effect, but a worse led road never was seen certainly, up and down hill by the steepest course that could be found,
according to the very old plan of making roads in England. Jolts,
too, we had in abundance, but, notwithstanding all that, I have
travelled many a worse road that has been less spoken of. We
changed horses twice; at Waterloo and at the "White House". The
whole distance was thirty-seven miles through very bleak, poor-
looking country, but we were fortunate in as fine a day as we can
expect to have at this season, for it neither rained, snowed, nor
froze. Eliza, as usual, was all fun and good humour, altho' she
slept only six miles of the journey. The rest of the time she either

read Cock Robin, that is to say had it read to her, or romped about the carriage, occasionally sitting quiet for a little while.

We have been in Washington between two and three hours and are quite charmed with the appearance of our lodgings and the small experience we have had of the goodness of the house in all respects. We have a large handsome parlour and two excellent bed rooms in a passage which leads to no other room, so that we can shut the door of it and be quite alone. The house is altogether well-furnished and just opened by the person who keeps it. The first appearance of Washington is exactly what I expected, as unlike the capital of a great country as it is possible to imagine, excepting the very first building of all, the Capitol, situated on an eminence and looking very commanding and beautiful on the first impression, but, except for that, one is tempted to ask even in the heart of the city, "Where is Washington?" We had a note a few moments ago from Mr. Vaughan to say that his engagements prevent him from coming to see us to-night and asking us to dine with him to-morrow. It is always more comfortable to be left to oneself the first night and to have leisure to turn the beds (Eliza's has already been shifted to three different positions), and to arrange the rooms according to what appears the best plan. We are here in the very heart of the city but not a sound is to be heard, and I could more easily imagine myself in a country inn than in a great hotel in a capital. And so to go on to a very different subject. I wish to tell you or any of my friends who may be oppressed with many or too bad peaches that one of the best pickles I ever ate is peach pickle. Some that we had at dinner to-day reminded me of this, for I have seen them before. It is more like mangoe than anything else, but better I think.

DECEMBER 31:—Sunday morning, the thirtieth, after waiting in vain for the warning sound of church bells, we set out in search of a Church and being directed to St. John's we proceeded to the smallest place of worship we have been in in this country. From the Church we walked to Mr. Vaughan's in hope of finding him at home, but as he had in like manner gone to us we missed each other. However, later in the day he called again. As he entered the room he said, in his cheerful voice which recalled old times to my mind, "This, I presume, is Captain Hall, but as for you," he exclaimed, taking me by the hand and leading me to the window, "I should not have recognised you in the least." I could have said as much of him but did not, for the change that I perceived was of a much more melancholy nature than any he could see in me. In fact, I could not trace the least remains of his former self. His hair which you remember brown and curling over his head was silvery and smooth, his cheeks yellow and sunken, in short, when he went away if it had not been for the folly of the thing I should have sat down and cried. It is the first striking example of the ravages of time that I have had so brought home to myself. The better part of him, however, I soon saw was unchanged. He is the same kind, agreeable person I knew him, and afterwards, when we went to dinner with him, even his looks gradually resumed their former character, and I returned from dinner in much better spirits than I went. We spent a most delightful evening, such an one as has not before fallen to our lot in this country. It was quite a family party, the Cornewalls and Mr. Bankhead, Mr. Vaughan and his two attachés, Mr. Ouseley and Mr. Doyle, a son of our old acquaintance, Sir Charles, a couple of very gentlemanlike young men. We staid for an hour after the others had all dispersed, talking of old subjects and new, and then walked home in a fine, moonlight night.

JANUARY 1: —Yesterday our visitors began at ten o'clock and continued without intermission until we went out at one o'clock to the Capitol to hear a discourse read by Mr. Southard, Secretary of the Naval Department. Miss Baker, sister of the Consul General, carried me there in her carriage. She was also kind enough to take Mrs. Cownie and Eliza in the carriage, and we took them into the Rotunda where Eliza was delighted with Trumbull's large, cold, flat, chalky pictures of the signing of the Declaration of Independence, Washington's resignation, and various other points of American history. The discourse was, as usual, what Basil has called a piece of self-laudatory cackling, puff—puff—puff—about themselves. The room was crowded to excess and hot almost beyond endurance, but a walk home from the Capitol was very refreshing. People told me before I came here that it was quite impossible to walk in Washington, but in fine weather I am sure there is no such impossibility. There is a broad footpath of bricks all the way from here to the Capitol and on the other side of us to Mr. Vaughan's, Mr. Bankhead's, and Mr. Baker's, a distance altogether of at least two miles. The weather is charming, dry, clear, and sunny, without much frost. Basil and Mr. Vaughan dined with the same institution as we had heard the discourse from, and in the evening we went to a ball at Mrs. Brown's, the wife of the Commander-in-Chief. This was the first specimen of a Washington party that we had seen, and if they are all to be like it I must say there is nothing very delightful about them. The rooms were small and crowded and low-roofed, miserably ill-lighted, and, in short, the whole thing was poor and shabby to a degree. We had seen the President and many other of the Ministers in the morning. Mr. Clay, the Secretary of State, was at the party and is a very agreeable person, but we are getting daily more out of humour with these disagreeable Americans, and they tell such absurd stories of us and misrepresent what we say in such a manner that it really wears out our patience. To-day everyone goes to pay their respects to the President. Mr. Vaughan calls for us at twelve o'clock to present us.

JANUARY 3:—Well, I still think that Washington is the best place we have been at, and yet when I ask myself where is the attraction I find that it is being with Mr. Vaughan that makes both Basil and myself like it better than any other part of the Union we have visited, so that the Americans have no share in our pleasure. One very essential point in our comfort is the great superiority of our lodgings over any we have had elsewhere. In every respect we are better off—attendance, rooms, quietness, cooking, and the expense by no means much greater, not so great indeed as at Baltimore. We pay six dollars and a half per day for ourselves, Mrs.

Cownie, and Eliza, and this includes board, lodgings, fires, and candles. This is under £1.10 per day. Mr. Vaughan would have us to dine with him every day if we would go, but we like being at home sometimes, especially as there is a party almost every night. He sent round our cards along with his own to the different members of the *Corps Diplomatique* and the Cabinet, which is vouching for us as proper persons to be received, and in return we have had multitudes of cards left for us. There are not any of my old diplomatic acquaintances here, but I hope to hear of some of them from their countrymen. There is a Baron Stackelberg, the Swedish Minister, whose appearance and whose valsing, more especially, reminds me not a little of Count de la Gardie, who, I understand, is now a great man in his own country. I have only just been introduced to Baron Stackelberg, but I shall meet him everywhere, of course, and I shall ask him about my old friend.

I have been out since I began to write. Miss Baker took me in her carriage to return some visits, fortunately at Washington it is the custom to leave cards instead of going in; many persons even send round their cards by their servants. Anything is better than having to go into every house and say the same thing twenty times over, and here where the distances are so great and the visits are so numerous, one's whole time would be taken up in this most uninteresting and profitless occupation. The hours at Washington are particularly well-suited to the style of life. Dinner is at five universally, and there is no sitting after dinner, so that by half past seven everybody is ready to go to the evening party wherever it may chance to be, and there are few evenings without one. They, again, are over by half past ten or eleven. Dancing is the universal amusement, with a couple of whist tables in the corner for those who are so disposed, of whom Mr. Vaughan is always one. A change since you and I knew him! The parties, to judge by the two I have been at, are of the most shabby description, small, ill-lighted rooms and bad, dirty-looking refreshments, carried through the crowded dancers by nasty black boys, on old japanned trays, to the great detriment, I doubt not, of the ladies' dresses. The music, too, is most defective; in short, nothing could be worse in all respects. I hope we shall find things better arranged at the Dutch Minister's, where we go to-night.

We went on the first along with the rest of the nobility to pay our respects to the President and Mrs. Adams. There was a queerish enough kind of medley of persons, tho', on the whole, not so many odd looking persons as I expected to see. The President is a short, elderly man with an expression of much care and anxiety. Mrs. Adams I could scarcely see, the crowd around her was so great. A suite of four or five rooms was thrown open and refreshments, smelling strong of gin, were handed round. Ice, too, there was, but the greater part of the eatables was devoured by the most ordinary of the company, who pounced upon the trays like those not much accustomed to such fare. The day was most beautiful, which was lucky as otherwise the smell of wet coats and boots would not have added to the pleasures of the squeeze. We remained upwards of an hour wandering about in search of oddities and then walked to various visits. We dined at home and then in the evening went to a party at Mrs. Pleasanton's, whose husband is in some public office or other. It was rather less shabby than that of the night before but still very poor; dancing and valsing carried on in the smallest possible space. I dance always, for there is no other way of amusing oneself. There is no room to walk about for the purpose of seeing people, and if there were there is no one worth seeing. You may say, perhaps, that dancing in a space no bigger than a cheese plate must be poor amusement for anyone out of their teens, but it is not quite so wearisome as standing crushed up to the wall. The President and Mrs. Adams never go into company, neither do they receive or pay visits. It is not etiquette to do so. Yesterday it rained till late in the afternoon, which was very convenient for us, as it kept away visitors, altho' many cards were left.

We dined yesterday at Mr. Vaughan's, the same family party as on Sunday, and Basil and I remained as before for an hour after all the others were gone, having a *talk,* which I think he enjoys as much as I am very sure we do. Even his appearance is not so much changed as I imagined it was when I first saw him, every day he seems to me to return more to what he was, except his hair. That of course remains white and has lost its beautiful curl. I never see him without regretting that he should be a bachelor and now, I fear, hopelessly so. I am sure he would be much happier if he were married, but I suspect it is too late. Mrs. Cornewall and I have great pocketting always at Mr. Vaughan's of the beautiful sugar plums from his dessert for the amusement of our respective children. He lives in very handsome style indeed.

JANUARY 4:—The comfort of a whole evening spent at home is not to be expressed. It is one we are at this moment enjoying, and very grateful we feel for it. Basil dined yesterday with a large party of the Vice-President and many members of the House of Representatives at Mr. Vaughan's, from which I was, of course, excluded, to the great sorrow of the master of the house who would very much have liked to have asked me, but I thought that a party of thirty gentlemen and one lady would not have been particularly agreeable. I went at half past seven to pick up Basil, but they had not yet rose from table, so I walked into Mr. Vaughan's very comfortable sitting room and amused myself with the newspapers until the party dispersed. Mr. Vaughan brought out a good deal of furniture from England, some exquisite Montagu chairs from Mr. Dowbiggin's make me quite homesick. They are the only truly comfortable seats I have met with since I left St. Colm Street. There is nothing in his house in the way of furniture that is at all splendid, altho' everything is perfectly comfortable, but his style of entertaining, Basil says, is magnificent and must surprise some of the members from the woods and wilds of the west, I should think. The party of the evening was at Madame Huygens's, the wife of the Dutch Minister and mother to Madame Neiderstatter, whom I met at Philadelphia. It was a much better party than either of those I had been at before. The ballroom was built for that purpose by the Baron de Mareuil, late French Minister here, and would have been quite perfect but for an immense fire which the servants in their wisdom had thought appropriate to the month of January, without paying attention to the thermometer, which must have been sixty at least, I am sure, for the weather is unnaturally warm for the season, damp and foggy and cloudy it is, accompanied by occasional rain, but anything is better than frost or snow.

This morning we set off from home in a coach by eleven o'clock, as previous to following our own pursuits we wished to arrange something about Mrs. Cownie attending the Sacrament upon Sunday next, so after going to the Presbyterian clergyman we drove to the Capitol from whence we sent home Eliza and her attendant whilst we proceeded into the Senate. There is rarely, I believe, much of interest in the Senate, and we went with the intention of merely seeing the opening of the House and the forms, but a debate arose on a bill abolishing imprisonment of persons for debt, and we remained to hear it until three o'clock, when the House adjourned, after having been occupied the whole day. It was proved to be of no use whatever, as the member who moved for an amendment in the Bill withdrew his motion. I was greatly more interested than I expected to have been and intend to return on Monday the seventh to hear the continuation, if not the end, of the debate. From the Capitol we walked home and as usual found the table covered with cards and invitations and have since, as I have already said, enjoyed our own company.

Last night at Madame Huygens the French Chargé d' Affaires, the Comte de Menou, asked particularly to be presented to me to renew his acquaintance which began at Madrid in the year 1815. I have not the smallest recollection of him, but he was there in such a time of confusion and numbers of persons that it is not surprising that I should have forgotten him, especially as he was only forty-eight hours there, but both the evenings he spent at our house. He came with Comte Henri de Montmorenci. What a different style of society to be sure we were then enjoying from what I am now mixing in! The beautiful women and their magnificent dresses and covered with diamonds, compared to the scarcely worthy to be termed *pretty* persons here, dressed as if their clothes were thrown at them. The splendid suites of rooms and superb suppers contrasted with the little ill-lighted apartments and bad refreshments of the Washington parties do not dispose me to view my present associates with very favourable eyes. We find numbers of persons whom we made acquaintance with now assembled here to attend Congress, and even foreigners and others who have no connection with that assembly officially are now congregated here to see its proceedings. Count Lillers, the Frenchman whom I have before mentioned, is here. This year there will be a long session, probably till May; in general it only lasts till March, and after that all the persons who remain here, except only those belonging to the executive and who cannot therefore get away, shut up their houses and live in some corner or other of them, saving their miserable salaries for eight months in the year on purpose to be enabled to make some sort of an appearance (though but a miserable one certainly) during the remaining four, so that really their bad lemonade ought to be accepted with gratitude and not to be abused, for they are most wretchedly paid.

I had a note to-night from a lady whom I had considerable curiosity to see, Mrs. Decatur, the widow of Commodore Decatur. I brought a letter to her from Mrs. MacTavish at Baltimore and sent it yesterday along with our cards. In this note she acknowledged the receipt of it, but excuses herself from calling upon me, "as peculiar circumstances attending a domestic affliction she has suffered make it impossible for her to come to Washington." She asked us to spend the evening of the tenth with her, or any other evening that suits us better, a very kind note, in short, and we have promised to go on the eleventh. I knew that she would not return my visit before I came. The reason of this peculiarity is that her husband was killed in a duel, and she fears if she were to go into company either morning or evening that she might meet either his second, who she considers as having been very much to blame, or his antagonist. Now all this is very natural, and I only object to it because somehow she appears to have made her reasons too much the subject of conversation, which is very unlike real feeling. She sees a great deal of company at home. Her note smells so detestably of musk that it quite perfumes the room and was like to make me sick, so we had sealed it up in an envelope, but it shall go along with the next of the scraps.

JANUARY 6:—We have had to-day weather much more like June than January, most extraordinary for this climate, where at this season there is generally severe frost and snow. I went out with a cloak on but speedily returned and exchanged that for a silk handerchief tied round my throat, which was as much as I could bear. Yesterday, the fifth, we walked off by eleven o'clock to visit Mrs. Decatur, who lives at Georgetown, which is separated from Washington only by a little creek, across which there is a shabby enough tumble-down looking wooden bridge. There was so thick a fog that we could not see three yards before us, "quite English weather," as our friends here tell us, but not disagreeable to my mind as it was very mild. At the door of Mrs. Decatur's house we met General Van Rensselaer, "the Patroon," who with his wife and daughter is now here. He went in with us and introduced us to the lady of the mansion, who we found dressed in very becoming weeds, and she gave us an extremely cordial reception. She is a pretty, pleasing-looking person and very animated, with no appearance of woe except the outward signs of cap and gown. We sat some time with her and then walked home, as Mrs. Cownie went to the Preparation Sermon, as they call the day before Sacrament Sunday in the Presbyterian Churches, and consequently the charge of little Miss devolved upon me.

We went last night to Mrs. Barbour's, the wife of the Secretary of the War Department; such a crowd and such heat I have seldom been exposed to. Mrs. Barbour told me that in consequence of the badness of the night, which was truly one of the blackest and darkest I ever saw, she had had innumerable apologies, which I am sure she must have been thankful for as I know not possibly how she could have stowed away any more people. Two of the lamps went out almost immediately and smelt the whole night in the most abominable manner, indeed, at these parties it is impossible not to imagine oneself at a three shilling ticket ball at a second-rate tavern, not that I ever was at any such, but nothing certainly can be lower than the style of entertainment, and you must bear in mind that Mr. Barbour is the Lord Palmerston of Washington! Talking of the weather having occasioned Mrs. Barbour receiving so many apologies, you cannot imagine what a fuss people make about a shower of rain in this country. Miss Baker tells me that she finds it considered quite sufficient reason for breaking any appointment. In the newspapers, too, I observe constantly notices given that such a sale will take place provided the weather be good "if not, on the next fair day." They marvel at me very much walking out in all sorts of weather as I do, even more than most English women, and all English women, which, of course means Scotch too, walk more than any other women in the world. I generally contrive to take a walk of three or four miles every day that it does not actually pour.

JANUARY 7:—Speaking of walking reminds me that I have the greatest difficulty in getting shoes, either for myself or Eliza in this country. As for a wellmade shoe, I have not seen such a thing. All that I have got are either too small or so large that my foot shakes about in them, to the great risk of spraining my ankle. The satin, too, of which they make them is the greatest trash that can be. At Philadelphia I got for Eliza the best shoes I have been able to procure for her, but still they are very inferior to what I should have got at home. I learned from some one lately that in London you can get nests of shoes for children from the age of one year upwards. If I had known this before I left home I should certainly have provided myself with some.

We dined yesterday at Mr. Baker's, the Consul-General's, for whom his sister keeps house. One or two foreigners were there and one or two Americans, quite a small party. It is not the custom here to spend the evening where you dine. The dinner hour is five, and by half past seven or eight one either gets home or goes to any party, and at ten o'clock we invariably order our carriage to bring us home. The distances one has to travel from one place to another are immense, and as the greater part of them there is no connexion between the houses and consequently no lamps, it is very dark indeed when the moon does not shine. Washington is not like one village but like several little villages thrown together with a small space between them. It is in all respects like a watering place, and the Capitol may serve as a huge hotel, public rooms and all. Those who know Tunbridge Wells say that Washington is exceedingly like that place.

JANUARY 9:—At length to my great sorrow but to the great joy of most persons, there is every prospect of cold weather. Yesterday there was some snow, or rather sleet, and to-day there is frost. On the seventh we set off between eleven and twelve o'clock to go to the Capitol. We went first into the Senate in hopes of hearing the continuation of the debate upon doing away with imprisonment for debt, but after waiting an hour, during which time we heard nothing but presenting numerous petitions, the House adjourned. We then went to the House of Representatives and there had the luck of hearing Mr. Randolph, a very much thought of speaker here, so it was well to hear him for once at all events, tho' I confess I was disappointed with his eloquence which appeared to me to be very much marred by the number of truisms he uttered. The debate was upon whether or not compensation was to be made to a man whose slave had been taken for the service of the government during the war and had been killed, and the question was whether slaves were considered persons or property. Anything regarding slaves always occasions a prodigious sensation in the House. It is a subject that the Southern members will not allow those from the North to touch, and they were going on very animatedly when a motion was made to adjourn, and we had time to walk home just in time to dress for a huge dinner at Mr. George Graham's. All the English Legation dined there and also the Brazilian *Chargé d' Affaires,* Mr. Rebello, one or two American gentlemen, Mrs. Rush, the wife of the Secretary of the Treasury (who was for some years in England either as Minister or Secretary of Legation, I forget which). His wife was with him and must have profited much by her English education for she is by much the most ladylike American I have seen. From Mr. Graham's we went to Mr. Dickin's who is married to a lady from Edinburgh, a Miss Arnot, I believe, and from thence we came to Madame Durant de St. André's, the French Consul General. The St. Andrés married at Madrid a very short time after we had left it, and from Madame I heard of many of our old friends, especially of the French Embassy. Comte d' Agoult and Baron de Caux are both married and both still in diplomatic life. In spite of all this gaiety we were home at half past ten.

Yesterday morning we were awoke by the firing of cannon in commemoration of the anniversary of the battle of New Orleans, where General Jackson commanded, and, as he is the rival candidate to Mr. Adams of the ensuing election of President and is the popular candidate, it was made quite a party business, as everything great or small is in this country even more than in England. We went as usual to the Capitol. At the House of Representatives we heard a discussion on passing a bill for engaging Mr. Allston to fill up one of the empty panels in the Rotunda with a picture of the battle of New Orleans. The member who brought forward this motion accompanied it by a most flaming speech which had all the appearance of being got by heart and repeated before the glass according to the most approved method of gesticulation used in the public schools. As usual, the house adjourned without coming to any decision. Mr. Everett of Massachusetts who has a great reputation as a public speaker said a few words, but I was disappointed in his manner.

At the next hotel to this and within half a dozen doors of us, there was a Jackson dinner which I was right glad to get out of the way of, as each toast was accompanied by firing cannon. Mrs. Cownie tells me that Eliza was delighted with the firing. The first time, she started, not being prepared for it, but then Mrs. Cownie told her about it, and they opened the window and the child watched each cannon that was fired with the greatest interest and laughed with delight every time. Basil and I dined at Mr. Bankhead's along with Baron Maltity of the Russian Legation, Mr. Lisboa of the Brazilian Legation, and Captain and Mrs. Kuhn. He is an American by birth, tho' by inclination, I think, somewhat more of an European. His wife is English, daughter of Mr. Hargrave who since the year 1811 has been consul at the Balearic Islands. She was in Spain at the same time that you and I were, but not at Madrid. She is a very pleasant person but has no love for this country, indeed, she said yesterday that if told at that moment that she was to set off next day for Europe she would undertake to be ready by nine o'clock. I can well understand that feeling in a person whose stay here is indefinite, it is only the knowledge that one may quit as soon as they please that makes the sojourn tolerable. The gentlemen all went to a whist party at Mr. Rebello's, and as soon as the toasting and firing in our neighborhood was at an end Basil came from the party to carry me home.

Count Survilliers and the Prince and Princess of Musignano are come to Washington. We met them walking near the Capitol on the seventh and to-day I mean to carry Eliza to visit her little friend. I never saw any man more anxious to see another than Mr. Vaughan is to see Joseph Bonaparte, which is natural enough considering that he was kept in hot water by him during three years whilst *"el re Bepe"* sat on the throne of Spain and Mr. Vaughan was Secretary of Legation to the Insurgents at Cadiz. It would not be etiquette that Mr. Vaughan should call upon him, so they have but a small chance of meeting, unless, indeed, the report he heard yesterday should prove true, that he dines to-day with Mr. Clay, which Basil and Mr. Vaughan also do.

JANUARY 11:—The ninth we went to the House of Representatives and heard the sequel of the debate upon the picture.

The motion was lost, and this was considered a triumph for the administration as it was made quite a party question. Mr. Randolph made a very amusing, sarcastic speech, but on the whole the business of the day was tiresome enough, as any member who wished it, proposed counting the House by ayes and nays, and this was done five times, each time occupying fifteen minutes. Basil dined at a male party at Mr. Clay's, the Secretary of State, and in the evening we went to the Drawing Room at the President's. Mrs. Adams has such a party on the alternate Wednesdays, Mrs. Clay taking the others. The night was bad, which made the party smaller than usual, for as I have before remarked, bad weather very soon turns the Americans from their purpose. At the President's we met the Prince of Musignano and were surprised to learn from him that he and his family are on the eve of embarking for Italy. They are to go in a ship of war, the *Delaware,* of one hundred and five guns. He seems to be quite glad to get away from this country, and he and his wife have certainly done their duty by their father with whom they came to stay a year, and have remained four, but I am sorry for the poor Count who will feel sadly desolate left alone in this country where he has actually no society and no pursuit. He and the Princess had set off that morning suddenly on hearing that their little girl who is dying was worse. The little Joseph was very unwilling indeed to go away without first coming to see Eliza. They will meet in Italy some day, I hope. We asked the Prince if he were not very glad to return to his own country. "O yes," he replied, "and you know after a little while one gets so sick of this country," a sentiment in which we cordially joined. He hopes to be in Rome in a month from this time. Good heavens, what a change! From Washington to Rome!

We were much amused with a conversation we had last night with the Comte de Lillers. He arrived at New York the very same day that we did and has been travelling ever since and has gone over a good deal more ground than we have. He describes himself as having arrived in America in very much the same frame of mind as Basil, totally impartial and unprejudiced, only if there was any leaning in his mind it was towards the favourable side as regards this country, and in this way he was willing to see all that was favourable, but it won't do, he has gone on daily liking this country and the people and the manners and the Government worse and worse, till now he has got so out of patience with the whole thing that he really got into a towering passion last night when he came to discuss the matter over with us, and Basil warned him more than once that he might be overheard. He said he did not care. He wished them to know, at least, that he was not their dupe. We contrive to become unpopular without expressing half so much as Count Lillers and many others do, but I believe this arises from Basil being known to be a writer and also because they have taken it into their wise noodles to believe and spread a report that Basil is employed by the Government to see and give an account of this country, and that he was selected *because* of his strong prejudice against it, which would lead him to give such an account as is wished by the British Government. This is complimentary, I think, both to the Government and the agent.

We took our usual three hours' dose of the Senate and House of Representatives yesterday, the tenth. We dined at home and before going to Madame Huygens's ball stepped into the Hotel next door to see a party of little creatures there assembled of whom Eliza was one, and the most delighted one of the group certainly. What with the number of children and the fiddle and the cat, she was in a perfect *embarras de richesses*. She went up to all the children, turned them round, and looked in their faces, taking great notice of those who pleased her.

At Madame Huygens's we made acquaintance with Augustin de Yturbide, the son of Yturbide, whose name and fate you are well acquainted with. He is a remarkably handsome young man. The Spanish Minister's family made their appearance last night. They have only just arrived, and with them came Mr. Wallenstein who is desperately in love with one of the daughters. He was introduced to me and made many apologies for not having recognised me when we met at Philadelphia. You know he was attached to the Russian Legation when we were at Madrid.

JANUARY 12:—Yesterday we paid some visits which we had long owed. We drove to Georgetown to call upon our fellow passenger in the *Florida,* Miss Wright, whom we found engaged in teaching a school. The sight of her almost made me seasick, so strongly was her countenance associated in my mind with the horrors of that suffering. Her dislike to the country does not seem to have diminished by her second visit. We dined at the President's with a party of nearly thirty. I sat next him and found him a quiet, mild man with very little manner, certainly, but a pleasing enough address. Mrs. Adams is a very ladylike person. The dinner was very showy, but no American ever understands doing those things really well, and there were strange inconsistencies and altogether a clumsiness very unlike the elegance of Mr. Vaughan's entertainments. We went afterwards to a party at Mrs. Decatur's but I have just heard that Mr. Vaughan has stopped the closing of his dispatches for our letters, so adieu.

MARGARET HALL.

LETTER XIV

WASHINGTON

The Halls visit the Supreme Court and dine again at the White House. Captain Hall asks to be allowed to present his daughter to the President. "This, of course, was graciously received" and Eliza, much curled and in a muslin frock, made her curtsey. Both the President and Mrs. Adams were kind, and the following day Eliza was sent a locket containing Mr. Adams' hair, a prize to be treasured with Mrs. De Witt Clinton's coral necklet and the Bonaparte doll. At dinner with Mr. Vaughan Mrs. Hall observes a pretty girl feeding herself with ice-cream from a steel knife and comments drastically on the provincialism of manners in the Capital. In spite of the endless parties to which she is invited by members of the Government and others, she feels that there is no heartfelt good will towards either of them. "Great dinners" and "squeezy" parties occupy all evenings and bring her but little pleasure.

WASHINGTON, January 15, 1828.

My DEAREST JANE,

I brought home a book to-day from the booksellers intending to indulge myself in a lazy evening, but I was not sorry to find it so uninviting that I speedily laid it aside, because, in fact, I feel at present as if I were doing something wrong when I read for mere amusement to the neglect of writing, wherein I can unite duty with pleasure. So I threw *The O'Briens and the O'Flahertys* on one side and seized hold of a sheet of paper, over which Miss Eliza shook the candle and threw a drop of wax, but I cannot for that condemn it as unworthy of bearing its share among my manuscripts, as really our consumption of stationery forms no small item in our expenses. In a visit to Mr. Vaughan this morning we made a prize of a quarter of a hundred prime, picked pens such as they use in the public offices in England, and

181

they will keep us writing for some time to come. I finished my last dispatch rather hurriedly; when Basil walked to Mr. Vaughan's he found that his dispatches were actually making up, but they were stopped on our account so we had to finish straightway and carry our packet with us when we went to dine at a huge party at his house, of about thirty persons. Those great dinners are always more or less of a bore, but the evil was increased upon this occasion by some of the party not arriving till an hour after the time they had been invited, owing to the gentleman's business having detained him, so, of course, the dinner was cold, as the cook happened to be more exact than the company and had dished at the proper time. Those who kept us waiting were two very pretty girls, the Miss Van Ness's, with their uncle, but, alas, the beauty of the one nearest me seemed to disappear when on looking round I found her feeding herself with very much-melted ice-cream with a great steel knife! I had the honor of the uncle's attentions at dinner, and a greater goose I have seldom sat near. One of his questions was how Washington compared to London, a comparison which I told him had better not be attempted. He next attacked me upon the society but saved me the trouble of replying by relating to me a conversation he had had with a certain Dr. Brown, an American who after having visited most of the Courts in Europe pronounced "what may be called the Court Circle of the United States" to be superior to any he had seen elsewhere. I could only answer that the gentleman was partial to his own country. You cannot conceive how difficult it is to keep within the limits of good manners and yet say nothing but the truth; the whole truth one is, of course, sometimes obliged to suppress. But, to be sure, to talk of the society here as compared to that of any part of Europe! I do wish you could see some of the *entrés* into a drawing room. For example, one gentleman with a couple of ladies, one pinioned on each side, a more unhappy looking animal you never beheld. The trio march up to the lady of the house, make their bows and curtsies to her, wheel round, and in the same way face and salute the Master, a third motion brings them to seats, where the unhappy man in question shakes himself free from his companions and is once more himself. Those little defects or absences of manner, however, might be overlooked did not the arrogancy and self-sufficiency of those people maliciously incline one "to spy fairlies," as we say at home. At times, indeed, we feel so disgusted that we are almost tempted to turn our backs upon the whole thing and start off home, but this would be cowardly, and we had better go through with it. There are some few persons, too, for whose sake one would fain think well and speak well of their country. I was with one of these to-day, Mrs. Rush, whose husband was for some years the Minister in England where they were both much liked. He is now Secretary of the Treasury here. Mrs. Rush is by far the most ladylike American I have seen. After Mr. Vaughan's dinner on the twelfth we went to a party at Mr. Obregon's, the Mexican Minister, where we had but a small portion of the *Corps Diplomatique,* as none but the English recognise the Republic of Mexico. The deficiency, however, was made up in natives, and such heat I never felt.

On Sunday we went in the evening to a quiet party at Mrs. Rush's. Yesterday the Supreme Court was to meet, we were told, at ten o'clock, and, accordingly, hurried over breakfast and proceeded with all speed to the Capitol, in one room of which the Court is held. On arriving, however, we were told that our informant was wrong by an hour, and that eleven was the time named. Accordingly, in spite of the mist we proceeded to employ our spare hour in mounting to the top of the building, from whence we had no view and on coming down found we had still another hour to wait, and in fact, their Lordships, as my Scotch habit inclined me to call them, did not appear till half past twelve, when all that took place was merely the opening of the Court, and in a quarter of an hour they went off to pay their respects to the President and Vice-President, and we betook ourselves home, the last fortnight's work by evening as well as by morning having totally unfitted us for any further exertion, particularly Basil, who invariably knocks up first, so we resolved to take a rest and, accordingly, sent an apology to Mr. Vaughan's dinner and Mr. Meade's evening party and indulged ourselves in laziness and idleness.

JANUARY 19:—In the course of a ramble we met some one who told us that the Attorney General, Mr. Wirt, was to speak in the Supreme Court on the sixteenth, not on any interesting case, but still to hear him was an object. Accordingly, we set off between ten and eleven to our destination and listened for an hour and a half to a dry point of law which, however, appeared to be very clearly stated by the Attorney General. We then paid a visit to our friends in the House of Representatives where after waiting another hour and a half in vain for a debate the house adjourned and we came home. We dined with our French friend Comte Lillers, who lives at the next hotel, within a hundred yards of us. The object of the dinner was that we might meet General Bernard, formerly a distinguished officer of Bonaparte's, but not choosing to accept employment under the Bourbon dynasty he came to this country where he has an appointment in the Surveying Department. He has been nine years here, and Count Lillers says that he has very intimate knowledge of it in all respects, and it was for the purpose of gaining information from him that the party was made up, but the Count destroyed his whole plan by destroying the *partie carrée* and adding to it Mr. Jared Sparks * of Boston, and so we came away no wiser than we went. It is curious that people will so mar their own plans. We have become very intimate with Count Lillers since we came to Washington, and we are to be great friends when we go to spend a winter in Paris, which is one of the pleasures in the anticipation of which we indulge ourselves as a reward for the sort of purgatory of a winter in American society.

The sixteenth was Mrs. Clay's evening. She and Mrs. Adams hold parties on the alternate Wednesdays. It was a ball, as usual.

*Editor of the *North American Quarterly Review.*

The same bad music drummed the same everlasting tunes in one's ears. There was the advantage, however, of large and airy rooms, and that is always something. The company, to be sure, looked queer enough, for there was such a preponderance of oddly dressed, vulgar-looking people that they seemed to put the more respectable part of the company quite in the background. The seventeenth we went to Mr. Clay's office, the Secretary of State, to see the original document of the Declaration of Independence and other things, but the office was shut. However, we found Mr. Clay in his room and an hour's conversation with him was infinitely more interesting than seeing any of the curiosities of the office. He is not what most of our associates here may come under the denomination of a commonplace man. We are told that in public speaking he is very eloquent. In private conversation he is certainly very animated and pleasing and extremely candid. There is a kindness and cordiality, too, about him which I do not think is a common characteristic amongst his countrymen, we generally complain of a want of heartiness. There is no want of great dinners and squeezy evening parties, and cards without number cover the table every day, but there is, or, at least, does not seem to be, any heart-felt good will. We have hitherto left every place in the country without a shadow of regret or a wish to return. Indeed, we are always more or less glad when the time of departure arrives. I never felt the same before and Basil whose experience is much greater says that it is quite new to him. It is by no means agreeable; I should infinitely prefer suffering a slight heart ache!

Yesterday we tried the House of Representatives again and heard some debating, but it was on a question that I have heard for so many days in that House that I am quite tired of it. It regards slaves, and that is a subject that always creates a ferment in the House; the Southern members are at all times violent upon it. Before going up to the Capitol we went to Colonel McKenney's office; he is at the head of the Indian Department, and his room is full of pictures of Indian Chiefs, implements of war, and articles of dress. We had a note in the morning from Mr. Vaughan asking us to dine *en famille* with him, the Cornewalls and Mr. Bankhead included. We went, accordingly, and, as usual, we remained for a couple of hours after all the others had gone away, always just going, but subject after subject arose and it is such a treat to converse with a man like him, so different either from the Americans or English by whom he is surrounded that it is quite an indulgence to get hold of him for a while alone. This is a weary country for a man of his mind to spend so many years in, but it is so far complimentary to be selected for the situation; that it is one which could not be entrusted to an ordinary man, for the Americans are very difficult people to do business with.

JANUARY 21 :—Here is frost enough now, I am sure, to please those who like it, of whom I confess I am not one. Yesterday and to-day there has been that clear bright, sunny frost with a piercing cold wind which chills me to the heart, and I fear the rivers will be frozen before the thirtieth which is our day of starting, and we shall have to go to Richmond by land, which we are told is the very worst road in the whole Union, and that is a bold saying. Another reason why we shall regret not getting to Norfolk is that a great ship, the *Delaware,* which has only just been launched, at least, this is her first voyage, is there, and Basil wishes to see her. It is in her that the Prince and Princess Musignano are going to Italy. I dined on the nineteenth at Mr. Bankhead's, Basil was, of course, invited also, but there was a meeting of the "American Colonisation Society" to which he preferred going and where we were very sorry not to know until he went there that ladies made part of the audience, but the knowledge came too late for me to profit by it. The objects of this society are to facilitate the disposing of manumitted slaves, for there exists a great difficulty in knowing what to do with them when they are made free. In some of the States there is a law against manumitting them, but I do not know whether that extends to prevent them being sent to Liberia, a track of land on the coast of Africa which has been purchased either by the government or by the society in question to colonise the black in. Basil says there was a great deal of most bombastical speaking, which, however, met with much applause from the majority to whom it was addressed. I was very sorry indeed not to be there instead of a dinner, merely the counterpart of many I have been at. One treat, however, I had. Mr. Ousely was one of the party and played (the piano) and sung most beautifully, but I tire sadly of the society of Mr. Bankhead and his guests. He and Mr. Cornewall have no conversation whatever except quizzing everyone and everything. Some few good stories Mr. Cornewall has, but they are not numerous, and I have already heard him repeat some of them three times, which is more than most stories can bear. Mrs. Cornewall looks out of health and out of spirits and captious, in short, not the sort of person that I could ever take to.

Yesterday, the twentieth, being the only day that Mr. Gales, editor of a paper here, could accompany us, we set aside going to church for once and drove out to visit Mr. Law, who as we had not previously met, we thought it best to have Mr. Gales, who is his intimate friend, to introduce us. He (Mr. Law) is brother to the late Lord Ellenborough. He spent many years in India and upwards of thirty years ago came to this country which has ever since been his home, altho' he has made more than one visit to England during that time. He is a very clever and agreeable man with a great many queer notions in his head and has, I believe, engaged in several schemes without profit either to himself or others. He lives about five miles from Washington at a place which, I dare say, is very pretty in summer but looks abundantly bleak just now, as everything pretending to be the country does at such a season. The old gentleman made me two presents, one, a work of his own, *Instinctive Impulses,* the other, a little belt of copper and zinc with a little piece of flannel between, which I am to wet with salt and water and apply to my forehead when I have a headache. I shall certainly try it upon the first occasion, but I do not feel particularly desirous that one should arise!

We dined at Mr. Vaughan's with a large diplomatic party, not so large, however, as it ought to have been, for just before dinner he received apologies from no less than four ladies, three belonging to the Spanish Legation and Madame Huygens, wife of the Dutch Minister. I was very well situated on one side, having my friend Count Lillers next to me, but on the other side, I had the Russian Minister, Baron de Krudener, who is as deaf as a post and, moreover, had his deafest ear next to me, so that I had to roar to him all the time at dinner and, what was worse, he speaks so indistinctly that I could scarcely understand what he said to me, but it was a pleasant dinner as such things go, tho' they are all disagreeable I think. Basil and I, however, are not quite agreed as to the comparative merits of the etiquette of English and French dinners. He, as he only eats of one dish, is bored by twenty or thirty being offered to him, but I think it is much easier to refuse the offers of the servant than to resist the solicitations of the master and mistress of the house. Besides, it is much more agreeable to see them enter into the enjoyment of the dinner than to see them wearing out both mind and body in doing the honours and carving large joints, and obliging your guests to go through the labor of cutting up is still worse. The only thing against the French style is that many more servants are requisite. So when I come to have a large fortune you shall see my dinners conducted *à la française.*

JANUARY 25:—Well, a great dinner is a very long business at any time, and to-day I have assisted, as the French say, at one of the very biggest, a great reunion of all the *Corps Diplomatique* at the President's. Thirty persons at least, O dear, I should dislike much to be obliged to give such huge dinners. I tire so much sitting so long. I had my former luck of the deaf Baron de Krudener; however, I tried speaking low and found that I succeeded admirably. On the other side I had Chevalier Huygens, the Dutch Minister, who is a very intelligent person. All the foreigners were in their dress coats, and you cannot imagine how gay the assemblage looked to eyes that have been accustomed for so many months to the blackness and badness and slovenliness of American dress.

We went to a particularly squeezy party at Mr. Southard's, the Secretary of the Navy. Those heads of departments are obliged to ask all the rag-tag and bob-tail, so that their parties are really anything but agreeable, more especially as their houses, generally speaking, are so low-roofed, and then the spitting! O the spitting! It seems to increase daily. One night lately as I was walking upstairs to valse my partner began clearing his throat. This I thought ominous. However, I said to myself, "Surely he will turn his head to the other side." The gentleman, however, had no such thought but deliberately shot across me. I had not courage to examine whether or not the result landed in the flounce of my dress.

On the twenty-third we walked off to the steamboat which plies between this and Norfolk once a week and secured accommodation for Wednesday, the thirtieth, in case of our going in her that day. She is very small and the prospect of having to pass a night in a small steamboat in a little low berth is never agreeable, but it is one of those prospects which we have realised, and still realise so often, that it would not do to take faint heart, but the berths are very, very low. Walking first to the Capitol and then to the Senate was pretty well for one day, and I was sufficiently tired to make my conscience easy in staying at home to read the *Red Rover* instead of going to the Drawing Room. Basil went late. The *Red Rover* is Cooper's, the American Novelist's, last novel and infinitely superior to anything he has before written. It is so very nautical that I was very often puzzled, but it bears that impress of truth which conveys conviction even to the uninitiated. Basil says that it is excellent. At the Drawing Room Basil said to the President that he was very anxious to present his little girl to him. This was, of course, graciously received and the twenty-fourth at two o'clock was appointed for the presentation. Mrs. Cownie was amazingly occupied with preparing her little charge for this interview with the " 'King of Washington,' or, at least," she added, "all that they have for one." Accordingly, the whole morning she was dressing Eliza, consulting which frock she looked best in and undoing her curls one tier at a time. I am sure that no young lady dressing for the first time to go to Court ever strove as much to make the most of her appearance as did Mrs. Cownie to bedeck Miss Eliza becomingly. She herself, poor little woman, was not at all conscious of the effect it was wished she should produce, but she was delighted with the various pretty things she saw in the President's drawing room and received both his and Mrs. Adams's attentions very graciously. They seemed to be very much taken with her, altho' neither of them have that sort of manner that shows it much. Mrs. Adams's niece Miss Helen, very kindly took Mrs. Cownie and Eliza thro' the different rooms in the house and after getting some cake and some bon-bons we came away. We went next to see all the shows in the Secretary of State's office where the only objects of interest were the original document of the Declaration of Independence and Washington's commission as Commander in Chief of the army.

JANUARY 26:—Before I could finish my story last night it was time to go to bed, so I shall take up where I left off. On the twenty-fourth there was a dinner of Judges at Mr. Vaughan's, Basil dined there, as did also Mr. Cornewall and Mr. Bankhead, and I dined *tête à tête* with Mrs. Cornewall, and we all went to Madame Huygens's ball which was a very pleasant one, as hers always are. They are so much more select than the others. Yesterday, the twenty-fifth, I did not stir out till dinner time and then went, as I before said, to the President's. When I was leaving him he put a little packet into my hand and begged I would take charge of a little memorial of him for my little girl, a locket with some of his hair in it. I really felt it exceedingly kind that he should have been so mindful of her and were the Presidential election to come on now, there is little doubt of which candidate would have our votes, particularly Mrs. Cownie's, who is much more gratified and flattered than if the present had been made to herself.

January 28:—Yesterday Judge Story sat an hour or two with us in the evening. He is certainly the most fluent man we have met with in America. He would be esteemed so anywhere, but here where people are so slow and make such dreadful pauses between their words the contrast is particularly striking. He is a generous open hearted man, too, such a one as helps to put one in a good humour with the country that he belongs to. His feelings towards England are very different from what we generally find them here. He is one of the Judges of the Supreme Court and is now here in the execution of his official duties.

Do you remember Mr. and Mrs. Webster at Boston? They were both to have spent the winter at Washington and left home for that purpose. She had been complaining through the summer and on arriving at New York they were both laid up by severe illness. He got better and came on here, but shortly was obliged to return to New York as his wife became so much worse, and a week ago she died. And now I must finish my letter and send it to Mr. Vaughan who is to forward it along with his dispatches.

Ever affectionately yours

Margaret Hall

LETTER XV

WASHINGTON TO NORFOLK

The last evenings at Washington were filled by a brilliant ball at the British Legation and an evening party at Mrs. Clay's. On the thirty-first of January the Halls set out by steamboat to Potomac Creek, landed there, and drove by Fredericksburgh to Richmond, "a beautifully situated and vilely dirty" town. The Eagle Hotel was condemned as detestable and filthy. Mrs. Hall found little to her taste except the views over the James River. She did not like seeing ten black faces for every white in the streets and found the slave-holding part of the Union very depressing. Visits were paid to the Capitol, which she describes as intolerably dirty and shabby, to the decaying Arsenal, and to the Penitentiary. The Editor of the *Richmond Enquirer* gave a party for them both, but otherwise Captain Hall seems to have been asked out alone. After six nights in Richmond they went by the James River to Norfolk where Captain Hall met old naval friends and inspected the *Delaware,* a newly built ship with one hundred and five guns. They found Prince de Musignano and his family on the quay, waiting most impatiently to sail in her for Europe. He invited them to drink tea and spend the evening watching a conjuror.

WASHINGTON, January 29, 1828.

MY DEAREST JANE,

I did not think I should have written you another word from Washington, but I must tell you of Mr. Vaughan's ball whilst the pleasure it gave is still so vivid in my recollection that I actually feel a little, a very little of that sort of regret that it is past that I used to experience in former days. It really was a delightful ball, a very different sort of thing indeed from any that we have seen in this city of Washington. Everything was so admirably managed and so beautifully arranged. We went before eight o'clock and were amongst the first. Before the door and about twenty yards along the pavements there was a set of stands with lamps, which were hardly required as there was moonlight, but still it had a good effect and looked very stylish. The usual drawing and dining rooms were appropriated to receiving company and to card tables, and the large dining room, at least fifty feet long, was the dancing room. In one corner of it there was an elevated place for the orchestra, which was much better than it usually is. The floor was chalked, a harp in the centre and round it a wreath of roses, thistles, and shamrocks. All the rooms were beautifully lighted, and the ladies knowing there would be something gayer than they are in the habit of seeing here, were in new dresses much handsomer than I have before seen them in. Considerable pains, too, had been taken in the selection of guests by Mr. Ousely and Mr. Doyle, who I believe cropped the lists a good deal. Below the dancing room was one almost equally large set apart for the eating part of the entertainment. Those arrangements were under the direction of Boulanger, the *maître d' hôtel,* who is always perfect in his department. There was a sort of stage at the end of the room such as you have seen flower pots upon in a drawing room, only infinitely larger, extending the whole length of the room in a convex form. At the back it was done up with evergreens, on the different shelves of the stage were placed on the top the ornamental china filled with all sorts of beautiful *bon bons,* lower down was every kind of French, cold meat dish, done up with the cook's very best skill, both as to the palate and the eye, and he must have been pleased to see that his trouble was not thrown away, for the company ate in a most satisfactory manner. Altho' there was a crowd for a while it was never so great as to impede the dancing, and there was charming valsing space. Of late I have almost given up dancing, I found it was too fatiguing to walk in the day and dance by night, but last night I made an exception and danced a good deal, particularly at the end of the night. Towards the end we had a German country dance. My partner was Monsieur Neiderstetter, the Prussian *Chargé d'Affaires.* This, I thought, was to have been the last of it, but the young gentlemen of the house were resolved not to give in so easily and we had two quadrilles, for the first of which I had the deaf Baron de Krudener who danced as merrily as any boy, and for the second, his young attaché, Mr. Ochando de la Banda, who tho' some twenty years his junior did not seem to enjoy the fun one bit more than his chief, who lamented to me most exceedingly not being able to give me a ball before my departure, but he has not yet got a house. By this time, past twelve, the company, who had since eleven been dispersing, had all gone with the exception of Baron Stackelberg, Baron Krudener, Mr. Ochando, Count Menou, Count Lillers, Mr. Cornewall, Mr. Bankhead, the gentlemen of the house, and ourselves, and off we went downstairs where we had a *petit souper,* talked over the ball, the ladies' dresses, and the ladies, and all were in such good humour with the amusements of the evening that everything and everybody was more or less approved of. Between one and two we got home, and so ends the ball.

FREDERICKSBURGH, VIRGINIA, JANUARY 31 :—You must now have recourse to your maps with greater diligence than ever or you will be quite unable to follow us, for at length we have begun our Southern tour, in comparison with which all that we have before travelled is mere child's play. Yesterday, the thirtieth, was our last day in Washington and consequently a very busy one. We took our last peep at the House of Representatives, paid some bills, and finally dined with Mr. Vaughan with what I may call the family party. We also went for an hour to Mrs. Clay's party that we might take the leave of some of our friends, and especially of Mr. Clay, who both Basil and I are quite fond of. He is so honest and generous and cordial that it is impossible not to like him. This morning there was no peace from half past four o'clock, as the waiter mistook an hour and began rummaging at the parlour fire at that time. From the time we got up there was nothing but bustle of one kind or another till we started for the steamboat in a fright for being too late. Our fear, however, was groundless, and we were on board half an hour before we left the wharf. The sky looked very threatening at first but brightened every hour, and before our day's journey was at an end nothing could be more lovely than the weather. We passed by Mount Vernon, which is the only opportunity we have had of seeing it as the weather had been so bad whilst we were at Washington that we could not think of going sixteen miles of almost impassable road even to see the place where Washington lived, died, and is buried. At half past two we landed at Potomac Creek sixty miles from Washington. We were obliged to get out of the large boat into a small one before landing, as there was not water enough in the Creek to admit of the steamboat going up the whole way. This is always disagreeable but was less so to-day than usual owing to the beautiful weather. After landing we had nine miles of a Virginia road, which are proverbially bad, but we made it out admirably. Eliza was so good, poor little body, altho' she was taken out of bed sound asleep and roused up by being dressed and knocked about, but she sung and laughed and played all day and then fell asleep during the land journey. She has become so laughably polite of late. It does not signify, however cross or tired she may be she never fails to answer "Yes, Maim" (for that is her mode of pronouncing it) and "No, Maim." She has picked it up entirely of herself. Just before reaching Fredericksburgh we crossed a ferry on the River Rappahannock, which if you have ever read Moore's poems on this country, you will remember to have seen mentioned as one of the unpronouncable names he met with.

RICHMOND, VIRGINIA, FEBRUARY 2:—The usual hour of starting from Fredericksburgh by the public stage is two o'clock in the morning, but, on remonstrating with the stage proprietor, he agreed to accommodate us as far as he could by delaying the carriage three hours. However, at four we were called, and at a quarter before five we were seated and off. We merely tied on Eliza's pelisse over her flannel gown, and wrapping her in a cloak carried her down, two thirds asleep, and a very short distance accomplished the rest. It rained hard when we set off but soon stopped and became so mild and pleasant that we had all the curtains up, which makes a great difference to the comfort, particularly when there are nine souls packed up together. We took the seats with our backs to the horses, which we found greatly preferable to the other side, altho' it is so popular, but the middle seat comes so close upon it that it is very choky indeed. The roads were in most places of clay and led along ridges, and the soil seemed everywhere to be slipping down, so that on both sides there were great gullies into which it would have been by no means agreeable to be overturned. We did not reach Richmond till near ten o'clock, but as it was near full moon we had plenty of light altho' the night was cloudy. We got very good private rooms in the Eagle Hotel, a large parlour and two good bedrooms. It is an immense establishment, and there is a great public dinner to-day, so it is doubtful, I think, that we shall be well attended to. I can hardly tell you yet what sort of looking place this is. I have been out, but the weather is so wet and foggy and dark that little is to be seen. The winding of the James River on which it is situated must be very pretty when seen to advantage. Yesterday we crossed the Rivers Mattapony and Pamunky, both Indian names of course. Richmond is the capital of the State of Virginia and at present the legislature is in session. We had several letters of introduction for persons here and sent them this morning after breakfast. One of the gentlemen came at twelve o'clock to take us to the Capitol, which is situated on an eminence commanding a very fine view. Our *cicerone* introduced many gentlemen to us, and we went into the galleries of both houses. One of the gentlemen remarked to me, in a way that showed that he wished to be contradicted, that the inside of the building altogether was quite republican, according to the general idea of want of neatness being a characteristic of republicanism. I could not contradict him in the application of it to what we were then witnessing, for anything so beastly (I really cannot use a gentler term and be correct) I never saw in my life. The gallery of the House of Representatives was an inch thick with dirt; the floor where the members sat was actually flooded with their horrible spitting, in short, the filth was beyond what I have seen anywhere. Both bodies hold their meetings in very shabby rooms, and the members, I must say, were quite in keeping. We went to the top of the building but little was to be seen from thence owing to the haze. We were surprised to see a sentry parading around the Capitol, and on questioning Mr. Lay as to the reason of it, he told us that they always had a guard of fifty men stationed there on account of the archives being kept there, and that they are afraid of them being destroyed by any rising of the slaves. This is the first specimen we have had of the constant dread that the Southern people suffer under from apprehension of their slaves. We have heard of it always but never came in contact with it before. Basil is gone to the public dinner; it is given to Mr. Tazwell, one of the Senators to Congress from Virginia. It is, in fact, a Jackson dinner, such being Mr. Tazwell's politics.

FEBRUARY 4:—I find I mistook in some degree the reason for having military quarters here. They parade a sentry round the Capitol merely as a pretence for having soldiers, but the reason for having them is in case of an insurrection amongst slaves of which the Southern people live in constant dread. What a miserable existence it must be! I think the masters are more to be pitied than the slaves, if it is really true that the soil cannot be cultivated by free, white labor and that the blacks are a necessary evil, but what a system that must be which renders it necessary to keep the slaves in such a state of ignorance that, altho' in this State, I believe, there is no actual, written law against establishing schools for them as there does exist in some others of the States, yet we are told by those who know well that if any such attempt were made a law would be passed forbidding it. It is necessary, in short, to keep them in total ignorance in order to prevent them from coming to knowledge of their own degradation. As I look into the street here I am sure I see ten blacks pass along for one white person. We went yesterday to the Monumental (!) Church, as it is called. It stands on the site of what was once a theatre which sixteen years ago was burnt down, and about sixty persons were killed. At one end of the Church there is a monument to their memories, but it is at present undergoing some repairs and is under cover. I must say what struck me most was the extremely irreverent manner in which people continued coming in during the whole time of the prayers being read, creaking the doors and walking, not with the air of persons accidentally too late but as if it were a habitual practice, as I suppose it is, for when we asked Mr. Lay the hour for going to church he said any time from eleven to half past eleven, and on getting him to explain what he meant he said that if you wished to be there at the beginning of service we ought to go at eleven. Of course it was what we wished and we hurried off accordingly. We had a good many visitors after church, and with one of them Basil is gone today to his plantation about twelve miles distant. We should both have liked that I should have gone, but it did not appear to suit, so I remained in this dirtiest of all dirty houses that I have seen.

Richmond is beautifully situated, but is a vilely dirty place and the hotel was detestable and very expensive. We went to a party at Mr. Ritchie's, the editor of the *Richmond Enquirer,* an anti-administration paper. There we had all the formality of an American party in its most formal shape, the ladies seated as stiffly around the room as possible without an attempt on the part of the gentlemen to separate them, but I think the most remarkable feature of the party was the number of cakes handed round with the tea.

NORFOLK, FEBRUARY 8:—I last wrote whilst Basil was absent on his plantation with Mr. Wickham. He did not return home until seven o'clock and then he had to dress for a bachelor party at Mr. Lay's, from which he came home very early. I had a good many visitors during his morning absence. On the fifth Mr. Lay called for us between ten and eleven o'clock and carried us to the Penitentiary, the most disagreeable sight of the kind that I have seen, not in itself, for there was a great deal of order and cleanliness in the arrangements, but the officer, as they called him, who went about with us, was the most savage animal I ever had the bad fortune to meet with at such an establishment. There was something in his manner that made one's blood run cold. He was, in short, to my imagination the *beau ideal* of a jailer, if I may so pervert a term, and I was right glad to get out of his company. We went from the Penitentiary to the Arsenal, a place now going very much to decay, but we had from thence a pretty view of the Rapids of James River. We were also to have gone to Powhatan, the residence of Mr. Mayo, and the scene of a piece of American, or rather Indian, romance. Captain Smith, who was the first person who visited the State of Virginia, was taken prisoner by the Indian chief Powhatan and was condemned to death according to the humane usages of Indian warfare, but just as his vanquishers were going to put their threats into execution, Pocahontas, the daughter of the chief, threw herself upon Captain Smith and declared that they should first sacrifice her if they did not desist from their purpose. This heroism of the lady's saved his life. Nevertheless, we were tired of sight seeing by this time and were willing to take the rock for granted and instead of boring ourselves any more, after one or two visits, dismissed the carriage and set off on a walk across a curious low bridge over the Rapids and strolled about in weather more like June than February. On the sixth, when we got up before daylight, we found that it was raining hard and looked so dismal that I thought we were to have a most wretched day. We went on board the steamboat that was to carry us down the James River to Norfolk and started a little before eight o'clock. There was rain and fog till near twelve o'clock and then it cleared up and was the first day that we have had for some time so warm that a great part of the day I sat on deck without my bonnet on. The river makes some pretty turns, and we saw many fine fields of wheat coming up, but there was no satisfaction in looking at cottages where you felt that the greatest degree of happiness experienced by the inhabitants must arise from apathy and indifference to their miserable condition. I have not yet got over the depression on my spirits which I have felt ever since I came into this slave-holding part of the Union. They are such stupid creatures, too, the slaves, that at every turn one is made to feel the effects of the degraded state in which they are systematically kept. The distance from Richmond to Norfolk is one hundred and fifty miles, which we accomplished in fifteen hours, paying twelve dollars for us all, which also included breakfast, dinner, and tea, cheap travelling enough and speedy likewise, a great contrast from our journey the other day from Fredericksburgh to Richmond when we were seventeen hours going sixty-six miles and paid twenty-three dollars, including two meals. To be sure, we took an additional place on Eliza's account, which added five dollars to our expenses.

It was near eleven o'clock when we reached Norfolk. There were no coaches waiting to carry the steamboat passengers to the hotels so off we trudged through the mud in the dark, Basil carrying Eliza who had one eye shut and the other open. At the Eagle Hotel we were refused admittance and recommended to Mrs. Housford's boarding house. There we were told that she had but one room with three beds to give us. That would never do, we said, we must have two rooms, but Eliza and Mrs. Cownie and I sat down in the parlour whilst Basil went in further search of lodgings. He returned unsuccessful, and right glad we were to put up with one room, which Basil by a contrivance (you know he is never at a loss for a contrivance) soon converted into two by the help of the bed quilts and one of the beds. Our principal motive in coming to Norfolk was to see a large ship, the *Delaware,* now lying in Hampton Roads previous to sailing for the Mediterranean, so before breakfast yesterday morning Basil went in search of Captain Downes who commands her and with him arranged our plans of operation, in pursuance of which he called for us at ten o'clock and took us in his gig to the Navy Yard where Commodore Barron commands. We went with those two gentlemen over the Navy Yard and to see the new ships that are building and then returned to Norfolk and at two o'clock came off in the steamboat to Old Point Comfort. We met the Prince of Musignano (Charles Bonaparte) on the Wharf. He and his family are waiting most anxiously for the sailing of the *Delaware* in which they are going to Italy. Parade was just commencing, and as soon as we had put ourselves a little to rights we walked off to look at the soldiers at Fort Monroe, quite a rare sight in America, at least, in the United States. The band is a very good one. Whilst we were at dinner the Prince came to ask us to drink tea with them and then to go with them to see a *conjuror* and a most amusing and dexterous one he proved, and there we sat, French, English, and Americans, the near relations of Bonaparte and those who belonged to the nation of his most deadly enemies sitting cheek by jowl together looking at the tricks of a charlatan. There are strange reverses in this life and none more striking than those which that family have met with. Had Joseph continued on the throne of Spain, in what a different style his daughter would now have been living! I question, however, if she would have been so happy, for they have a very good fortune and her husband, at least, never played any part in the royal game which the rest of his family (except his father Lucien) acted. They are waiting most impatiently for the sailing of the *Delaware*.

FEBRUARY 9:—I was interrupted yesterday by Basil coming to tell me that the boat from the ship had come for us, so I had to hurry on my bonnet and shawl and be off. We went first to a fortification erecting on the opposite side of the Roads, or rather in the middle of it, for there has been an island formed in the middle of the water by stones being thrown in in the same manner that the breakwater at Plymouth has been made. From thence we went on board the *Delaware*, where we found Captain Downes waiting for us. We went all over the ship with great pleasure to me and still greater to Basil, of course, as he felt quite at home, and I shall leave it to him to tell you all about her as he is much more competent to do so than I am. Captain Downes is living at Norfolk, but the first lieutenant came with an invitation from the officers for us to dine in the Naval Room, which we should have liked very much had it suited, but as it did not we came off with Captain Downes in his gig and had a most delightful partly sail, partly row, back to Norfolk, a distance of twelve miles from the ship. We set out on our travels again to-morrow. We cannot get an "Extra" and must therefore make a good deal longer day's journey than we like. To-day Basil is gone with Mr. Thompson, a gentleman here who remembers him at Norfolk three and twenty years ago, to see the commencement of the Canal through the Dismal Swamp. We should have liked to have seen the Lake of the Dismal Swamp, but this would have required more time than we have to spare at present.

Ever affectionately yours,

MARGARET HALL.

LETTER XVI

NORFOLK TO CHARLESTON

The four-horse mail from Norfolk carried the Hall family to Winton, Stantonborough, and Fayettesville. Mrs. Hall describes the dismal landscape and the wretched appearance of the population, white and coloured. A note of gladness comes into her narrative at Fayettesville, when she discovers it to be the centre of a colony of Scotch Highlanders. At Montpellier, another Celtic oasis, she was pleased to find that the landlord spoke Gaelic. A three nights halt at Columbia enabled Captain and Mrs. Hall to dine with Governor Taylor, attend the Washington Birthday Ball, and to spend an evening with Judge de Saussure.

Fifteen days after leaving Norfolk they reach Charleston. Mrs. Hall watches a slave auction from the balcony of the post-office, goes to the races and see the gentlemen clearing the course with whips, dines with the Editor of the *Southern Review,* and attends the Jockey Club Ball.

FAYETTESVILLE, NORTH CAROLINA.
February 13, 1828.

MY DEAREST JANE,

We have got pretty far South since I finished my last letter to you at Norfolk. We have in the interval had three days' hard travelling, by which I think Eliza is much the least fatigued of the party, and she is to-day running about looking as lively and as little heated as if she had not gone a mile, instead of having been bumped and banged and thumped about in a stage in a way that you may form some idea of if you remember the state of the roads across the Pyrenees. No such thing as an "Extra" was to be had from Norfolk, so that we were obliged to come in the mail, the only carriage on the road, and which comes in a four horse stage only three times a week. There is so little travelling in this part of the

States that comforts of all kinds are very rare. After travelling twenty-eight miles we stopped to dine at Suffolk, and there paid for a much inferior dinner to what we should have had in the Northern or Eastern States, nearly twice as much as we should have been charged there. We grumbled somewhat at this but our experience since has taught us very practically the truth of the saying that you may go further and fare worse. We got on very pleasantly with delightful weather and tolerable roads till we stopped to change horses for the last time. The driver asked Basil if he had a pistol and mentioned certain fears of robbers cutting our trunks from the back of the stage, and a little boy in charge of the mail told us a story of such a feat having been performed only a few nights previous. Mrs. Cownie was in a prodigious quake for the trunks and kept a sharp lookout upon every passer by, but we rambled and jolted along undisturbed by anything except a violent shower of rain. The road during the whole day lay through a miserable country, pine barrens and swamps, with here and there a field of tobacco and cotton which showed us that we had got into a warmer latitude. But the most characteristic and the most disagreeable features were the immense numbers of blacks everywhere along the road, for being Sunday they were idle and straying about the roads. A more miserable looking race I never beheld, with hardly a rag to cover them, and they are so stupid and so slow that really one's patience is severely put to the test by them. The white population over that part of the country through which we have passed is almost as wretched in appearance as the black and, in my opinion, far more degraded, not one of them, as far as we have been able to learn, ever works. Most of them own two or three negroes whom they send out to work and pay them so much a day which they spend in brandy, for drinking is carried to a greater excess in the South even than it is in the North. The houses they live in are the most wretched hovels I ever saw in my life, log hovels not even weathertight; I am sure no Irish cabin can be poorer, and the people themselves look squalid and miserable. Their manners we found gruff and uncivil, and as for the universal intelligence that is so much talked of in this country, it is not in the South, at all events, that it is to be found.

On the eleventh we slept at Stantonborough, all four in the same room, but we think nothing of such things now-a-days. At four next day we were up again and drove eighteen miles to another uneatable breakfast and fifty more for a dinner little better, for which the unconscionable woman made us pay three dollars, or about thirteen shillings. Another eighteen mile stage brought us to Fayettesville, but such a road I thought the stage would go every moment to pieces. Any other carriage would have been demolished at the first blow, but at length we crossed Cape Tear river and got to this excellent hotel where we ate most enormous suppers and went to bed half dead, and altho' a good night's rest in part recruited us, we resolved to remain some days, as we are in no hurry.

FEBRUARY 15:—This is the third day of our sojourn here. It has rained almost without intermission since we arrived and we have felt thankful to be so well housed. We brought no letters of introduction to this place, but Mr. Mallett (the stage proprietor) has brought various gentlemen to call upon us and has threatened me with a cargo of ladies, which evil I have hitherto escaped thanks to the badness of the weather. We had a stout argument with a man to-day who contended that the slaves in this country are better off in all respects save that of being able to change their employer than the working classes in England. You may say that it is absurd to enter into such an argument, but it makes one's blood boil to hear such impertinent assertions and made by persons, too, who know nothing of the matter, though that of course must be the case or the assertion would never be made. I wish you saw the wretched, ragged, stupid, ignorant creatures whom their oppressors so impertinently hold up as better cared for, fed, and clothed than the labourers in England. We have learnt a curious thing here. There are so many Highlanders settled in this town and for four and twenty miles round that they are obliged to have a clerk in the Post Office who can speak Gaelic. Now did any of you ever in your lives before hear of such a place as Fayettesville? The further we have come South the more universal have we found that disgusting practice of chewing tobacco. Every man we meet has constantly an immense lump in his mouth, which he keeps munching at as if it were a bit of bread, and the spitting that ensues is beyond what I can describe. It makes the *gentlemen,* as they style themselves, so very offensive. Really, between tobacco and brandy they are intolerable. The greatest good fortune attending our last journey was that we had not a single companion the whole way, as far as that goes we had all the advantage of an "Extra" without the expense, but then we had to travel each day much further than we liked.

MONTPELLIER, NORTH CAROLINA, FEBRUARY 18:—Yesterday at the end of a fifteen mile stage we stopped at Mr. Nelson's. His wife's parents were Scotch, and she appears to have inherited a Scotch heart as well as countenance from them, for nothing could exceed her desire to please when she learnt that we were Scotch, and after giving us by much the best dinner we have had at any place on this road, she charged us only a dollar for the whole lot instead of three, as a landlady upon a former occasion that I mentioned. There was a kindliness and a desire to please, too, which we found to be infinitely more valuable than a good dinner. The number of Highlanders in this neighbourhood is so great that Mr. Gilchrist, our landlord, altho' he has never been out of the States, speaks Gaelic tolerably and understands it perfectly, having been in the habit of hearing it all his life.

COLUMBIA, SOUTH CAROLINA, FEBRUARY 20:—This is the capital of the State of South Carolina. We arrived here at dusk. In the course of our journey yesterday we met two parties emigrating to the South. The first consisted of about fifty persons, black and white. They had four waggons, large, covered vehicles like the eight horse waggons in England. It was between twelve and one o'clock when we overtook them, and they had stopped to dine. They were scattered along the road in groups seated on the ground, numbers of little children amongst them, with whom Eliza made herself very popular by distributing cakes. They had come from near Cheraw and were travelling on into Georgia. They travel at the rate of twenty miles a day, starting at day break and encamping for the night before dark. The second party that we came up with later in the day was not so numerous, but their journey was longer. They had come from Maryland and were going on to Florida. The slaves were walking, and we observed two in front with their wrists chained together. Mr. MacLean, the Stage proprietor of this place, was with us, and we asked him what he supposed to be the reason of this. He said that one of them had probably left a wife behind and that they feared his running away. This frequently happens, even without any wish to be cruel on the part of the master, but the slaves often marry women belonging to other plantations, and, of course, altho' the master may carry away his own property, and indeed must, because in the Southern States they are not allowed to emancipate them and no one else in the neighbourhood may choose to buy them, he cannot make off with the property of his neighbour. In the same way they are often separated from their children, and all the people I have heard talk on the subject speak of the sufferings of those poor wretches with a degree of callousness and indifference that makes one's blood run cold.

FEBRUARY 22 :—It was our intention to have set out to-day for Charleston, and we were actually all packed and ready, but it occurred to us early this morning that we were running away from the capital of the State with rather too little ceremony, and that we ought to bestow another day upon it. This has been the most perfectly beautiful day that I have seen for months, serene and clear with a bright warm sun. We went by appointment at ten o'clock to call at Dr. Cooper's, the President of the College; he is an Englishman by birth and was one of those who left his country at the time when the French Revolution caused so many disturbances in England. His wife's parents were also English, but they are both thorough Americans. The people here are very hospitable, which is indeed the character of all the Southern States. The Coopers wished us to make their house our home and Chancellor de Saussure sent his carriage to me this morning to make what use I pleased of it the whole day. After sitting an hour with Dr. and Mrs. Cooper, they took us to see the College and the Lunatic Asylum, which is just finished, but is yet untenanted. Several gentlemen joined us whilst we were there and we staid a long while talking to them. We were asked to dine at the Governor's, Mr. Taylor's, to a military ball by some officers, and to a party at Judge de Saussure's. All this we were resolved to accomplish as well as we could. To the dinner we went at half past four, and I must say that in spite of all my experience of the strange arrangements of American dinners I confess this style did astonish me, and what any of you who have never seen such would have thought I cannot say. There was a huge party invited to meet us, all gentlemen with the exception of four ladies belonging to the house. I ought to promise that I had before been informed that both Mr. and Mrs. Taylor belonged to the old stock families in South Carolina, families who pique themselves on their ancient standing, quite the old aristocracy, in short, and possessing immense wealth. There was the same fuss before dinner of calling the mistress of the house out of the room and so on, and finally she and another elderly, female relation disappeared altogether and we found them standing ready placed at the upper end of the table, and then with one consent the gentlemen fell to carving the dishes nearest to them with a degree of dispatch and eagerness that I never saw equalled anywhere out of a steamboat. The top dish was a ham which Mrs. Taylor herself showed her power of carving upon by beginning to cut it in pieces from the knuckle upwards. The rest of the entertainment consisted of turkeys, roast and boiled, chickens, roast ducks, corned beef, and fish, together with various dishes of sweet potatoes, Irish potatoes, cabbage, rice, and beetroot, to demolish which we were furnished with two pronged forks, and if you were troublesome enough to call for a second knife you were furnished with one merely half wiped. For second course we had *eight pies* down the side of the table, six dishes of glasses of syllabub and as many of jelly, besides one or two "floating islands", as they denominate what we call whipped cream, and odd corners filled up by ginger and other preserves. I was fortunately well placed next an exceedingly agreeable old man, Judge De Saussure, a most gentlemanlike person. On the other side I had one of the young ladies of the house, for ladies in America have a vile custom of crowding all together at dinner tables and leave the gentlemen likewise to herd by themselves. We had neither tea nor coffee after dinner and at seven o'clock went off to the ball, but if the dinner was queer, what was the ball! Thank goodness no one was with me that I am intimate with except Basil, and you know he has no great genius for quizzing, but even his gravity could scarcely stand it. However, I did not laugh, for which I take the greater merit to myself than for anything I ever did or left undone in my life. It is quite out of my power to describe it to you. The day was Washington's birthday, and I suppose that the ball was in honour of the occasion. The Military, that is to say the Militia, Yeomanry, and Volunteers, were all in uniform, which made the *gaucherie* of the individuals all the more conspicuous. Then the ladies I can compare to nothing I ever saw except girls at the circus or strolling players at the Dundee Theatre, dressed in my cast-off finery fitted up according to their own taste. Such heads, such fabrications of silver muslin and tinsel, such feathers and such flowers it would require the pen of a poet or the pencil of a painter to do justice to. I was asked by the Captain of the Troop to dance, but the honour I declined, fortunately, for I should have been strangely thrown out by what they imagine to be quadrilles but which a Frenchman, I think, would have scarce recognised. An hour of this was, you will believe, enough, and we were glad to exchange the ball for a party at Judge De Saussure's, where I had as tough an argument regarding slavery with some ladies as ever Basil had on any subject with gentlemen, and by ten o'clock we were at home.

All the best society of Columbia, with a very few exceptions, is at present at Charleston where the races which are to take place next week have attracted great crowds, so that the ball must have consisted of very second rate company. We crossed the Congaree River this evening on leaving Columbia by a covered bridge which is not yet finished overhead.

CHARLESTON, SOUTH CAROLINA, FEBRUARY 26:—I went to see one sight to-day which I had not before had an opportunity of witnessing—an auction of slaves. There was an immense collection of them gathered together near the Post Office, from the balcony of which I saw it. A table was placed in the centre on which stood the auctioneers and the different lots as they were set up and knocked down to the highest bidder like so many books, chairs, or bullocks. There were multitudes of infants, little unconscious things, sleeping in their mothers' arms or smiling and laughing merrily, quite unaware of their own degradation. They were sold in families, which so far it was pleasant to see, but still it was a horrible sight. Close by were auctions of horses and carriages going on, so near indeed that it was impossible to distinguish whether the last bid was for the four-footed or the human animal. There was an expression of dogged indifference about the poor blacks, but I am told they do not at all like to be removed from the place where they have been brought up. We took a walk this evening thro' Charleston, a very pretty place it is. All the houses are built, apparently in reference to the hot weather only, with deep verandahs round. Some of the verandahs are fitted the whole way round with Venetian blinds, but altogether the houses look very pretty. Charleston is situated on a peninsula formed by the sea in front and on each side by the Rivers Ashley and Cooper, which names mark who the soil originally belonged to. We were invited to a ball this evening and until two hours ago had resolved to go, but neither of us have yet got over the fatigue of our late journey, and the nearer the time approached the more reluctant did we feel to encounter the additional labour of dressing, going out, and, more especially, talking. So we put on our dressing gowns and sat down to write, which many persons perhaps would consider the greatest fatigue of all, but I find it quite a refreshment.

MARCH 2 :—On the twenty-seventh we went to the races, where there was but a small show of company, and I did not admire the free use the gentlemen made of their whips in trying to keep the course clear. I am sure that an Englishman would not have submitted to one half that the foreign people put up with very quietly. I know nothing whatever about horses so that the interest I take in a race is not very great. In walking that evening we strolled into some of the fruit shops where we saw all sorts of West Indian fruits and sweetmeats and great lumps of sugar cane. We have had bananas every day since we came here and yesterday where we dined, asparagus and pease. The asparagus very poor, certainly, compared to what is to be had in London at this season, but then it is without forcing. The pease were excellent. On the twenty-eighth we took a family dinner at Mr. Stephen Elliott's, the editor of the *Southern Review* in this country, of which you have probably never heard, altho' the good folks of Carolina say that it has made a good deal of noise in England. It would be totally out of the question to make them understand the degree of ignorance and want of interest that prevails in England regarding everything in America, indeed I always feel that it is uncivil to tell them of it, altho' truth obliges one to do so sometimes. The party at Mr. Elliott's consisted of four in his own family, the Attorney-General, Mr. Pettigrew, Judge Huger, Mr. Legaré, one of the writers in the said *Southern Review,* and Mrs. Nott, an unfortunate little French woman whose unlucky stars have transplanted her from Paris to Columbia! She, in a mistaken hour, having married an American, who is now Professor of Belles Lettres in the College of Columbia, and most bitterly does she feel the change; indeed, I cannot fancy one more intolerable, and she has no hope of ever bettering herself. A family dinner in Charleston is a very plain affair, if we are to judge by the specimen we had at Mr. Elliott's, there was not a bit of second course of any kind, not a pie nor a pudding, and no apology for the absence of it, so I suppose it is the usual style, for people in this country are apt enough to make apologies for what ought to be there, instead of letting the deficiency pass without comment.

On the twenty-ninth there was a ball given by the Jockey Club, to which we were invited and went. The room is good and was well lighted, nevertheless, it was a very dull ball, much too thinly attended and too small a proportion of gentlemen. They do not invite any of the gentlemen of this State except those belonging to the Club, and many of the ladies whose husbands or brothers are not members do not choose to go. There were awful pauses between the dances, and the music was really insufferably bad. I had thought the young men much more gentlemanlike when I saw them in the morning than those generally to be seen in this country, but in the evening they looked very second-rate, indeed, more vulgar, I think, than most I have seen elsewhere. As for the female part of the company, I never in my life saw so many ugly women gathered together, there were but three pretty women in the room, two of them from Philadelphia, the other a French girl. There was a supper, a very handsome one as far as quantity and quality went, but such an absence of taste, such a contrast to be sure from Mr. Vaughan's beautiful set-out at Washington, such heavy ornaments and great lumbering, long, two-pronged forks to eat one's rice with.

Yesterday we had another stroll about the town which I admire the more I see of it, and when the trees which ornament the side of the streets are quite out the effect must be very pretty. It is a remarkably cheerful looking place, Charleston. The dinner at Mr. Pettigrew's consisted of thirteen gentlemen and three ladies, Mrs. Pettigrew, Mrs. Nott, who is living in the house, and myself, the others were all gentlemen without their wives, according to the fashion of the place and of many other places in the Union. Women are just looked upon as house-keepers in this country, and as such are allowed to preside at the head of their own table, that they may see that all goes right. The evening party was at the house of a

From a drawing
by Capt. B. Hall, R. N.

THE BRIDGE ACROSS THE CONGAREE IN SOUTH CAROLINA

Mrs. Thomas Lownde's and I think there was a greater number of pretty women than on the preceding evening but most of them dressed so ill that they would mar even real beauty. I must in justice say one thing in favour of the South Carolinians, they are remarkably hospitable, not only in inviting strangers into their houses, but lending their carriages, which is a much less common piece of hospitality. By the bye, I was asked by one of the lodgers in this house the other day one of those puzzling questions that the Americans are so apt to put, how the American ladies compare in point of information and acquirements with those of Edinburgh. I was obliged to refuse to make a comparison, as I should have been obliged to sacrifice either my conscience or my politeness in comparing them with any ladies that I know, English, Scotch, or Irish.

MARCH 5:—To-morrow is our day of starting. For this reason we mean to cut a ball we were invited to to-night in order to have good time to finish our preparations. I begin to find that the only time of rest for us is when we are actually on the roads travelling some forty or fifty miles a day. One is so fatigued when one only stops for a week or ten days by the multitude of parties, the innumerable visits to be returned, and here, I mean in America, harassed by the tiresome way they press you to prolong your stay, even after demonstrating that by doing so whole weeks of plans would be deranged and the risk of encountering the unhealthy season be incurred. This is very different from the kind, considerate letter we had since coming here from Mr. Couper of St. Simon's Island, the old Scotch gentleman of whom you have heard so much. We had been hesitating about going to visit him, but the style of his letter is so considerate and shows him to be a man of so much sense and real kindness that we at once resolved upon it. Instead of being hurried along by the public Stage we have engaged a private carriage with four horses to take us on leisurely. On the third we dined with a party of twenty at Dr. Tidyman's—the proportions were fifteen gentlemen and five ladies. We had a very grand dinner as could possibly be, and heaps of it, as there always is. Everything, however, was really handsome, and there was less appearance of effort than usual. Dr. Tidyman was long in Scotland but returned from there many years ago. He was intimate with Baron Hume, the Mackenzies, and many others, and still corresponds with Mrs. Dugald Stewart. He has been remarkably kind and attentive to us, really most particularly so, and, therefore, it is with pain that I am obliged to confess to myself and you that he is one of those intense bores who make life a burden to those on whom they bestow their company. The Americans are all given, more or less, to speak in parentheses, but this man's parentheses are so numerous and so involved that it is almost impossible to connect the different parts of his sentence and to disentangle the substance from the branches right and left and in every direction.

We went after the dinner to a Military Ball given by the Officers belonging to the different Militia corps. There was no one present without uniform except Basil, but I don't think the change of dress improved the appearance of our friends here, who may for aught I know be very effective in the field, but they are certainly not drawing room soldiers. I must do the Charlestonians the justice to say that I have not seen any chewing amongst them nor spitting. I am *told* that even smoking is in disrepute. They are very hospitable and make you as welcome to their carriages as to their dinners, but there is the same apparent coldness of character and feeling as about all their countrymen, an absence of heartiness and cordiality which is the chief charm of such attentions. The fact is they hate the English, and there is no sincere feeling of friendship or kindliness towards them, and all the attention is merely a sort of bribe to make us speak well of them. We did up all the sights in Charleston yesterday, Work House, Poor House, Jail, Orphan Asylum, and Rice Mill, which last was the only thing much worth seeing. All the others are much inferior to the establishments of the same kind in the Northern States.

De Witt Clinton, the Governor of New York, whom I have mentioned so often, died very suddenly on the eleventh of Febru-

ary. He was conversing with his two sons when he laid himself
back on his chair and expired. He was one of those whom we have
known in this country whom we have liked best. His loss will be
much felt in his own State.

Ever affectionately your's,

MARGARET HALL.

LETTER XVII

CHARLESTON TO SAVANNAH

This letter opens with a few parting shots at the barbarism of the dancing
and the dirtiness of the servants in Charleston, and goes on to describe the
new adventure of staying on plantations. After enjoying the comforts
and cooking provided by Mr. Skirving, Mr. Nathaniel Hayward, and Mr.
William Hayward at their respective homes, Mrs. Hall is inclined to revise her opinion as to the stupidity of slaves.

JACKSONBURGH, SOUTH CAROLINA,
March 6, 1828.

MY DEAREST JANE,

We breakfasted between seven and eight this morning, but
as there were many little arrangements, as usual, on first starting
it was nine before we first got off. We shall probably use the
carriage we now have for a month, and therefore it is of considerable consequence that it should be as comfortable as we can make
it. You know Basil's genius for contrivances, and of course he
adapts many a one to increase our comfort in travelling. We have
a multitude of small things, too, which require sorting at first
setting out, though once they find their proper berth they are easily
arranged. Mr. Wallace in his short, tight jacket worked away in
his province and at nine, as I said before, we left Mrs. Kerrison's
boarding house, and I must confess that, with one exception, I
should not care though I did not see any of the Charlestonians again.
That exception is Mr. Pettigrew, the Attorney-General of the State.
He sat a couple of hours with us last night and is a very intelligent,
sensible man, tho' he has never in his life been out of South Carolina.
There surely is a greater want of interest in American society than

in that of any other country I ever was in or heard of. My conscience too smites me for speaking so of persons who have shown us so much attention and civility, for somehow I cannot call it kindness, but I cannot help it. I cannot like their society and I cannot like themselves. Mrs. Clough, the English lady I met the other night, says there is no tenderness in this country. She meant as applied to *love,* but the same want of . . . I don't know what to call it, for tenderness is too soft a word to apply to the intercourse of general society, so, as I cannot explain myself, you must try to do so for me.

I forgot to mention that at all balls and dances at Charleston a favorite dance is the Spanish dance, as they call it, and in *plan* it certainly is a Spanish country dance, but in execution, Oh Heavens! To me it was actually excruciating to witness such barbarism and to remember the contrast of beautiful Spanish women with their graceful figures and sparkling eyes, instead of the dowdies and their clumsy partners I now saw handling and elbowing each other about, for their propriety will not allow them to valse, so they *poussette* and hold each other by the elbow instead of the side. I respect all scruples on the score of propriety, and if people don't like to valse they are quite right to let it alone, but why murder a pretty dance by substituting most ungraceful alterations for the prettiest part of it? Why not leave it undone? One thing that assists in depriving their parties in the South of any appearance of style is the nasty, black creatures whom they have for servants. It is true that many of them are dressed in livery, but of such coarse cloth and so ill made, and then they all look so dirty. You can't imagine how disagreeable it is to have so many of those creatures going about. They are so stupid and so indolent, always in the way when not wanted. In a country tavern like this, for instance, there are heaps of them, children of twelve and fourteen years old without stockings or shoes, so that one does not hear them glide into the room, but this evening every time I raised my eyes there was a new black face staring at me as if I were a wild beast. They are like a species of constant waking nightmare to me, and you have to desire them to go away more than once before they will stir. But in summer I am told they are offensive beyond what can be described. A lady in Charleston told me that she knows each one of her servants who come up stairs without seeing them, merely by the smell. Her family quizzed her for saying so but they have tried her half a dozen times and she has always been correct. Only fancy such a misery!

A mile from Charleston to-day we crossed the Ashley River in a horseboat. It is a very fine wide river, of whose existence I had never heard till within three or four miles of Charleston. After that we travelled thirty miles to this place. On each side of the road for the greater part of the way there were well cultivated looking farms, and we saw the slaves forming the ground into ridges with large hoes, in place of having horses to plough it. Varieties of beautiful flowers were in the swamps and numerous live-oak trees in every direction. We passed through but little pine barren. The live-oak is in form very like the English oak, but not so in leaf. The leaf is like that of the myrtle, but larger, and it hangs on the branch not unlike the willow. The timber is used in this country for building ships for the Navy, and the Americans think it superior to any other wood in the world for that purpose. Within a mile of this place we crossed the Edisto River, the most rapid we have seen since we left the St. Lawrence. Before arriving at the ferry the road was covered for about a quarter of a mile with water about a foot and a half deep. At times it is so deep that people are obliged to go the whole way in a flat, as you may remember we had to be boated over part of the high road at Richmond some years ago when the Thames got so high. It must look so strange to be ferried through the forest. We arrived at Jacksonburgh between five and six, having stopped an hour on the road to rest the horses. We dined in the carriage upon provisions of our own supplying.

MR. SKIRVING'S PLANTATION ON THE COMBAHEE RIVER (PRONOUNCED CUMBEE) FIFTY MILES W. OF CHARLESTON, MARCH 8 :— That is a long date, but this place is well worthy of being noted in as particular a manner as possible, as you will allow when I tell you of all the comforts we have found here. Mrs. Skirving is a lady with whom we made acquaintance in Charleston, and when we talked of travelling to Savannah she begged that we would make use of her house as an inn, and as we were desirous of seeing some plantations we resolved to accept her offer, altho' it increased our journey several miles by taking us off the direct road. Accordingly, yesterday morning we left Jacksonburgh at eight o'clock, after having breakfast. It was a lovely morning and the hoar frost which had covered the ground gradually melted beneath the hot sun. The road was very interesting, partly through forests of pine and live-oak and partly through nicely cultivated fields and the whole way covered with innumerable beautiful flowers and shrubs. The road was most excellent, and after a drive of eighteen miles we found ourselves at Mr. Skirving's gate. We had previously had no idea of what sort of a place a plantation house might be, and not having conjured up anything very delightful in our own minds, our plan was to take some dinner, walk a little, and then go on five or six miles further to another plantation, the owner of which was, we understood, at home. At the door of the house we were met by the head man, or driver as he is called, a black man of the name of Solomon. The overseer is always a white man, but there is none here at present, and it was to Solomon that Mr. Skirving directed us to apply. The more we saw of the house the more did our inclination to remain increase. Everything looked so clean and comfortable. The bed rooms, especially, were such as we have not been used to of late, with their snow-white quilts and draperies, delightful arm chair and sofa, nicely set out toilet tables, and, in short, everything that is luxurious, and before we had been here an hour we had resolved to remain all night. The house is small but very comfortable. On the first floor is a small drawing-room and dining room opening upon a deep piazza, as they call them here. From this piazza a few steps lead down to a delightful garden filled with all sorts of flowers in full bloom, and close to the piazza is an orange tree covered with the flower and fruit in all stages. They are bitter oranges; the sweet do not ripen here. Having settled ourselves a little, we proceeded with Solomon to see the Negro huts about five hundred yards from the house. They are twenty-nine in number, very neatly arranged. In each hut there are two apartments, one for sleeping in. Some of the huts had windows but very few, most of them having no light but what was admitted by the open door or an occasional separation between logs. In one of the largest were assembled all the children under the age of fourteen, whom they consider too young to work. They were under the charge of one woman who prepares their meals for them and takes care of them whilst their parents are at work in the fields. The children, as well as the men and women, are fed upon Indian corn which is served out to them at the beginning of each week; to each man and woman a peck in the week. The children have their allowance measured daily. After dinner we went to see them at their work, making a dam to prevent the Combahee from overflowing the rice fields to a greater degree than is wished, for they are always kept under water, which is what makes a rice plantation so peculiarly unhealthy during the hot weather. Indeed, even at this season when there is no such danger, it is quite easy to imagine how deadly it must be to inhale the noxious vapours rising from such immense beds of stagnant water. All the way that we have come from Norfolk, were we to travel it in the months of May and so on, we should meet with certain and sudden death, for the swamps are as pernicious as the rice fields. Along with those at work there were two other drivers, each with his wand of office in his hand, that is to say, a cart-whip with which to keep their human cattle under subjection. The slaves on this plantation are, I believe, as well used as any that we could see. They have a doctor to attend them when they are ill, and tho' not sumptuously fed and clothed they have both food, clothing, and weather-tight houses, but still it makes one melancholy to see them, even at their best. There was no laughing or talking in the field, no sign whatever of merriment or happiness; they seemed to work on mechanically, aware that the slightest relaxation was watched by the driver and would be followed by the infliction of his cart whip. The scene looked out of place on such a heavenly day when everything looked smiling and happy except the human beings. Solomon is an intelligent man, for his caste, and we have asked him many questions, but frequently he stops and says that he does not like to answer such and such a question, a man may get into trouble by saying too much. He told us that he has belonged to four masters in succession. It sounded very strange to hear a man tell that formerly he used to sell for from six to seven hundred dollars but that now he does not suppose he would fetch more than four hundred.

Mrs. Cownie and Eliza walked about the place with him whilst we were writing this morning, and he spoke more freely to them than to us. He told Mrs. Cownie that he cannot read nor write but that his wife who can is teaching him, but when he hears his mistress coming he hides the book because he knows she would be so angry if she detected him. Of course, the policy of the planters is to keep their slaves in a state of ignorance, that they may not come to knowledge of their own degraded situation. In the mean time Solomon keeps all his accounts in his head. But I must now tell you of our own treatment. At two o'clock we found a most admirable dinner prepared for us, boiled turkey, roast chicken, asparagus, pease, potatoes, rice custard, and sweetmeats, all admirably dressed and nicely served. Tea was brought in the same good order and the whole establishment is apparently under the most excellent management; all the servants, altho' slaves, born and bred, a race whom we have generally found so stupid, understand their business perfectly. Mrs. Skirving is an English woman altho' she has been long in this country, but she still speaks of England as home, and certainly the arrangements of her house and household have a very English air. We slept sound in our beds till seven o'clock, but if the dinner was good, what shall I say of the breakfast! Such a breakfast! Such admirably boiled rice, such hashed turkey, broiled quails, and Indian corn flour which heretofore I have thought so bad, made into cakes of every description, each one more delicious than the other. I am sure you must think us very great epicures, but if you had been exposed for as many months as we have been to wallowing in grease you would know how to value a clean and good meal when put within your reach.

Mr. Nathaniel Hayward's Plantation, March 8:—This is the gentleman's house I mentioned we had thought of coming to last night from Mr. Skirving's before the comfort of everything there tempted us to remain. We left our excellent quarters about eleven o'clock, and with a guide to show us the way proceeded to Mr. Hayward's. I ought to mention, however, that at the door of Mrs. Skirving's all the house servants and Solomon were assembled to bid us good-bye. Solomon shook hands most cordially with each of us, as did likewise an old woman who keeps the keys, and the others all bowed and smiled and looked quite pleased with us. I believe we treated them with more civility and kindness than they are used to, and this gained their goodwill, I think, much more than the dollars and half dollars that we gave them. We had only five miles to come to this place, and on stopping at the door found that we were expected, although the master was out to superintend the work. Whilst we were sauntering about in the garden Mr. Hayward made his appearance, and with him we proceeded to walk about the grounds, the rice fields, that is to say, for his whole plantation is rice with the exception of the corn that he cultivates to feed his slaves upon. His plantation is considered one of the best regulated in this State. At dinner we were joined by one of his sons who had been out hunting. We were not much the better of his conversation, nor that of his brother who came in in the evening, neither of them spoke a word. I have heard of sisters being no greater use at a party than to fill two chairs, but I never saw the case so completely identified as in the case of those two brothers. The old gentleman himself is much more willing to talk, but neither is he a man of much information, and when we had got all out of him that we could relative to the cultivation of rice and the treatment of slaves, the conversation flagged so much that we were glad to make our escape to our own room.

We walked to the slave huts and looked into one or two of them, each of which consisted of two sleeping apartments and one hall, as they call it. Here, as at Mr. Skirving's, one old woman was employed in looking after the children whilst the parents were at work. Mr. Hayward does not interfere with his slaves in any way further than is necessary for the good of his own interest. They may have two or three wives apiece so long as they do not quarrel about them, but if they quarrel he interferes. He says they have no morals nor principles whatever, and are all the most notorious thieves. The masters have power of life and death over them. If a slave were, for instance, to be caught on Mr. Hayward's plantation cutting our portmanteaus from the back of our carriage, his master would call together two magistrates and five freeholders, and if it were proved that he was guilty they would forthwith string him up to the nearest tree. We have been very well used here, but on the whole commend me to the house where the mistress is absent. I still think Mrs. Skirving's English education is seen in the arrangements of her establishment which is vastly superior in all respects to this one, altho' the proprietor here is by much the richer of the two.

This pretty place is quite on the Combahee River. The laurel in this State grows to the size of a large tree, and there is every species of the laurustinus, both in the gardens and in the woods. The weather already is almost sultry, altho' in the morning there has once or twice been frost. We crossed the Ashepoo River yesterday, the seventh; all the rivers we come to now retain their Indian names.

COOSAWHATCHIE, S. CAROLINA, MARCH 9:—This a little bit of a village on a river of the same name. We left Mr. Hayward's this morning at ten o'clock, crossed the Combahee, and stopped here between one and two, after a drive of eighteen miles, to rest the horses and to dine, as we thought, upon our own provisions, but at the tavern we found a roast joint of venison and upon that we made an excellent dinner.

OLD HOUSE, 10½ MILES OF COOSAWHATCHIE, MARCH 9:—On leaving Mr. Nathaniel Hayward's this morning he gave us a letter for his relation, Mr. William Hayward, whose house, he said, was a good distance for a day's journey, and that the owner would be most happy to receive us. Accordingly, on we came, altho' at Coosawhatchie we were told that Mr. Hayward was from home. However, by the time we reached his gate it was half past five o'clock and there was no place where we could put up, short of nine miles further on, which would have obliged us to travel in the dark, so we boldly drove up to the door. The servant told us that his master was from home but that he could with ease accommodate us for the night. This was too hospitable to be rejected, so we had our things taken out of the carriage, walked in, had fires lighted in the sitting room and two bedrooms, and in half an hour were as much at home as if we had lived all our lives in South Carolina. Eliza appears to enjoy the comfort we meet with as much as any of us, and as she is now quite independent in being able to go up and downstairs alone, she makes a survey of the house and premises in a very short time. But I must do her the justice to say that she is equally merry under all circumstances, and however poor her fare and accommodation may be she is quite as gay as if they were of the best. But only imagine our luck and our delight in finding ourselves in full possession of a gentleman's establishment without the *gêne* of the company of the gentleman himself! Imagination could not have conceived a more perfect piece of luck. Assuredly we must allow the virtue of hospitality to its full extent to these planters, for it is quite common for strangers to go to their houses in the way we have come here. Dick, the head servant, has given us tea and is to give us breakfast to-morrow before we start for Savannah, which is still about thirty miles distant. Already we are plagued by mosquitoes. I have just had the peculiar satisfaction of killing one; it is the only living thing I ever took pleasure in killing, but there is satisfaction in demolishing those creatures, which none except those who have been exposed to torment by them can understand. They began their attacks on Eliza at Charleston and she has a great bite on her cheek to-day which reminds me of what she suffered last summer, poor infant. There has not been cold enough this winter to kill them and this swampy country is a glorious harbour for them. We have passed by numerous plantations today, but none of them I think quite so nice looking as those we have visited. You must know that amongst the talents that this journey has brought to light in this party, is Basil as a singer. Eliza is quite pleased with his music, with which he almost daily sets her to sleep, but the name by which she designates it is characteristic enough, and the moment he stops singing she says, "More diddledy dum." The mosquitoes are biting her sadly, poor child, and every bite rises in a blister. The weather is so hot that we are glad to sit with all doors and windows open and, when out, to avoid the sun. Indeed, I do not allow Eliza to walk out. The only medicine she ever gets is castor oil, and altho' she seldom gets even that, the impression it has made on her mind is so strong that every time she sees a spoon she calls out partly in fun, partly in earnest, "No oil, not a dop o' oil!"

SAVANNAH, GEORGIA, MARCH 12:—I must tell you how we got to Savannah and what we have been doing since we came. We left Mr. William Hayward's after an excellent breakfast on the morning of the twelfth. We found our rooms most comfortable and the servants as attentive as if their master had been at home. We had thirty miles to travel to the Savannah River, all excellent road with the exception of the last two or three miles which was most execrable. From the ferry we came up in a canoe to Savannah, a distance of three miles, and were landed close to the City Hotel to which we had been recommended to come. We had our dinner and then walked to the Post Office in search of letters. Whilst walking along a gentleman on horseback overtook us and introduced himself as Mr. Molyneux, brother to the consul who is at present in England and for whom he in the meantime does duty. From him we learnt that our non-arrival on Saturday had excited quite a sensation. The fact was that at Charleston we had mentioned to a gentleman of this city that it was our intention to get to Savannah that evening. This we said without the least intention of fixing our selves positively to a particular day, but he, I suppose, being one of those who keep to a minute fancied that we were the same and wrote to desire that his carriage might be in attendance for us, so there it waited for three whole days and finally, as we landed close to the hotel, we did not need it. The coachman, poor man, made hourly reports to a certain Mrs. Wardrobe, and at last brought word that we had broken down, so that altogether there was no little interest astir about us. Before we had been an hour in the house we had an invitation from the said Mrs. Wardrobe for a party that evening, and as Mr. Molyneux told us that the party was given on purpose for us, of course, we resolved to go. But first of all we walked to Mr. Anthony Barclay's, one of the sons of old Colonel Barclay, formerly the British Consul in New York. Anthony Barclay was one of Basil's companions in former times. He married a widow, a native of this state, but he is not on this account going to spend his life in this country and has been making enquiries of us about living in Edinburgh. Well, to Mrs. Wardrobe's we went and found a large party dancing quadrilles. She proved to be almost a Scotch woman, for tho' born in Georgia she was educated in Edinburgh, married a Scotch man in the British army, and lived for ten years in East Lothian at the house of her brother-in-law, Mr. Gray of Southfield. She is a cheerful, pleasant little woman who tries to be contented here but longs sadly to return to settle herself in Scotland, which she hopes one day to do. She has two daughters who are no less desirous than their mother to exchange the new for the old world. Savannah is a very pretty place, quite like an English village with its grass walks and rows of trees on each side of the street. The gardens, too, are in great beauty and I have actually seen sweet oranges growing. There are some very fine houses and one most beautiful church. It is elevated about thirty feet above the river. I went yesterday evening with Mrs. Wardrobe, a drive of about three miles, to a place called Bonavento where there was formerly a house which has been since burnt down; it is a very pretty situation on the Savannah River. Basil dined with a bachelor party at Mr. Molyneux's but afterwards joined me at Mrs. Wardrobe's where I drank tea quite alone. The old lady was delighted to get hold of anyone who could talk about home to her. Our visitors, of course, have been innumerable, and I am sorry it is out of our power to remain longer, but with the immense journey before us we must be careful not to give more time to each place than we can conveniently spare. The greater number of our associates here are English or Scotch or connected with them, and this has made the society particularly pleasing to us. To-day we drove all over the town returning our visits. The place is so small that this was soon done, more especially as the people were all very sensibly out. We have dined with Mr. Barclay with a large party, but not like the American dinners, all gentlemen and no ladies; there was an equal proportion of each, which is certainly more agreeable and looks infinitely better.

SAVANNAH, MARCH 13:—And now I must tell you of our travelling arrangements. When we arrived at the other side of the river on the tenth Mr. Wallace said that his horses were almost dead, that the roads were much worse than he expected, that the expenses are great, and a great many etceteras, which all went to show that he did not wish to go further. This was a considerable disappointment, for altho' we had made no positive engagement further than Savannah we took it that he was to go as far as Montgomery with us; however, of course we could not urge him against his inclination, so have parted company. The next thing to do was to seek out another carriage and driver and this with the assistance of Mr. Barclay we soon got, and I hope we shall do better this time as the man who goes with us is an old servant of Mr. Barclay's, with whom he has been acquainted upwards of ten years and has travelled with him a great deal. We are to have a carriage and pair and a little one-horse waggon for our luggage. We go about fifteen miles to-day and to-morrow, the fourteenth, we hope to get to Mr. James Couper's, the son of the old gentleman on St. Simon's Island, and who lives within a few miles of Darien.

I shall just give you one instance of the good treatment of slaves and then conclude. The night we came here Mrs. Cownie rang the bell for the chambermaid, but in place of her there came a little girl who said that the chambermaid could not come as the mistress had been whipping her and she was not fit to be seen. Next morning she made her appearance with her face marked in several places by the cuts of the cowskin and her neck handkerchief covered with spots of blood. Mind, I am not so ridiculous as to say that all gentlemen and ladies are continually beating their slaves, many of them I know are extremely well used, but the number of gentlemen and ladies is comparatively small and the secondary and lower classes, with exceptions of course, have no feeling whatever for the unhappy wretches.

Ever affectionately yours,

MARGARET HALL.

LETTER XVIII

SAVANNAH TO MOBILE

From Savannah the Halls drove to Darien, "a city of the dead," and were
rowed to St. Simon's Island to stay with Mr. Couper, a Scotch planter, who
entertained them and passed them on to his son, James Couper of Hopeton.
Mrs. Hall watches slaves working in cotton fields and enquires into the
process of preparing cotton for market. Returning to Darien the party set
out to drive by compass reckoning to Macon, a city three years old, and
thence to Columbus, a town still in "the forest stage". Mrs. Hall notes
the parcelling out of the land into town-lots by Government Surveyors, the
lanes pegged through the forest, the shacks being erected for settlers and
bidders at sales, the hotel signs swinging on trees, and the whisky drinking
loafers. Bored and wearied the party pushed on to Montgomery. Mrs.
Hall describes the journey over rutted tracks and tree stumps, the sleepless nights, the execrable food, the dreadful taverns. Both husband and wife
were on the point of collapse when they reached the Alabama and clambered
on to the steamer for Mobile, where they are lent a comfortable house
and Mrs. Hall makes friends with Mrs. Erwin, daughter of Mr. Henry
Clay.

Mrs. Fulton's Tavern,
24 Miles South of Savannah,
March 13, 1828.

My Dearest Jane,

I have mentioned more than once how much time morning visits
occupy in this country owing to the bad habit the ladies have of
never being ready to receive company. I have found this to be the
practice invariably except at Washington where company alone is
their occupation. English persons who have lived many years in
this country say that they too have observed this want of being
ready to be quite universal. Mrs. Wardrobe, of Savannah, whose
experience of the ways of this country is great, says that when any-

one calls the lady called upon is probably lying down quite in *deshabille* and has to dress, from her stays inclusive. She also confirms what I have before heard of the active part they take in kitchen and other menial duties. The other day, for instance, in Savannah we drove past a house where there had been a great dinner on the preceding day, and thro' the windows saw the ladies, with their white aprons on, busy washing up the glasses and tea-cups. If this were really necessary it might be all very meritorious, although even in that case I should think a better plan would be not to give parties, but Mrs. Wardrobe says that it is only bad management and that she never finds it necessary to give herself so much trouble. Another opinion which she also confirms is the low estimation in which women are held. She says that when a man marries the only qualification he looks for in his wife is that she should be a good housekeeper. There appears to be no sort of sympathy between the sexes. They have no subjects of conversation in common and at a dinner table, for instance, instead of sitting alternately even if there be but three or four of them to a dozen gentlemen, all get together. This, I think, a very great bore and always take care to avoid as much as I can. Hitherto I have observed in the slave-holding States the most utter disregard to religion, more especially on the part of the gentlemen; not only to the spirit but even to outward forms and observances.

St. Simon's Island, Georgia, March 16:—We are now at the house of Mr. Couper on a low island bound on three sides thereof by different branches of the river Altamaha and on the fourth by the sea. You may possibly have heard of the sea-island cotton which in the cotton market has a great character. This is the largest of those islands on which it is cultivated. The first settlement was made by General Oglethorpe about the year 1730, which is as early, I believe, as any settlement was made in the State of Georgia. The little town of Frederica which was built by General Oglethorpe is now quite in ruins. It is about six miles distant from here. We drove there yesterday in company with Mr. Fraser, and on the way saw the slaves at work in the fields planting cotton, which is a very light part of their work, but no part of the process of cultivating cotton is so laborious as that of rice, but as I do not thoroughly understand it as yet I shall not say anything of it at present. There is no beauty whatever in this island, which is as flat as all the rest of the State that we have hitherto seen and covered with many swamps. There are several families resident on St. Simon's, part of each of which dined here yesterday. Captain Wylie, an old half pay officer of the time of the Revolutionary War but in the English service, and his two daughters, two more of whom are married, one to Dr. Fraser and the other to Mr. James Couper. We had also Colonel Hayward, a fierce looking *militaire,* at least so far as a light-coloured pair of moustachios could make him so, and his brother, a doctor by name, though I don't know whether or not he is so by profession, Mr. King, the manager of one of the plantations, and a Mr. Geikie, a Scotchman by birth as well as name; besides those there were Dr. Fraser and Dr. and Mrs. Tunno from Darien and three additional children, so that altogether there was a very numerous party mustered. With the exception of the Tunnos and the Miss Wylies they all went away at night, and such a night, to be sure, I never heard, such a tremendous storm of wind, rain, thunder, lightning, the whole house shook as if it would have fallen and the lightning was so vivid that, although the blinds and the curtains were shut and there were also curtains drawn all round the bed, the lightning flashed into it as tho' it had been illuminated by a dozen candles. The wind continued to blow with unabated force during the whole night, and altho' it has now lulled in some degree, it still blows pretty fresh.

HOPETON PLANTATION ON THE ALTAMAHA. MARCH 17:—This is the plantation of Mr. James Couper, the eldest son of our old friend on St. Simon's island. It is at present almost all under water in consequence of the "fresh", as they here term the rise in the rivers. The weather was considered too bad to admit of our going to the little church, about five miles off. The clergyman was living in the house so that we knew there could be no service without our knowing of it. The old gentleman was of opinion as much as the other members of the family that the weather was sufficiently inclement to make it advisable that we should stay at home, and we had church in the drawing room instead of five miles off. All the negroes about the house were ranged in the adjoining lobby, to which there were two communications from the room, both left open, so that we made a large congregation. This, you will think, does not agree with the remarks I have made in the first part of my letter about the want of observance of even the forms of religion in these slave States, but in this case the clergyman was a resident in the house so that the omission would have been very marked, besides I do not mean to say that they make a point of being so very careless. The sky cleared and the wind fell so much in the afternoon that we kept an engagement we had made conditionally on the weather to drink tea at Captain Wylie's near Frederica, and by ten o'clock we got home.

DARIEN, GEORGIA. MARCH 19:—I am sorry it has not been in my power to write as I went along during these last two days, for we have been with a man of a very different stamp from those we are in the habit of meeting. I mean our host Mr. James Couper at Hopeton. He is a person of very formal manners, but it is merely manner and goes no further than the very surface. He is not at all reserved and has great information upon all subjects. Of course slavery was that on which we were most anxious to get his opinions and he entered into the most minute details as to his treatment and regulations on his plantation, much too detailed for me to relate here, but you will hear about it some day. It does you good to meet such a man, not to reconcile you to slavery on principle, but to show how much the evil which appears to be irremediable at present may be softened by proper management. We talked on many other subjects also, and altho' he is a staunch American and republican there were many points on which he agreed entirely with Basil, particularly as to the low estimation of the women. He says that the only chance a man has for a rational companion in his wife is to marry her when very young and cultivate her mind. It is singular enough that he should make this confession, as it happens that he married not three months ago a girl of sixteen. He appears to me to have a most promising subject to make his experiment upon. Mrs. Couper is a ladylike pleasing young woman with excellent sense, as far as an acquaintance of two days can enable me to judge, and even in that length of time there are considerable differences of character to be seen, in the arrangements of a house even. Now their house is the very smallest that we have been in, a mere pigeon-hole, and yet everything was in better order and with less appearance of effort than many a large establishment that we have been in. Instead of the bare naked-looking room, which an American parlour generally is, apparently only intended for receiving company in, there are books of all sorts and sizes lying about in every direction. We arrived so much earlier, on the seventeenth, than they expected that there was no company invited for dinner that day, which we considered a piece of great good luck. We had left St. Simon's at eight o'clock on a frosty morning and with a cold wind which made us resort to all our coats and cloaks. We rowed up seventeen miles to Hopeton in four hours. Soon after arriving we set out to see the process of preparing the cotton from the time it is brought in from the fields till it is packed in Dundee bags ready to be shipped for Liverpool. We also visited the hospital for the negroes and various other things connected with the establishment, all equally worthy of commendation. Mr. Couper plants both cotton and rice but mostly cotton. We spent a very agreeable evening, and yesterday, the eighteenth, passed over equally agreeably. At dinner our numbers were augmented by the addition of Mr. Spalding, Dr. and Mrs. Troup, Colonel Troup, and his daughter. The Colonel was late Governor of the State of Georgia, and owing to the part he then acted in opposing the General Government, which the Georgians considered as interfering unwarrantably with their State rights, he is at present looked upon as the great lion of this part of the country, and certainly his outward man goes far to maintain his claim to such distinction, for I certainly never saw any mortal more like a wild beast, a red head, bushy eyebrows, and little eyes, added to a most uncouth dress, a sort of surtout or greatcoat with three little capes or tippets, and a shabby sort of black stock round his neck, which by no means concealed it, and yet there is something mild and melancholy in his appearance that half makes you forget what a strange looking being he is. The other members of the party had nothing peculiar in their appearances or manners either. They did not leave us till it was nearly dark and not in time to save themselves from a thunder storm which commenced soon after they left us.

In coming from Hopeton to Darien we stopped at Butler's Island, the most valuable plantation on this river. We walked across the island on which there is the greatest number of oranges, sour oranges, that I have ever seen. There are also lemon trees in abundance and sweet orange trees, tho' they have at present no fruit. We did not reach Darien until after three o'clock, and then we dressed for dinner at Dr. Fraser's. Eliza is in high health after all her aquatic excursions. She was much pleased with the number of children at St. Simon's, and not five minutes after her arrival went scampering about the passages with them, as much at home as any one of them. Dr. Fraser, with whom we dined to-day, came out about nine years ago and is settled as a physician in Darien. He married the daughter of Captain Wylie and consequently sister to Mrs. James Couper, but she is in bad health and I have not seen her. Darien is a pretty little village altho' dignified with the name of city, and was formerly a thriving place, tho' it has now lost that character and looks like a city of the dead. The streets, like most of the southern towns we have been in, are lined on both sides with rows of trees, which have a very pretty effect.

RICEBOROUGH, GEORGIA, MARCH 20:—We have dined, and I am now seated in the piazza writing whilst Basil makes a sketch with the *camera* and Eliza is looking after her favourites, the pigs, and a large black bear which is chained in the court yard. Mrs.

The Village of Riceborough, in Georgia

From a drawing
by Capt. B. Hall, R. N.

Cownie appears to be under no small apprehension that the animal will break loose to feed upon such a delicate morsel, but her Papa ensures her life and limbs. To-morrow we commence fairly to get out of the civilized world, and we look forward with much interest to our journey. In the course of this day's travelling we saw, not "stuffed" but all alive, two very large snakes, one of a poisonous kind called the yellow mocassin, and one black, not venomous, also two terrapins.

MR. GALDEN'S, 20 MILES WEST OF RICEBOROUGH, MARCH 21: —I think our landlady at Riceborough was one of the kindest persons we have met with. She saw that we were anxious to have some breakfast for Eliza before starting, and she made one of her girls milk the cow an hour or two earlier than usual on purpose that there might be some for her. She had a pot of coffee prepared for me likewise, and having seen that Eliza was much pleased with an apple pie that she had for supper last night, she put up a huge piece of it for her to carry off this morning. I think I hear some of the Mamas exclaim, "Apple pie for supper! What a strange way to feed a child!" but I suppose that most of your children have apples with a little of the crust many days in the week, or some other sort of pie or pudding, and whether it be ate at dinner or at supper makes little difference. However, I allow that her mode of feeding, like all other ways of her life is somewhat of the strangest. All I can say is, "Look at the result!"

In this part of the country there is a large part of the population termed *Crackers,* persons who do not trouble themselves with procuring title deeds, but, emigrating from other States, settle themselves here on the first piece of land they think will suit them. By and by, perhaps, the rightful owner of the land comes and then either a bargain is made between them or else the cracker moves off to some other spot, where for a time, at least, he remains undisturbed. On the Mississippi the same character of persons are called *Squatters.* I hope to see some of them by and by. We stopped three-quarters of an hour on the road after leaving Galden's and did not arrive here till after six o'clock, hungry enough for our supper as you may believe, which I hope will shortly make its appearance. Mrs. Cownie and Eliza are to sleep in this room after we have supped. The little wooden bedstead stands in one corner of the room, our supper table in the middle, and the side board at one side. There is no carpet or curtains, of course, and no glass on the windows, nothing but wooden window shutters to shut out the weather, whatever it may be, so that if it be very furious the light also must be excluded.

MRS. O'NIEL'S, 29 MILES WEST OF MR. RICKS'S, MARCH 25:— This is a superb house, in our eyes, after the accommodation we have been used to during the last five days. There are actually glass windows and we have had as much milk as we could make use of. As to the sheets being of check, blue cotton we have got quite used to that, and are not to be daunted by such trifles. Besides we carry our own sheets and, therefore, are independent so far, but what is most agreeable is that the people seem willing to make us comfortable as far as lies in their power and appear to make us welcome, which is not what we often meet with, particularly in these Southern States, where the manners of the secondary classes are more disagreeable, gruff, and boorish than anything I ever saw elsewhere. There is such an absence of all kindness of feeling, such unbending frigid heartlessness, that I am always surprised how Basil has patience to wheedle and coax them in the way he does, but I believe that if it were not for him we should never get anything at all, for my part I feel so disgusted with them that I am inclined to turn my back upon their disagreeable countenances and take my chance.

MR. WELLS'S TAVERN, BETWEEN FLINT AND CHATTAHOOCHIE RIVERS, MARCH 30:—This is a queer life that we are leading, I say to myself a dozen times a day, nor does habit make it appear less so, nor make it more agreeable. I am sorry that I have omitted writing for so many days, but the truth is that by the end of the day and after everything is put right for the night, I am so completely tired that I have not strength left even to write, and in the morning we get up by candlelight and are off as soon as we have swallowed our breakfast. My last date was at Mrs. O'Niel's on the twenty-fifth. I think, on the whole, that that was the most comfortable house we have been in, altho' there was the usual complement of fleas and bugs, but we have ceased to expect anything else and even the travelling bed is not an antidote for them. Every night I am awakened by Mrs. Cownie striking a light to commence her search for her tormentors. We bring them along with us in our clothes and when I undress I find them crawling on my skin, nasty wretches. After four hours and a half of weary driving and crossing sundry crazy bridges we reached Macon, a town three years old, not unlike in appearance to some of the new towns in the Western part of the State of New York through which we passed last summer, but exceedingly unlike them in appearance of activity and thriving, and in a year or two I suppose it will begin to fall off. There is not a single town or village through which we have passed south of Philadelphia which is not on the decay. From the moment the slave system commences, so does the decline. We had a busy day at Macon, all of us. Middleton, our driver had to get the perch of the carriage mended and various other little jobs to arrange about and to put the waggon to rights. We had sheets for Eliza's bed to buy and have made, our stores to renew, clothes to get washed and numerous other etceteras, so that, altho' it was a day of stopping, it was no day of rest.

The twenty-eighth we were ready to take our departure from Macon and away we went up hill and down dale across a ferry and over innumerable fords where bridges had been but were broken down either by "freshes" or by mischievous persons. When we were still twelve miles from the end of our day's travelling the rain commenced with great violence and the thunder rolled most awfully, and whilst this still continued we arrived at a place called the Old Creek Agency, having been formerly the boundary line of the nation of Creek Indians who have now gone further to the West. Here we were to have made our halt for the night. It was a miserable looking place, a collection of small wooden houses consisting of one room each and apparently quite rotten. We had to splash through the wet, dirty yard from one nasty hovel to another before we got to our resting place, and, in short, it appeared wretched in the extreme. By and by, however, appearances became better, the rain ceased, and the clouds both in the sky and in our prospects began speedily to disperse. The people at the house were abundantly willing to make us comfortable as far as they had the power. We got out our rice and the chickens we had brought with us from Macon, made our tea, had a blazing fire lighted in the room where we were to sleep, and got on famously in spite of the open logs all round our room and the looseness of the planks which prevented Eliza from walking three steps without falling. We put up a mosquito curtain that we had had made at Savannah and, drawing a table close to the bed, placed ourselves under our curtain to write. Without this contrivance we could not possibly have sat, for the mosquitoes and the flies exceed anything I ever saw. On the last page is the blood of one I chanced to murder some few minutes ago. Before I had been here five minutes my feet were in a perfect fever, and heaven knows what state we shall be in to-morrow. The room in which we are lodged is open all around with holes big enough to throw one's whole person through and there is no small danger of Eliza twisting her little foot between the planks. There is no window in our room, but there is abundant admission both of light and air through the holes I mentioned.

COLUMBUS AT THE FALLS OF CHATTAHOOCHIE, GEORGIA, MARCH 31 :—Basil says that he has seen a town without inhabitants, but that he never before saw inhabitants without a town. To such a place we have got now, as I shall tell you in the course of my narrative.

On crossing the Chattahoochie we got into the Creek nation, the portion of country still in the possession of a tribe of Indians called Creeks. Till about two years ago their territory commenced at

From a drawing
by Capt. B. Hall, R. N.

Engraved by W. H. Lizars

EMBRYO TOWN OF COLUMBUS ON THE CHATAHOOCHIE

Flint River, and you will find on most maps that it is still called so, but two years ago the United States Government purchased from them that part between the Flint and Chattahoochie Rivers and they are now all on the western side of the Chattahoochie. Great numbers of them have gone over the Mississippi; poor wretches, they will no doubt soon vanish from the earth. At Colonel Crowell's we saw numbers of them flocking about his house in eager expectation of supplies of food which were arriving from the State of Alabama. They are in a state of starvation, and their habits are of that idle, wandering nature which makes labour too irksome for them to submit to. Colonel Crowell is the agent on the part of the government of the U. S. through whom all business between that government and the Indians passes. He met us at the door of his house, a very comfortable one compared to those we have of late been used to, and the sight of a blazing fire was very cheering on a morning as cold and raw as any March morning at home. He also gave us some breakfast altho' his own was long past, for it was nine o'clock before we arrived. Our next enquiry was as to the easiest and best way of getting to Columbus, and we were informed that there was a carriage road to it and that we could from Columbus get into the main road again without retracing our steps. This was all very satisfactory and we resolved upon going.

When the United States purchased the land lying between the Flint and Chattahoochie Rivers from the Creek Indians, they made a lottery of it, dividing into lots 202½ acres each, and every one over age in the State of Georgia had a right to draw. A man with a wife had two draws, or chances, and one with a wife and family had three. But at the same time a certain portion was reserved five miles square for the purpose of erecting a town, and this portion is at the Falls of the Chattahoochie, a very beautiful situation indeed. The lots for the town consisted, some of an acre, and others of half an acre, and around are some larger bits of ten and twenty acres which will make nice villas. All this you will observe *is to be,* for as yet the town is a thick forest, with the exception of some temporary wooden buildings erected to shelter the numerous bidders from all parts of the Union who are waiting for the sale of lots which is to commence early in July. Our companion pointed them out to us as we walked along, for we had an hour's walk from the water side along streets staked out amongst the trees. "And now," he said, as we were on the most rugged beshrubbed part of the path, "you are in the heart of the city." The little temporary streets at which we at length arrived presented a very strange appearance, little log and frame houses, most of them intended to be moved to some other situation a few months hence, but in the meantime exhibiting very imposing signs such as T. Gordon, Attorney-at-Law, "Bake House," and so on. Crowds of gentlemen, American gentlemen, remember, in large cloaks and beards of a week's growth lolling about with the forefeet of their chairs in the air according to custom, and some of them showing symptoms that whisky has already found its way to Columbus. Hotel signs swung among the trees, and we were very well accommodated at the principal one. There are several commissioners on the part of the United States Government residing there for the purpose of arranging the sales. To one of these, Dr. de Graffenreidt, we had a letter, and he introduced all the others, and a whole host of people besides, to us. It was four o'clock when we reached Columbus, and after walking down to visit the Falls, or rather Rapids, Basil took advantage of the remaining daylight to make a sketch. This, as usual, brought all the idlers to stare, and he soon had a mob round him. Two long hours passed before there was a morsel ready for us to eat, and we had had nothing since ten o'clock, however, at last our supper was ready and having dispatched it we walked off to one of the adjoining houses, for each room was a separate house, to see the plan of the town, and there we sat talking with numerous gentlemen till I got so sleepy that I could sit no longer.

LEWIS'S TAVERN, IN THE CREEK NATION, APRIL 1 :—The Indian chiefs allow white men to establish taverns in their territory for the accommodation of travellers. We are this night at a most excellent one kept by a man of the name of Lewis, who has a squaw to wife. We are in a closed house and have got blazing fires, which the change in the weather rendered very necessary. I suffered badly from cold last night, so much, indeed, that I could not sleep, and there was sufficient talking and snoring all round me to keep me awake independently of the change of weather, for we occupied a room containing four beds out of which had been thrust four gentlemen who had to be put up in the little places close to us. Altho' I have groaned over each day's journey with the feeling of one whose every bone aches from ill usage, our longest distance has been very little over thirty miles and more commonly under it, and as there are only certain houses that are tolerably decent to stay at, we are obliged to go on from one to the other, according as we learn which are the usual stopping places of other travellers. Then, too, we are generally so uncomfortable in the house that we are anxious to get out of it as early as possible, tho' we are just as desirous by the end of the day to quit the carriage. In spite of the various discomforts we have experienced, there has been great interest in the journey, but I shall rejoice most truly when we arrive at Montgomery. What I have felt the greatest suffering is the dirt that we have to put up with in everything, even in our food. This is an appearance of dirt that is very disgusting. One thing we have to be thankful for is that we have all enjoyed such perfect health throughout the whole journey, as for Eliza, she is as hardy as a wild Indian and nearly about as wild. She has never caught the slightest cold in spite of all the exposure she has had.

CAPTAIN TRIPLETT'S CABIN, CREEK NATION, APRIL 2:—We are now within twenty-seven miles of Montgomery, which terminates our land travelling for the present, and it was our intention to have pushed on there very early to-morrow morning, but the landlord here has told us of a ball play that the Indians are to have to-morrow, and as we may not have another opportunity of seeing such a sight we mean to delay our journey a few hours for the purpose of being present at it. They dance all this night previous to the ball play, and Basil is gone with Captain Triplett to see them. Had there been any mode of conveyance for me I should have gone likewise, tho' I am abundantly tired and sleepy.

I think I have mentioned more than once that we were astonished that more questions were not asked of us by the Americans, whose inquisitiveness is so proverbial, but I find that, altho' they do not interrogate us, Mrs. Cownie is bothered to death by their questions and highly indignant at the ignorance and stupidity displayed by many of them. Of course they always ask where we come from and after telling that we are from England, she has been asked whether we have learned to speak English since coming to America. At Columbus the landlady asked when told we were from England, "What England?" Is there more than one England? She was not at all pleased with me and said to Mrs. Cownie that I was very "stingy."

"Stingy," said Mrs. Cownie, "what do you mean?"

"I mean stingy in her talk," rejoined the good lady. "I sat by her for half an hour and she hardly spoke a word to me."

Now I had exerted myself to be particularly civil and had made one or two commonplace remarks with a very good grace, as I thought, but only fancy the misery of travelling in a country when, weary and hungry tho' you may be, you are expected to make conversation to every ignorant low-bred mistress of a tavern you may chance to lodge with. The *camera* continues to excite its own share of wonder. "I suppose you mean to publish a geography of the country, from your being so particular," said a gentleman two evenings ago.

The same day we stopped at a house in the forest to rest our horses a little and Basil, as usual, began to sketch. The sun was so hot that I took shelter from it in the house opposite to him and which he was drawing. A half-drunk black man belonging to the place came to converse with me and remarked, "That man there wanted me to look through that thing he has got, but I was afraid he would ask me more money for the sight than I have to give, so I said I didn't want to look. Of course, it gives him some trouble to let me

look and he must be paid. It's his business, is it not?" evidently
supposing him to be a raree-show man by profession.

MONTGOMERY, STATE OF ALABAMA, APRIL 5:—We are at
length at Montgomery, which finishes our land travelling for the
present, and in an hour we are to embark on board of the steamboat which is to carry us down the River Alabama to Mobile, a
distance of nearly five hundred miles, which we shall be two or three
or four days in accomplishing. We were very anxious to have
reached Mobile before Easter Sunday, for at Montgomery there is
no Episcopal Church, so it was not worth our while remaining here
for so many days.

Yesterday morning we remained at Captain Triplett's till we
heard the Indians begin to yell in the woods, which was a sign that
they were assembling. This was at ten o'clock. The horses were
then put to the carriage, and pioneered by our landlord we proceeded
about a half a mile through the very heart of the forest and where
none but a thoroughly good driver could have ventured to drive a
carriage. There we stopped on a little eminence overlooking the
valley where the Indians were to play. We were the first persons on
the ground and had upwards of two hours to wait before what we
went to see commenced, but we were interested by various groups,
some of whites in waggons, but mostly of Indian women and children
in their best attire, who collected in the mean time. All this time we
heard strange yells from the opposite parties, and at length one party
rushed on the ground throwing themselves into all sorts of fantastic
attitudes, like nothing I ever saw except the plates of Captain Cook's
Voyages, and with no more dress on. Their bodies and faces were
painted with various colours, they wore feathers in their heads, and
some of them tails of beasts. In short, it is impossible to conceive
anything more thoroughly savage, but it was interesting to see such
a sight totally unsophisticated by any mixture of civilization, and on
the ground that has belonged to the Indians from time immemorial,
tho' probably it will not belong to them much longer. The first party
then seated themselves on the ground and the others made their

appearance in the same manner and garb, or no garb, to speak more correctly. Each party consisted of fifty. The game I cannot pretend to describe, for there was so much danger of being knocked over in the course of their sport that I was advised to retreat into the carriage which was placed at too great a distance for me to be able to judge of anything except the extraordinary agility with which they run, which appears all the more extraordinary when contrasted with their usually very indolent, lounging habits. We remained till two o'clock, and then fearful of being benighted on our way to Montgomery we set off and soon regained the high road. Six miles further on we crossed the Old Line Creek, which divides the Creek Nation from the State of Alabama, and nineteen miles more brought us to Montgomery. The last seven miles it was quite dark and we had to creep along very cautiously as neither the driver nor the horses were acquainted with the ruts and other dangers of the road which altho' quite perfect when compared with what we have lately travelled over had still a sufficient number of defects to require careful driving. We got to Montgomery about eight o'clock and learnt that a steamboat starts for Mobile to-day.

ON BOARD THE STEAM BOAT *Herald* ON THE ALABAMA RIVER, APRIL 5:—It is not much our habit to like steamboats, but so great has been our fatigue of late on land that we actually find the dirtiest, most unpleasant steamboat we have been in in all our water travellings quite luxurious when compared to the labour of travelling through Georgia, and we enjoyed to a degree having our meals prepared for us without our having to look after the catching of chickens, boiling of rice, and many other etceteras. Then the bad roads, early rising, without comparatively early going to bed, knocked both Basil and me up completely. I was so unwell that I am sure I could not have stood three more days of the same fatigue, and I am now only recovering it. Basil, too, when there was no further call for exertion, quite gave in, but he also is recovering. Mrs. Cownie had her share of suffering and, in short, all of us paid for our journey on the score of health except Eliza, and she showed no symptoms whatever of fatigue, unless sleeping thirteen hours without stirring be one, and certainly she never did such a thing in her life before.

The signal gun from the *Herald* was fired yesterday at one o'clock. We found the Captain waiting only for us to set off, and in a few minutes we were running down the Alabama at a great rate, but the river winds so much that the distance which by land is only one hundred and eighty miles is by water nearly five hundred. We make so many stops, too, to take in bales of cotton, and things are so clumsily managed that we expect to be a long while in making the voyage. Yesterday, for instance, we stopped about twenty miles from Montgomery about four o'clock in the afternoon and there we remained till this morning at seven o'clock. First of all there were numerous bales of cotton to be got on board in their clumsy fashion, then they waited for the owner of the said cotton, who chose to be absent when he ought to have been present, and finally the fog became so thick that it was impossible to proceed.

In the South they are far, far behind their Northern neighbours, backward tho' they may be in all that regards the elegance and refinement of life. I must just give you one little instance of the advancement and improvement that they boast so much of in this part of the world. Yesterday morning at Montgomery we begged a black man to go out and get us some fresh bread, being a thing we had not tasted since leaving Macon, but presently he returned, and poking his oily countenance into the room announced that there was no bread to be had, as the baker had left the town the morning before!

MOBILE, APRIL 7:—This morning we landed at Mobile at ten o'clock. There was a great fire here in October last in which most of the hotels were burnt down. We were recommended to-day to go to Mr. White's as the best. We did so, accordingly, and had our things carried there, a nasty, dirty house it appeared. We were shown first into a parlour where sat the mistress of the house at work whilst Miss White strummed her lesson on the piano under the guidance of a foreign teacher. There was no private parlour to be had, and the only bedroom they could give us for the whole party was one in which there was no fireplace. Now you must know that the weather has been bitterly cold. The deck of the boat yesterday morning was covered with ice. Under such circumstances it was not agreeable to have the prospect of sitting in a room without a fire, and as for subjecting ourselves for the whole evening to the company of Mrs. and *Miss* White, more especially Miss, with her music and her airs, not forgetting her gold chains, and her numerous seals, that was not to be endured. So I made up my mind to be frozen and wished myself back in the dirty steamboat, from whence we had issued such figures that anyone of us from Eliza upwards might have been mistaken for the engineer. However, there appeared to be no remedy, and Basil went off with a letter of introduction he had for a certain Mr. Robertson to enquire about the steamboats for New Orleans. In about half an hour he returned with a much brighter countenance than what he had set out with and told me that Mr. Robertson had begged that we would remove from the hotel up to his house which is at present unoccupied, all his family and his wife having gone to New York and he himself, as we understood, living somewhere else. This was an offer not to be rejected, and I rejoiced to think of the comfortable fire poor little Eliza would gain by the exchange. So having merely staid to dine at the noisy, bustling public table where sixty persons dispatched their unchewed dinner in the course of twenty minutes, we bundled off, bag and baggage, to Mr. Robertson's very comfortable house where I now sit beside a blazing fire and with the prospect of reposing on the most delicious large, firm mattress that I have seen since leaving home. Eliza is sound asleep in a room equally comfortable, and, in short, we are all in the height of enjoyment and only think of the consideration of our host. A short time ago we discovered that he is in the house, but supposing that we must be tired and not wish to be disturbed he did not come near us, and it was only accidentally that we found out that he is upstairs.

SAVANNAH TO *MOBILE*

APRIL 9:—We thought that when we should get to Mobile we were actually at New Orleans, but it appears to be no such easy matter to get there even from hence. Owing to accidents of various kinds there is now but one steamboat plying between this place and New Orleans, and there is no certainty of her time of coming and going. She has not yet arrived, and so here we are still in a state of uncertainty as to our time of departure, however, we are so comfortably lodged that we don't fret over the detention tho' we shall be glad that it does not continue much longer. It is just a year to-day since we left Edinburgh, a busy year it has been. In half that length of time, I trust we shall be tolerably near home. Yesterday we had a visit from Mrs. Erwin, the daughter of Mr. Clay, the Secretary of State. Mrs. Erwin lives at New Orleans, and I brought a letter of introduction to her from her father, but she is at present on a visit to her husband and husband's sister, Mrs. Hitchcock, who with Mr. Hitchcock also called upon us and we are to dine with them to-day. Yesterday, the eighth, we dined at Mr. Pole's, the cashier of the Bank of the United States. Mrs. Pole is sister to Mrs. Robertson, our host's wife. Mrs. Erwin has sent this morning to ask me to take a ride with her, as they universally call a drive in a carriage. I remember how we used to quiz Miss Douglas in Edinburgh for talking of riding to Church, but the Americans contend that driving means actually driving the horses.

Mrs. Erwin called for me, accompanied by Miss Porter, a very pleasing, elderly, young lady, either English, Scotch, or Irish, I could not make out which, who has been several years in the State of Louisiana. We drove out about five miles amongst our old friends the pines to a place called Spring Hill, which is the spot to which the inhabitants of Mobile fly for refuge during the season of yellow fever. They consider any place safe a little elevated, with a sandy soil and running water. This is not peculiar to this part of the States but all over the South, and going to the sand hills is reckoned a perfect security against the certain death that would probably be their portion not a dozen miles off. I found Mrs. Erwin very agreeable and we got on famously during our two hours' drive, which is saying a great deal, I think, especially as one of the party, viz. myself, hates speaking in a carriage.

We dined at Mr. Hitchcock's, the brother-in-law of Mrs. Erwin and where Mrs. Erwin is living. I don't think there is anything peculiar in the arrangements and providings of a dinner table here except the quantity of French wine that is drunk instead of Madeira, which is elsewhere the universal beverage in the way of wine. Here they drink claret in tumblers, not strong, English claret but the *vin du pays* unadulterated by spirits, and a most delicious drink it is in hot weather. For the rest there is the same frequent disappearance of the lady of the house before the guests are at length summoned to the dining room, the same overloaded table, bad cookery, and worse attendance, but it is very kind of them to ask one at all, for I am sure it must be a great bore to them. The dinner hour is three o'clock, but you do not remain the evening so we took a walk and then came home to drink tea and sit comfortably. This morning our first question was as to the arrival of the steamboat, which was answered in the negative. We have sat at home all day receiving visitors and writing letters. We have breakfasted alone every morning as our kind host, Mr. Robertson, in the absence of his wife and family, boards at his brother-in-law's, Mrs. Pole's, whose early breakfast hour suits his habits of business better than our lazy hours do, but to-day we thought he would certainly dine with us. However, to our astonishment there was a most ample dinner provided, but no Mr. Robertson to help us eat it. He seems to be resolved that we shall consider the house entirely our own without the smallest interference on his part further than to provide everything of the best for us.

Ever affectionately yours,

MARGARET HALL.

LETTER XIX

MOBILE TO NEW ORLEANS

Rested and refreshed by the luxury of Mr. Robertson's house at Mobile Mrs. Hall and her family embarked on a steamer for New Orleans. Crossing the Bay on a rough night made the "miseries" of the land journey a "joke" by comparison. At New Orleans they put up at Mrs. Herries' well-known boarding-house where they found two Scotchmen who could act as guides to the city. They were taken by Governor Johnson to the Ursuline Convent, by Vincent Nolte to the battle-ground, and by M. Pilié, the Surveyor General, to inspect the Levée. Justice Porter, the British Consul Salkeld, and others entertained them during their stay of ten days.

NEW ORLEANS, LOUISIANA,
April 16, 1828.

MY DEAREST JANE,

At length we have reached the extreme point of our journey, and from the moment we leave this place I shall consider that we are returning home, and a very delightful feeling that will be. I sent a letter of nine sheets to you from Mobile containing a history of our rough journey through Georgia and Alabama during the preceding three or four weeks, but all that we then suffered is a mere joke compared to the miseries of the voyage from Mobile. When I finished my letter we were still waiting the return of the steamboat to take us to New Orleans. On the tenth I was woke at twelve at night by the groans of the high-pressure engine as it puffed off its last breathings at the wharf within a few hundred yards of our house.

We took a very pleasant drive with Mr. Pole to a point where the Bay of Mobile looked to particular advantage, but the pleasure of the drive arose more from his agreeable conversation than from any charms of scenery. It is so rarely that we meet in this country

249

with anyone whose feelings, I should say rather whose opinions, accord with our own that when such a meeting does take place we enjoy it in a very peculiar degree. Mr. Pole is a native of Connecticut and removed to Mobile as cashier of the Branch Bank of the United States only a year and a half ago, since when he has married a young girl very little older than his eldest daughter. He is no great admirer of things in the South nor, I think, of the political state of the country in any part of the Union, but the Southerners are far behind their Northern brethren in all respects, backward as those also appear to us.

On the twelfth we had dined and were in readiness to move by two o'clock, but it was four before we found it necessary to go on board. The preceding passage from New Orleans had occupied fifty-two hours, and I had many misgivings that we should not be much less, altho' the usual length of passage is considered from twenty-four to thirty hours. We had ladies on board, Mrs. Erwin and two children, and Miss Erwin, her sister-in-law, Miss Porter, and her niece, a girl of eleven, and a French lady with two children. These, with two black female attendants, were more than enough for the ladies' part of the establishment. The cabin, however, appropriated in general to their use was such a wretched place below that we were unanimous in our protestations against subjecting ourselves to the additional discomfort of such accommodation, and as there were not gentlemen sufficient to fill one half of the berths in the principal cabin, which was large, we had a part of it screened off for us. The evening was beautiful when we left Mobile, although the breeze made the water rather rougher than suited the construction of some of the female stomachs. Poor Eliza was the first to give way, but her sickness is so different from that of an older person, for she smiles in the midst of it and the next moment calls out for something to eat. Not so Mrs. Cownie, who is more completely subdued than anyone I ever saw; before tea was ready she was as pale as death and had thrown herself on the berth in a manner that looked as if she would never lift her head from it again. Basil and I undressed Eliza, and he soon put her to sleep and then laid her down in the berth in the gentlemen's part of the cabin where he lay on a mattress beside her, and till eight o'clock next morning she never stirred but once, which was a great ease to us.   Between eight and nine in the evening the motion became so great that I made the best haste I could to bed. At ten o'clock we came to anchor.   We had attempted going outside Dolphin Island, but the sea was too high to admit of our going on during the night, or even anchoring, so we put back to a safer place, but altho' we anchored we continued tossing the whole night in the most wretched manner possible throughout a violent storm of wind, lightning, and some rain. Indeed, I believe those in a schooner which had left Mobile the day before us entertained considerable fears for our safety.   The morning came, once more we moved on against a violent head wind which made a sea fit to tear anyone's stomach to atoms.   Mrs. Erwin and the French lady, Madame Perault, never suffered a moment; the rest were all more or less subdued but not as bad as Mrs. Cownie and myself.   I never passed a more thoroughly miserable day.   Basil tried scolding me to make me exert a little and get up, but all in vain.   I do believe if I had been told that there was danger of the boiler bursting I should not have moved.   This was the thirteenth; towards evening things quieted a little and we were going on tolerably smoothly, when scrape went the boat, and we were fast aground.   They made such a row trying to get her off that I took it into my wise head that we were in some danger altho' the night before when there really was cause for apprehension I had suffered none, but the truth was I had not then judgement sufficient to form even a wrong opinion, much less a right one.   We remained hard and fast till the tide got us off, and this was the last interruption we had.   The rest of our voyage was performed pleasantly enough, and at four in the afternoon we landed at the Piquets, a place six miles distant from New Orleans, and had a very pleasant drive indeed along the Bayou or Creek by which vessels come up from Lake Pontchartrain to the city.

We had been recommended to go to Mrs. Herries's boarding house as the best, indeed, the only tolerable establishment of any public kind in New Orleans. Some of our fellow passengers were going there, and, accordingly, we drove to her house at once through a long, narrow, Spanish looking street totally unlike anything to be seen elsewhere in the United States. We found Mrs. Herries willing and able to accommodate us with two good bedrooms but no private parlour, all our meals to be swallowed in public amidst the clatter of thirty pairs of knives and forks, at the rate of six dollars a day with the chance of higher terms being exacted should she be obliged to refuse admittance to anyone in consequence of Mrs. Cownie and Eliza occupying one of her best rooms. Everything in the place is equally extravagant, why I don't know, as there is ample and easy means of obtaining the best supplies from all quarters, both at home and abroad. Basil's first expedition was, of course, to the Post Office from whence he returned with forty-seven letters. He ran also, before returning to the house, to take a look at the great Mississippi, the "Father of Waters", as its name denotes, and its magnificence shows its claim to. I deferred my first visit to it till yesterday, the fifteenth, and found each successive view increased my veneration. The river is particularly high at present, and at New Orleans you must change your phraseology and instead of talking of taking a walk *down* to the river, say that you are going *up* to the River, the water being in fact considerably higher than the town. This causes the inhabitants to keep a sharp look out for crevasses, as they term breaks in the *levee,* or bank, which is formed to keep the river from overflowing the city and for many miles up where there is cultivated country. At one part of the river lay thirteen steamboats of which we went on board several and found some of them really splendid with three decks, one on top of the other, for different classes of passengers.

There is something in the short view I have yet had of Orleans that pleases me particularly. There is an air of cheerfulness and gaiety and, withal, an old Continental aspect which is peculiarly pleasing after being for so long teased with the newness and rawness of all American cities. The mixture of lively, French tone heard in the streets, too, adds to the interest, and the forests of

From a drawing
by Capt. B. Hall, R. N.

THE LEVEE AT NEW ORLEANS

Engraved by W. H. Lizars

masts all around beget a feeling of connection with more distant and far dearer countries. Then the appearance of the houses with their queerly-shaped, high roofs and iron balconies instead of the pitiful wood things universal elsewhere, for which I have not yet got over my contempt. The delightful dark *portes cochères* and Spanish *patios* round which this house, at least, is built with rooms with borrowed light from the corridors beyond, look deliciously cool for summer use, as do also the women walking along the streets with nothing but a veil over their heads. We did not send out any of our letters of introduction till this morning, the sixteenth, and denied ourselves to any visitors that might call, tho' none did, I believe, as we wished to have time to read our letters and ramble about the town undisturbed.

We took Eliza and Mrs. Cownie with us to where the vessels were lying and amused ourselves for a long time with the bustling scene. Amongst the boarders in this house are two, primitive-looking, old ladies from Dumfries, the Miss Maclures, who arrived a few days ago on their way to the State of Indiana, or Illinois, to visit a mad sort of brother of theirs, an elderly gentleman who, when about the age of sixty, took it into his head to join with Mr. Owen in his wild scheme of changing American nature by teaching and surrounding men and women by circumstances, as his phrase goes. I think the undertaking of the old ladies at their advanced period of life not much less extravagant, for they are a couple of as fragile looking beings as I ever saw. An Irish milliner sits at the top of the table next to Mrs. Herries and one other lady from Alabama completes the female part of the boarders. The rest are all gentlemen, merchants from Liverpool, and elsewhere. We see nothing of any of them except at meal times as we sit constantly in our rooms. The weather here is delightful, cool and pleasant, and New Orleans at this season as healthy as any place in the world.

APRIL 20:—With one of our fellow lodgers, Mr. Duncan, as *cicerone* and accompanied by another, Mr. Dennistoun, from Glasgow, we sallied forth on a walk through the town, and by the advice of our guide we mounted to the roof of one of the hotels, from whence we had an excellent view of the city. New Orleans is a much smaller place than I had supposed. I don't know why I had taken it into my head that it was nearly as large as New York, instead of which it is not above one fourth of the size. I suppose I had formed my judgement from hearing so often repeated what an important place it will one day be. Everything in this country is in perspective, but New Orleans is already a place of much importance. We were pretty well fatigued by our walk and our climb and were preparing to go to bed when we were informed that the Governor of the State of Louisiana, Mr. Johnson, was below waiting to see us, and, accordingly, down we went and found a quiet, modest-looking man of between thirty and forty. He sat an hour with us and is certainly the most attentive and polite governor we have met with since poor De Witt Clinton. He told us that he had that morning received an invitation from the nuns of the only Convent here inviting him to be present at the ceremony of two young ladies taking the black veil. He had just got our letters of introduction and immediately wrote to ask leave of the Superior that we should accompany him, which was granted. This, we have since learnt, was a greater piece of good luck than I, at least, was aware of, for those nuns of the order of Ursulines are very strict and rarely admit even ladies within the grate. The ceremony was to take place very early, and at eight o'clock on the seventeenth the Governor accompanied by Judge Porter, an Irishman by birth but now an American citizen, called for us to go to the convent, which is about two miles distant. Here we found a good many ladies assembled and were introduced to the nuns, who as I have always seen persons of their calling, were delighted to have strangers to talk to. They occupy a delightful house charmingly situated down the river and have abundance of rational occupation, having no less than one hundred and seven young ladies as boarders, whom they educate with the assistance of a few masters. We soon adjourned to the chapel, where we had Mass and then the ceremony took place. No one can forget that part of it when the funeral service is said over them as they lie extended on the ground under a black pall, figuratively buried to the world, but I am afraid my days of romance have gone by, for I felt no emotion altho' both the young women were pretty and only nineteen years old, but in this country it is impossible to connect any idea of force on the part of friends with the sacrifice made, and it is very well known that at any time, even after pronouncing the last vows, they may quit their retirement and return to the world if they have the smallest wish to do so. More than one lady has availed herself of this privilege and one married after having been a nun for ten or twelve years. After the ceremony we were shown through all the house, and finally had cake and wine before going away. The Superior is a fine, old lady nearly eighty years of age, a native of France but who has been in this country forty-two years.

We went in the evening to the French Theatre and saw *Marie Stuart* very well performed by Madame Clausel, but she was miserably supported, and "Queen Elizabeth" was a complete virago.

We dined at Mr. Byrne's on the eighteenth, an English merchant married to a Creole lady. The style of table here appears to be a mixture of American and French with all the sins of American attendance, of course, because there is no service but that of slaves, than which nothing can be worse. We suffer much from it in this house, which is the most uncomfortable of the kind that we have been in, altho' we are told it is the best in New Orleans. One of the greatest discomforts of a boarding house, to me at least, is the difficulty of finding fault when the lady sits at the head of the table as one of the company and makes me feel as if I were her guest instead of paying an enormous sum for middling fare and uncomfortable lodging.

We dined at the British Consul's, Mr. Salkeld, who has a pretty Chinese-looking house about two miles out of the town down the river, to which he has lately imported one of his daughters, a chubby, English-looking girl, and with her an elderly, maiden cousin to superintend his *ménage*. He has a wife and numerous other children in England. We had a regular English party of ten persons, Mrs. Briggs, to be sure, is a Creole, but she is married to an Englishman, and when that is the case an American woman soon ceases to be American. It is to us like escaping from school to get into a party of English unmixed with Americans. We feel that we may speak all we think and feel without restraint or fear of misapprehension, and it really is quite a holiday to be for once off our Ps and Qs. Another great charm, too, consisted in the small dinners in place of the oppressive load of an American table.

APRIL 21 :—This has been our busiest day since we came to New Orleans. Our expedition began soon after nine o'clock with Mr. Pilié, the Surveyor General. I have told you of the levée or bank which confines the river for many, many miles both above and below, as well as at the town. In this levée there sometimes occur holes which admit the water and soon cause whole plantations to be submerged. These holes are termed crevasses. On the first suspicion of such a thing in the town all the citizens are put in requisition to lend their aid towards remedying the evil, for after it goes a certain length it is impossible to stop the water, and it is necessary to wait patiently until the fall in the river draws it back again. A few years ago all the back part of New Orleans was for a considerable time under water. There are several at this time, but the nearest is sixty miles up the river, and as there are none in the immediate neighbourhood Mr. Pilié said that he would take us to where there had been one and explain the nature and effects of it. Accordingly, we crossed the water by the ferry-boat and were there for the first time fairly upon the Mississippi, which like the Falls of Niagara begets increased respect upon acquaintance. It is, indeed, a noble river, boiling and bubbling in a hundred whirlpools as magnificently as the River Niagara. There is a feeling of awe felt, too, on the Mississippi, arising from the knowledge of its immense depth and from knowing that no one, however well he may swim, is ever known to rise after the first and last fatal plunge. We walked up the opposite bank about a mile and a half, and I must say that I should not like to live there. There is an appearance of insecurity in the bank which would render such a residence very uncomfortable. There were no striking remains of the torrent, a few minutes satisfied our curiosity, so we walked back and recrossed the river. We then again set out on the second excursion to the Field of Battle or Battle Ground, as they term it here, taking Eliza with us. Mr. Vincent Nolte, who was one of the actors in the scene, went with us and pointed out the positions of the two armies and all the manœuvres. It is like all fields of battle very shortly after the battle is over, a quiet, new-cultivated field without a trace of anything extraordinary having taken place. How sadly all those who lost friends here must have grudged their fall after escaping in safety from the long and toilsome campaigns in the Peninsula, to come to be mowed down by a parcel of American Militia. Mr. Nolte, altho' a citizen of New Orleans, is a Prussian. He said that until the day of that battle he had not imagined it possible that men could march up to certain death with the coolness with which the British troops did. We concluded this day's entertainment with a sumptuous dinner at the governor's, who is the most attentive and the most modest of men, has a handsome house, and, I am told, entertains a great deal.

APRIL 23:—Yesterday was a busy day what between visiting, writing, and being engaged to dine at Judge Porter's at the barbarous hour of half past three, which is universal in New Orleans and cuts up one's time sadly, for it is nonsense to argue that if you go to dine early you will return home early. The hours in the evening are not the hours of business, and if you go out at half past three you must begin to dress soon after half past two. We had a large party at Judge Porter's and a prodigious dinner, which appears to be the fashion at New Orleans. The first course, of soup and meat, was followed by a second course, also of as many dishes of meat and vegetable as the first. Then came a course of pies, custards, strawberries and cream, and other kinds of fruit, and I fancied this was to be the last act when, to my astonishment, on the removal of the tablecloth a fresh set of plates was put down and another dessert of oranges, apples, and so on.

From habit, the singular *table manners* of our friends here are not so constantly apparent to me as when we first arrived, and I was less used to them, but I am still sufficiently alive to them to amuse myself from time to time in thinking what would be the surprise of anyone of you were you suddenly transported to an American dinner table, especially in the South. The moment any gentleman is requested to carve the dish nearest to him, up he springs to his legs, seizes his knife and fork, and hacks and hews the unfortunate joint or fowl into great junks. Then follows the question as to what you will eat. "Governor, will you take a piece of this turkey?" "What part will you take?" (In England we suppose no part is to be eaten whilst the breast remains.)

"A piece of the breast, anything that is most handy," whilst your plate is covered to the exclusion of the possibility of discovering that it is a plate or anything but a mass of turkey and vegetables.

Your neighbour says, "Madam, allow me to give you a piece of this stewed duck?" They put the most extraordinary mixtures on their own plates, and nearly altogether realise my ideas of the servants' hall. By the time we had got through Judge Porter's dinner it was time that we should be off home to put on travelling dresses and get into the boat. At half past six Mr. Briggs called for us and accompanied us to the boat wharf where all the vessels lay and across three or four of which we had to walk and to step over planks between them, a service of some danger, I thought, but one which we accomplished in great safety. On either side of the steamboat we found a vessel attached, the one bound to Hamburg, the other to Havannah, having on board a cargo of wretched Spaniards driven from Mexico by those who have acquired the upper hand there, but altho' their fate is wretched their appearance was not so, and I would defy the drawing-rooms of any town in the Union to produce as many gentlemanlike men even with their coarse blankets thrown round them. I felt a strong interest in them, but the night soon closed in and I saw no more of them, for this morning we had cast off both vessels before I got out of bed. I would have got up earlier but in crossing the bar it was so rough that the only way to keep myself tolerably well was to lie still. We soon got into smooth water and running down another of the passes found ourselves by nine o'clock at the Balize, a place where the pilots who bring vessels up the rivers live. And such a place to be sure! It cannot be called land for there is nothing but a deposit of mud and logs brought down by the river on which are built about twenty houses of different sorts and sizes having logs placed all along from one to the other, for it is out of the question to put your foot upon anything except a log without the danger of sinking knee deep, at least, in the swamp. For a great distance along the coast it is of the same nature. Nothing but marsh and reeds, but it is interesting to have seen this great river emptying itself into the Gulf of Mexico, and it is something, too, to have been actually in the Gulf of Mexico altho' but for a few minutes. We stayed two hours at the Balize, Basil hunting, pretty much in vain, for points of view from which to take sketches, and then returned on board, and now are only forty miles from New Orleans having in the interval run nearly two hundred miles.

NEW ORLEANS, APRIL 25 :—Eliza has been most popular during our absence, and all the gentlemen were so kind to her, but it would make your heart bleed to see the cruel manner in which the mosquitoes have destroyed her poor little legs which look as if they had been burnt or had had the small pox or anything most dreadful. She is so healthy that everything heals upon her directly, otherwise I should be quite uneasy about them. We went yesterday evening to visit the old Spanish priest, Padre Antonio, who has been in this country fifty years. He looks the character admirably, with a long, flowing, white beard and his friar's habit. He is eighty years old.

Believe me very affectionately your's,

MARGARET HALL.

LETTER XX

THE MISSISSIPPI

Before leaving New Orleans Mrs. Hall bought a pair of mosquito trousers for Eliza whose legs were "mangled" and swollen with bites. The child seemed sick and miserable when they embarked on the river steamboat, but soon was romping about again to her parents' delight. Mrs. Hall gives an account of the river in flood, the isolated houses, the waste of water, and her husband made sketches of the drowned country and the towns of Natchez and Memphis. They landed at Shippingport and installed themselves in a hotel at Louisville "half as dear and much more comfortable" than the boarding-house at New Orleans. Audubon had given them letters to his sister-in-law, Mrs. Berthoud, so with her help and that of Dr. Johnson, a friend made in Philadelphia, they were inducted into Louisville society.

S. S. "PHILADELPHIA,"
MISSISSIPPI, April 27, 1828.

MY DEAREST JANE,

We left New Orleans with a growing moon, the most comfortable time for ascending the Mississippi, as the bright moon is as useful as the sun in enabling the pilot to steer, but a foggy night succeeded the sultry hot day we had had and obliged us to come to anchor when only twenty miles from New Orleans.

I never spent a more uncomfortable night. The heat was oppressive beyond anything I ever felt, the mosquitoes swarmed and made it necessary to keep the mosquito curtains down, which in those little berths increase the heat to an intolerable degree, the engine was kept working at intervals during the whole night to keep the boilers full of water, and to add to this poor little Eliza was sick the whole night and of course indulged in an occasional fit of crying. Towards morning she fell into a sound sleep from which she awoke comparatively well. Before leaving New Orleans we got her a pair of mosquito trowsers to save her poor little legs from being mangled in the way they have been during the last week, when they have been in a state really shocking to look at, and I have no doubt very painful. The whole of yesterday was as hot as the preceding day, and the temptation to remain on the upper deck for the purpose of seeing the scenery on both sides of the river was so great that we wore ourselves out by exposure to the burning sun.

For one hundred miles up on both sides is a continued succession of rich plantations with rich houses upon them. We had also the good fortune to pass by two crevasses, or breaches, in the levée, or artificial bank, caused by the overflowing of the river. They have a very singular appearance, the water rushing through the crevasse with the impetus of a rapid and running along into the forest much further than the eye could penetrate. Several houses that we saw were nearly thrown down by the violence of the torrent. We have passed innumerable places where altho' there is no crevasse, the water has overflowed everything leaving the houses each morning a little island by itself without the possibility of neighbours visiting each other except by boats. The unhappy cows, too, I saw penned by twos and threes into a little place eight or ten feet square with a few logs to stand on, but of course not a morsel of anything like vegetation near them, looking very miserable indeed. Nevertheless, the scenery on the Mississippi, so far at least, is by no means of the dismal order, further than the consciousness felt that all the nice, fine fields are the result of slave labour, which always takes from enjoyment in seeing them.

There are few passengers and they appear to be of a quite unobtrusive caste. Four of them, Mr. and Mrs. Reed with a son and daughter, were some days at Mrs. Herries's boarding house with us and they leave us to-morrow at Natchez. There are only two more ladies. Besides those mentioned there are ten or twelve gentlemen, but the cabin is so large that this looks like nothing, and we all sit in our respective corners and read our books and write our letters without seeming to know that there are other occupants of the cabin than ourselves.

APRIL 28:—This morning broke gloomily enough and about nine o'clock there was a slight thunder storm; at ten we came to Natchez where the captain told us he would remain two hours, so Basil and I resolved upon a walk up the hill to the town. We were warned against the hill which the people belonging to this flat country describe as of most formidable ascent. Knowing the dead level to which they are accustomed we paid no attention to their protestations but trudged on. We found we were quite correct as to our contempt for the climb, but they had not told us that we should find the soil after rain, of a substance like dough in which I fairly stuck, lost my shoes, and, in short, but for the cowardice of such a proceeding I believe I should have turned back. However, we strode manfully through it and did gain the summit. Natchez is a very pretty little town of new-looking, brick houses and rows of trees along the streets. There is an old Spanish fort close to it which I am told is the scene of a novel lately published by Chateaubriand. At Natchez we put out Mr. and Mrs. Reed with their son and daughter and took in a cross-looking woman with two children, one of five years old and the other apparently of as many months. I do not much like to allow Eliza to associate with American children. They are kept in such a state of filth. Being all of us of course "intelligent and observant travellers" we each take most notice naturally of what belongs more particularly to our own department. Mrs. Cownie is most curious as to the arrangements in nurseries and all that regards the management of children, and the result of her observations makes her very unwilling to allow Miss Eliza to come much in contact with the rising generation of little democrats. Sir Walter Scott says in his life of Napoleon that to wear foul linen and ragged clothing became all that was necessary to constitute a good republican. I suppose dirt and rags are always in part the emblems of this wild state of society, at least here, altho', the children are not in rags and their outer garments, altho' of the worst make and most unbecoming fabric, are still whole. All that is below the upper part of the apparel is dirty and slovenly to a degree that the lower classes in England would scorn to allow their families to wear. At Washington, even, I saw the children of a lady whose husband is high in office, and she has been much in England too, who under their frocks wore nothing but red flannel, not even a chemise of linen. But this is nothing in comparison to their heads, which I must beg your pardon for mentioning, but I suppose you wish to hear all how and about these people we have got amongst, who claim to be English in all that is most admired in England and far more enlightened in many respects, and so you must take your chance of being shocked sometimes. Their heads then are absolutely crawling! Two in particular I can name—Mrs. Erwin's little girl who came from Mobile to New Orleans with us, where Mrs. Cownie saw her mother catching them according to the method depicted in an engraving of Pinelli's of a similar proceeding in the streets of Naples. The other case, which came immediately under our observation, was in the little girl about ten years old who left the boat to-day, and whom Mrs. Cownie saw undergoing the same operation in the hands of the stewardess yesterday. The rudeness of their manners, too, disinclines Mrs. Cownie to allow Eliza to be much with them, for she is so much given to romp even without such example that she fears she will be totally ruined if exposed to their influence. One of our correspondents remarked that altho' we complain of want of polish and refinement there must be a great pleasure in feeling that all the Americans express and do for us is at least sincere, but this is a great mistake, as we have frequently experienced, and I should say on the contrary that I never met with people on whose good offices I would less rely in time of need. Of course, there are exceptions to this as to all rules, but even in the simplest forms of courtesy there is an insincerity that is very disagreeable. Mrs. Reed was all smiles and smoothness during the two days we were on board together, and we were perfectly good friends altho' there was no intimacy between us, and when she went on shore she expressed many regrets that we had given up our plan of remaining some days at Natchez. However, it appears that when her husband told her that I had set off to walk with Basil up to the town, she replied that she hoped I would get a good ducking for my pains. Those Englishers are always full of curiosity and she hoped I "would get something for my travel." A most ladylike manner of expressing herself you must allow. This little anecdote is nothing by itself but I could tell innumerable similar ones.

To-day both sides of the river have been overflowed except at Natchez and some distance above and below, where there are bluffs. Last night we passed a most singular looking dwelling, a small, frame house about fourteen feet by ten, including the verandah, as completely surrounded by water as ever the Ark could have been. At the door of this little island mansion sat three grown persons and two children. There was no other house to be seen within miles of them, and neither could I discover cattle of any kind and this is the state in which they have been for weeks. It is marvellous to me how they exist at all.

APRIL 29:—We find this voyage on the Mississippi very agreeable. We were told that it was extremely monotonous, that we should tire to death of it, and many other prognostics, none of which as yet, and this is the fourth day of it, we have found true. There is certainly an endless forest on each side of us, but it changes its character frequently and is of the most beautiful description, a delightful exchange from the interminable pine barrens that, I must confess, I was thoroughly tired of. To-day we have observed immense numbers of the trees covered with the most luxuriant creepers. Occasionally we come to one or two small houses half-drowned by the unusual height of the water, and we passed one very pretty little village this morning, Vicksburgh, situated on a bluff, the highest land we have seen for some months.

APRIL 30:—We heard magnificent tales of the splendour and good cheer on board the Mississippi boats while we were still at a distance from them, which a knowledge of them has not altogether confirmed. The cabin of this one is very spacious certainly, and the crimson curtains and gilt mirrors have an imposing look which is not altogether of a piece with the couple of tin basins chained to the board which are all that the passengers, excepting those in the state rooms have to wash in. I must do the stewards the justice to say that they keep things much more clean in the cabin than is usual in steamboats. The fare is very indifferent, altho' very abundant and served now no less than five times a day; breakfast at seven, luncheon soon after ten, dinner at one, tea (at which there is as much meat as at breakfast or dinner) before six, and a sort of supper without table cloth about nine. We have had very little milk since we have been on board, for the last two days not a drop, but Eliza does not appear to mind it but drinks the tea very contentedly without. She has got complete possession of the gentlemen, who are her most humble servants and at her command at all times to do exactly what she pleases. She keeps them running about most actively, for the openness of the sides of the boat is such that whoever has charge of her for the time is obliged to be most vigilant not to let her run out, as there would be much danger of her falling overboard. She is such a cunning, frisky little thing that she delights in keeping them moving, and she is quite aware that she is watched.

MAY 5:—We have come up this river very pleasantly to-day enjoying the change of scenery after that of the Mississippi which was so flat and watery and swampy that the banks of the Ohio although generally not more than three or four feet above water are comparatively quite high and the pretty little villages and the occasional houses give it an air of great cheerfulness. In the afternoon we passed Henderson, a village in Kentucky, where our friend Audubon built Steam Mills. The Mills still stand but they are no longer used by him, nor by anyone else I believe. It was a bad speculation, as I should suppose anything he undertook in the way of business would probably prove.

LOUISVILLE, KENTUCKY, MAY 7:—We reached Shippingport last night between eleven and twelve o'clock by which time we were all in bed altho' not many of us asleep, I believe. This morning at six o'clock Basil walked up to Louisville to engage lodgings for us and brought down a hack in which to convey us to the town. Breakfast was provided for us in the boat, and that over we set off. Before breakfast Basil had also been to the house of Mr. Berthoud to whom we brought letters from Mr. Audubon. Mrs. Berthoud is sister to Mrs. Audubon and they have a house at Shippingport on the bank of the river. On leaving the boat we again called there and then proceeded along a very pretty common covered with cows feeding off such grass as we have not lately been used to see, to Louisville, a small town with the worst paved streets I ever saw but beautifully situated on the left bank of the Ohio, and all round this town we have already seen finer trees than any that have before come under our notice in any part of the Union that we have visited, for altho' America abounds in forests I have not till to-day seen what would be considered really fine trees in England. Arrived at the Washington Hall we found things neat and clean, without pretention, most excellent fare, very tolerable attendance for this country, and for all we pay exactly one half the money that Mrs. Herries at New Orleans made us pay for everything that was bad and uncomfortable, but in the South the charges are everywhere exorbitant and the comforts small. In the Western country, on the contrary, everything is plentiful. The only drawback to the comforts of this house is that we cannot have a parlour to ourselves, but there is an improvement on the usual plan of public tables. The married couples and all the ladies, as well as the gentlemen who may be with them, have a dining room and a drawing-room quite apart from the single men, who rush to their meals like so many wild beasts. The smaller party conduct themselves in a more leisurely manner, tho', of course, with a large portion of American haste. I wish you could have seen the perfect satisfaction with which Eliza sat eating some of the best, I may say the only, really good roast beef we have seen since we left England, nor did she enjoy less some nice young gooseberries in a pie.

Having finished our early repast, for dinner was between one

SHIPPING-PORT ON THE OHIO IN KENTUCKY

From a drawing
by Capt. B. Hall, R. N.

and two o'clock, we sallied out in quest of Mr. Bakewell, brother to Mrs. Audubon and Mrs. Berthoud. Basil had called to deliver a letter to him before, but not finding him at home we made a second attempt, as we were desirous of consulting him about our plans, of which I shall say nothing as yet as they are still undetermined upon. We then took a walk along the river bank thro' a most beautiful avenue of beech and elm and returned home at five o'clock supposing that long ere that time Eliza must have finished her walk. But no! Whilst we had been thus soberly engaged the young lady had been exciting a much greater sensation in the place than her Papa or Mama are likely to do. We had all gone out together but after walking about a hundred yards Mrs. Cownie and her little charge parted with us and turned into a shop in search of something they wished to purchase. This proved to be a milliner's shop, and the old lady was so delighted with Eliza's frock—one which her Aunt Katherine worked for her—that she begged Mrs. Cownie as the greatest favour to let her see some more of her dresses. Mrs. Cownie very good-naturedly returned home for three of the child's prettiest frocks and nothing could exceed the admiration, not only of the milliner, but of the numerous ladies for whom she sent to see these beautiful things. Now you must know that they have all been worn and washed for a twelvemonth, and I could not but imagine what would be the amazement of the Louisville ladies could they have seen the clothes of the children of some of my friends who understand the subject so much better than I do that my little girlie's modest equipment could not possibly bear comparison with their's. However, as those ladies knew no better they were sufficiently astonished with what they saw. Patterns were taken and a request made that one of the frocks might be sent to a lady at some distance, but Mrs. Cownie not liking to lose sight of her property could not carry her good nature so far. They had seen Basil and me walk past and the next petition was for the loan of my bonnet to copy, a bonnet which I got the beginning of last summer, but the milliner says that a thing being made from an English pattern or from what is worn by anyone well known gets sale so much better and sooner than on account of intrinsic value. The party assembled then went on to ask many questions, according to custom, but as they were of a more flattering nature than are sometimes put Mrs. Cownie answered them with greater suavity than is her wont. She was asked if I were not a nobleman's lady, but to this she was obliged by the mortifying truth that my husband was not a lord! But seeing that they attached some value to connexion with nobility she proceeded to state that his mother was a lord's daughter. Being told what lord, one of the ladies said that she had read books published by a Lord Selkirk, and another remarked that she had heard of a Lady Selkirk having passed through this country some years ago, whilst the old lady said she had often read of Captain Hall in the newspapers. And so the visit ended by her requesting Mrs. Cownie to help herself to a pair of gloves as a compensation for her trouble, which she refused, altho' she allowed Eliza to accept a little parcel of barley sugar kisses.

MAY 9:—I had an assemblage of all the beauty and fashion of Louisville to visit me yesterday, and really there were amongst them some very pretty persons. The northern climate shows itself in the increased brilliancy of complexion in place of the sallow faces we have of late been in the habit of seeing. I believe I have already mentioned that the great tide of immigration in this country flows to the West, so that here there is a large proportion of the population who have come from the East and the North. I should think many also would be tempted to come from the South, for this is really a land of promise when compared with that miserable country. You cannot imagine with what pleasure our eyes rest upon the verdure of everything here, so different from what we have of late been used to. It really looks quite English. I have not seen much grass anywhere else in the Union. The ladies, I think, managed their visit very well, no fewer than six came together, accompanied by four gentlemen which was much more agreeable to me than if they had occupied my whole morning by dropping in one at a time. This large detachment was brought by Dr. Johnson, a gentleman whom we met at Philadelphia and then at Washington. We walked down after dinner to Shippingport and on returning had to get ready to drink tea at Mr. Talcot's where we met half a dozen persons and spent a very pleasant evening. Mrs. Talcot is of French parentage and spent some years in England where she says she should wish much to go again were it but for the comfort of having good servants, for that the torment of servants in this country makes housekeeping a perfect labour and that she thinks it quite beneath a lady to pay the degree of attention necessary to the most menial arrangements in order to get them done, not well but done at all. Last night we were just seven persons at her house and yet before tea and coffee and a tray of cakes and bread and butter could be brought in to the room she had to go at least six times out of the drawing-room to see things got ready!

This hotel is one of the very best managed houses I have been in in any part of the Union. The master of it appears to understand management thoroughly and everything goes on smoothly and well as if by machinery, for no effort nor management is visible, and to persons so long exposed to the rough ways of the South the change is very agreeable. Some few gifted individuals can make good servants even of slaves, but the talent is a rare one.

LOUISVILLE, MAY 11 :—We dined on the ninth at Mr. Berthoud's at the very inconvenient hour of two which cuts up the day entirely. Only imagine having to begin to dress for dinner at one o'clock, for we had two miles to go to Mr. Berthoud's who, I have before mentioned, lives at Shippingport. The annoyance of beginning the engagements of society at so early an hour is by no means counterbalanced by the subsequent early period of returning home from dinner. I, at least, for one feel so completely tired by the result of dressing, driving, talking, and making company during the hottest part of the day that when I get home at seven o'clock I am fit for nothing but going to bed. I wish the people would grow a little more civilised. We had a pleasant party, however, at Mr. Berthoud's in spite of the unchristian-like hour at which it was brought together. Mr. Berthoud is a Frenchman by birth and altho' in appearance rather coarse, his manners are gentlemanlike and pleasing and tho' he has been in this county since he was eight years old he is still completely alive to the strange, messy way in which the Americans eat. Probably his parents, with whom, of course, he was brought up retained their European customs and taught them to their son, and to French persons the American mixtures must appear still more revolting than they do even to us, for they think the English eat too many things together, such for instance as vegetables and meat on the same plate. There were three ladies and five gentlemen at Mr. Berthoud's, independently of ourselves and those of the house. We walked home, and he accompanied us so far to point out different things about the canal now making between Louisville and Shippingport to divide the rapids of the Ohio. It was as fine an evening as if it had belonged to English summer, and that is very rare in this country early in spring. Altho' the days are so hot that it is impossible to walk out with comfort the evenings are chilly and in summer the ardent heat generally continues till sunset when unless there is moonlight it becomes dark almost immediately, as there is scarcely any twilight.

Yesterday, the tenth, we made an expedition to the country in company with Dr. and Mrs. Johnson, and Mrs. Caldwell whom I had no hesitation in pronouncing to be the most pedantic woman I ever met with. Her husband was one of the professors of the University at Lexington and I suppose she thinks it necessary to be as learned as the professor. She paid me one compliment, however, which I must not omit to mention, that I speak such pure English that she mistook me for an American! The speech was longer and much more circuitous in its form, but the sum and substance was as I have given it. Only fancy what a nasal twang and what a cargo of vile Americanisms I must have acquired! The house we went to was distant about five miles over a most shocking road but thro' a rich and well cultivated country. The proprietor, Mr. Hunley, is a rich, sickly bachelor, aged about fifty, I should think, who has built himself a capacious and commodious house which he occupies in solitude, or the next thing to it, having no other companion than a very dull brother. He has the more need, you will say, of a good conscience, but that he enjoys this appears to me doubtful. He has made every dollar he possesses by buying and selling slaves. He is, or was, in the most literal sense of the term a slave dealer, one who scruples not to separate mothers and children, husbands from their wives; such is the account given of him by a person who has known him since he began his career by working for a dollar a day and having by that means acquired money sufficient to purchase one slave he went off to the South where having sold him for a sum large enough to enable him to buy two on his return to the West, he again went off to the same ready market. There is something particularly cruel in this traffic, for in the Western States, owing to the difference of climate, the approximation of free States and divers other causes slavery becomes much softened. To transplant the poor wretches from such comfort down to all the miseries of the South must require a heart of a harder material than I can imagine to exist. He is mighty religious in his talk, too, and never alluded to his intentions of making a new walk near his house nor removing the pigeon house from the yard without adding, "If it please God that I live so long." The dinner was not in the first style of elegance. There was pork in three shapes, ham, roast pig, and pig's face, and after the course of meat was over we each had a portion of gooseberry and another portion of apple tart on the same plate given to us like so many good little boys and girls at school, and a custard apiece was in like manner handed round. With a little English taste the place might really be made a pretty one, but it is allowed by its present possessor to remain very untidy about the doors and not at all ornamented save by the wild geese, rabbits, and other pets running about, if indeed such creatures can be termed ornamental.

We have been very comfortable during the quiet week we have spent at Louisville. Indeed, I believe the goodness of the hotel has induced us to remain longer than we should otherwise have done, for we have seldom been out of it. We should not have liked to have gone much sooner on Eliza's account likewise, for she has had the worst cold since she came here that ever she had, she was so hoarse that we were quite alarmed about her one night so we sent for the doctor who prescribed sugar candy and balm tea and said there was nothing the matter with her! And such is the opinion given by every medical man who has at any time been consulted about her. The first exclamation always is, "That's a fine child. Why! She is the picture of health."

Ever affectionately your's,

MARGARET HALL.

LETTER XXI

ST. LOUIS, CINCINNATI, PITTSBURGH

Having admired the confluence of the Mississippi and Ohio Captain Hall
decided he must also inspect the confluence of the Mississippi and Missouri.
The travellers set out for St. Louis by water, stayed there at Mrs. Paddock's
boarding-house, then went up stream to the Portage des Sioux and drove
to St. Charles, "a poor, miserable looking place".

Returning to St. Louis they engaged seats in one of the new fashioned
stages with leather flaps all round and set out to drive to Vincennes (Indiana), an uncomfortable experience. Eliza sang most of the way and
appeared to enjoy the bucketting, but her parents were glad enough to get
to Louisville and take ship for Cincinnati. A violent home-sickness, overcame the travellers at this point. They hurried round the sights of Cincinnati, rushed on to Pittsburgh, and then crossed the Alleghanies to
Philadelphia. One thought only was in their minds—escape from America.

ON BOARD THE STEAMBOAT "CAVALIER" ON THE OHIO.
May 16, 1828.

MY DEAREST JANE,

A year has now elapsed since we landed in America. It has
not been an idle one, and certainly not an uninteresting one either,
but I have no wish to spend such another. I mean not in this same
country, for I should have no objection to pass a year of as much
bustle and variety elsewhere. All yesterday we continued descending
the Ohio at a great rate, and by eight o'clock this morning we were
once more at the confluence of the two rivers and turned up the
Mississippi to continue our course to St. Louis. The distance from
the confluence is I believe not two hundred miles.

ON THE MISSISSIPPI, MAY 17:—Whilst we were at Louisville
we were free of the pest of mosquitoes but during the last two days

we have had them in full force. And they have been, as usual, merciless in their attacks upon Eliza. I never saw anyone on whom their sting has such an effect, her trousers save her legs and by much watching we have contrived to keep her face clear of all but one bite. But in spite of all our care they have found their way to her hands and where they bite on the bone the effect is really frightful. To-day on one of her fingers there was a blister as large as a moderate-sized strawberry. Poor little thing, when she got over her distress about it she called it "a plum". The pain ceases as soon as the blister finishes rising but she must suffer a great deal before it reaches that point.

St. Louis, Missouri, May 19:—We arrived here yesterday evening after a very hard struggle against the current the velocity of which is so great that at times we could not only make no way against it but we actually went a little way down the stream again on several occasions. All that part of the river which we ascended yesterday has high, bold cliffs on either hand which give a very picturesque appearance to the scenery, very different indeed from what it is lower down. About ten miles below St. Louis we passed Jefferson Barracks, a military station most beautifully situated. After that the rocks gradually disappeared and so did the fine trees that we have admired so much in the Western country, but in the vicinity of a town they are cut down for fire wood and to supply the steamboats. There were some magnificent trees at Louisville and the roots of some still larger, which on enquiry we found had been cut down to make cogs for wheels, or some such purpose, for which a smaller tree could have answered quite as well. Those trees which I have seen in the West are the only ones in this country which would be thought worthy of a place in a gentleman's park in England, for altho' trees are really a weed from their profusion they are not generally very fine. We went out this morning soon after breakfast to deliver one of our letters of introduction to a person we thought might be of use to us, Mr. Wahrendorf. So in we walked to Mr. Wahrendorf's Store—*anglicé* shop—containing a great variety of articles with as little room to show them off as any shop in a small village in England. The fact is that in those new places in wild countries which we visit the letters are generally for persons in the line (at least apparently) of Mr. Atchison, at Cockburnpath, the village near Dunglass, where you may suit yourself with a woollen nightcap or a tin cannister, according to your wants. As our plans are uncertain we have not yet given any of our letters, but by and by we shall go and call upon General Clark, the Indian Agent here, for whom we have three. We have already dined altho' it is now just two o'clock. Our meal was dispatched with the usual haste, indeed an American breakfast or dinner never fails to remind me of the directions given of old for the eating of the Passover, "With your loins girded, your shoes on your feet, and your staff in your hand; and ye shall eat it in haste"; and truly if the Israelites obeyed the command with a strictness equalling American speed it must have been a strange scene. We are lodged here in the boarding house kept by Mrs. Paddock, who tells us that Lord Selkirk lodged with her when he was at St. Louis on his way from Upper Canada to New York to embark for England. I cannot say that her house has much to recommend it, but we did not expect to find anything better at St. Louis. Mrs. Cownie and Eliza have been out exploring, as usual, and have come home full of stories about some Indians they saw whose painted faces frightened poor Eliza; however, after she became a little more composed Mrs. Cownie took her back again to where they were and she walked backwards and forwards coaxing them saying, "No touch Eliza, the little darling." Poor body, she is not old enough to consider that her fair face is as strange a sight to them, tho' I should think more pleasing, than their painted cheeks to her.

ST. LOUIS, MAY 22:—We learnt late on the evening of the nineteenth that the steamboat *Illinois* was next morning to set out for some place on the Mississippi about nine hundred miles above St. Louis. Our wish was to see the confluence of the Missouri and Mississippi and also to visit St. Charles on the Missouri. How we were to see the confluence was a difficulty which was obviated by this fortunate occurrence of the *Illinois* starting in the morning instead of the evening as she had at first intended, and as we were to return by land we resolved to take a carriage in the boat along with us. Accordingly on the twentieth we got up at four o'clock in the morning and by five were on board the *Illinois,* having been previously warned by the Captain that we should certainly be off at daylight. The Missouri empties itself into the Mississippi eighteen miles above St. Louis. It has two mouths and the view up both is very striking, tho' neither of them of the imposing magnificence of the confluence of the Ohio. The most remarkable circumstance is the instantaneous change in the character of the water of the Mississippi below and above its meeting with the Missouri. I have often mentioned the muddy nature of the river all the way from the Balize, but that part of it from the mouth of the Ohio up to St. Louis is doubly dirty, indeed the mud accumulates so fast in the boilers of the steamboats that they were obliged to clean them out every day. The innumerable logs and other driftwood were also proportionately increased, and the strength of the current was such that we had the greatest difficulty in making way against it. All those circumstances arose from the approximation of the Missouri, and as we continued to paddle up from hence they increased, and when we got near the confluence the mixture of the two waters was very distinct. Had you been in the United States I could have told you what it resembled, but you have never seen a dish containing American gravy and, therefore, my simile is lost, but you must know that the said gravy is always of two colours, a lighter and a darker and of a thicker and a thinner substance, if liquid may be so termed. Such was the water of the Mississippi until we got above the confluence and then all at once it was as pure as the sea and quite the same colour. The scenery on both sides all the way to the Portage des Sioux, thirty-three miles from St. Louis, was highly picturesque, so different from the swampy marshy Mississippi we left below. Here the cliffs surmounted by green and grassy knolls were much more pleasing to the eye, and we enjoyed the day's excursion extremely.

At the Portage des Sioux we landed and disembarking our carriage proceeded in it along the prairie to St. Charles. I thought it resembled what in England are termed downs and in Scotland, links more than anything I ever saw. That which we passed over was covered with cattle and pigs, some little patches of it were cultivated, but this part of the country is as yet so thinly inhabited that thousands of acres of fine land are allowed to lie idle. I thought as I stood looking down upon it what a pity it was that some part of our own overpopulation at home could not be transported to such fine land by which both they and the soil would be so much benefitted.

Within a couple of miles of St. Charles we diverged a little from the road to visit the Mamelles, two little nobs of between two and three hundred feet high which have strangely stuck themselves up in the midst of this great extent of plain. We walked up one and across and down the other and about sunset reached St. Charles, a poor, little, miserable-looking place on the left bank of the Missouri and which bears every appearance of going to decay. We found a tolerable tavern kept by a very intelligent Virginian and his wife, two of the civilest and most obliging persons we have met with in our travels. It was our intention to have returned to St. Louis early on the morning of the twenty-first, but Basil made some sketches, and as ill-luck would have it, just as he had finished one and we had both turned our faces in the opposite direction, there was a rumble such as I fancy must be like the noise of an earthquake at a distance, and crash and behold part of the bank he had not a minute before finished drawing had tumbled into the river. It was really mortifying to miss seeing such a sight, but the sound was to me very awful, and my first impulse was to run away. It was nearly one o'clock when we reached St. Charles and then we had to wait half an hour for the ferry-boat which was, as ferry boats always are, on the opposite side of the river. By this delay we had the whole of the contents of a black cloud discharged upon us as we sat in the little skiff, but we had cloaks and umbrellas and cared not for the rain. A pretty drive over a baddish road until we got on to another prairie within eight miles of the end of it brought us back to St. Louis at six o'clock in the evening. We had left Mrs. Cownie and Eliza here, as our absence was to be so short. They were out when we came home, but in half an hour they returned, Eliza bringing in her hand a pretty, little purse which she had got from General Clark. In the course of their walk they had stopped opposite to his house to look at some Indians; the family saw them from the window and, as in a small place like this strangers are immediately known, they guessed who Eliza was and sent for them to come in. They went, accordingly, and saw all the Indian curiosities in his collection. You may possibly have heard of Clark and Lewis's *Travels Across the Rocky Mountains*. General Clark is the person who made that journey. He is now agent for the northern part of the country. Of course, there were long and interesting details to listen to of all that Miss Eliza had said, looked, and done during the period of our absence, interesting, at least they were to us, more so than all we had seen whilst away from her. We have been teaching her to say Mississippi and have succeeded perfectly, as she now says it very prettily. Missouri, too, she can say but Ohio rather puzzles her.

St. Louis, May 23 :—We were last night at a gayer party than I thought could have been mustered in St. Louis, for after all it is the furthest Western point where anything like civilised society is to be found, and if you look at its position upon the map you would hardly expect to find such a nice house and well-lighted rooms as Colonel O'Fallon's, with ladies dressed in silks, satins, and artificial flowers. The Americans and those who have lived most part of their lives here are quite enchanted with the wonders they have done in the way of improvement and ask what you think of them with countenances radiant with the anticipated pleasure of the certainty of your unqualified admiration and approval; but alas for those who have seen better things, young women whom the well-intended folly of their parents sent at an early age to be educated in

278

all the accomplishments and refinements of France and then brought them back to be really household drudges where, as a lady said to me last night, "I have to attend to the washing of my cook's face as if she were a child of five years old." The same lady told me that when she gives a party she is confined to bed for a week after from actual fatigue of superintending her servants, "and after all," she added, "what is the result? After I have laboured in this way to attain the least and lowest degree of order, things are in such a state that were an English servant to come in she would lift up her hand with horror." This lady is Mrs. Biddle, wife of the Democratic major with whom Basil had a conversation at the same moment. Our entertainment consisted of a succession of trays, the marshalling of which cost Mrs. O'Fallon no small trouble, to judge by the various exits she made from the apartment. I have often thought what would have been our astonishment had we been transported all at once from England to this part of the country instead of becoming gradually accustomed to it by commencing with New York, which altho' it then appeared so different from what we left resembles England so much more that returning to it now we should wonder how we had ever found it different. This boarding house, taken all in all, is the worst we have yet been in. There is not the bustle and confusion of Mrs. Herries's at New Orleans and it is cheap enough certainly, or rather I ought to say we pay little enough money, for really we get no more than the value of it either in food or comfort. Three dollars a day is the charge for which we have three bad meals, positively not enough to eat a dinner. The whole attendance in the house consists of two, dirty, black boys, the one eight and the other twelve years old, and they have everything to do, so you may imagine how it is done. I am told there is a woman in the kitchen, but she apparently confines her range of duties to that spot and three strapping daughters attend to the laying of the table. The daughters are really very civil, but they have little in their power and the mother is a little, blunt, niggardly Yankee who seems desirous of squeezing all she can out of her boarders without giving them a just equivalent.

SALEM, ILLINOIS, MAY 25:—On the twenty-third we secured places in the United States Mail Stage, as it terms itself. The last evening of our stay at St. Louis we spent with a French family, Colonel and Mrs. Shoto, with whom Lord Selkirk was intimately acquainted during his stay there, indeed he spent eight days in Colonel Shoto's house. The old gentleman is now past eighty. He is one of the earliest settlers at St. Louis when it belonged to the French government, and I believe it was he who gave the site for the town. The old couple have a large portion of their children and grand children settled in St. Louis and they were assembled quite in patriarchal style the evening we were with them. They entertained us with a regular supper which by no great stretch of imagination we could convert into a dinner being between seven and eight o'clock, a good London hour, and Mrs. Paddock's one o'clock dinner took the place of a bad luncheon. Yesterday the stage came to the door. It is of a different form from any we have before travelled in. It is open all round with only leather curtains to exclude the sun or rain from entering by the sides, but there is a roof to it. There are three seats, each calculated to hold two persons comfortably, but the front one is appropriated to the driver so that leaves room for only five passengers. Well, we got ourselves and our baggage snugly stowed and on we drove through the street, but at a gay-looking shop door we were brought up by signals from a gentleman and lady holding most formidable looking band boxes in their hands and themselves of no trifling bulk. Our party consisted of three and there was already another gentleman seated beside the driver. However, as to resisting two passengers and their two bandboxes that was a thing not to be thought of, especially as they comforted us by the assurance that they had only seventeen miles to travel, so they were squeezed in and we proceeded on without further stoppage across the ferry on the Mississippi which took us from Missouri into Illinois. Well, we took leave of the Mississippi as we have done with the greater number of our American acquaintances without any regret, and, dashing through the forest as if we had been pioneers, jumbled along, passengers, trunks, and bandboxes inclusive. Our road lay chiefly through prairies but sometimes through forests, and the day being pleasantly cool we had an agreeable enough drive, particularly after we got quit of our fat friends and had elbow room. Mr. Scott's house at Sugar Creek we found a remarkably good one as houses go in this part of the world and we were well pleased to get some good food and plenty of it after the starvation we had experienced at Mrs. Paddock's. By 7.30 today we were once more on the move. Our journey was almost entirely over prairie. I think those prairies remarkably pretty, the last we crossed yesterday extended twenty-three miles. In fact it runs away up to the Michigan Territory and is called the Grand Prairie. Their appearance is very like the ocean and the single trees in the distance are easily converted into ships. It looks so strange to see such immense tracks of good land lying idle, but the objection the settlers have to them is the distance at which they are from wood for fuel and fences, and as long as they do not enclose their land anyone is entitled to send cattle to pasture upon it. We got to Salem, forty-five miles from where we set out in the morning at six o'clock, having had nothing to eat since six o'clock breakfast, but, as usual, we had a weary hour and a half to wait for a single, boiled fowl and some of our own black tea.

MACAULAY'S TAVERN, MAY 26:—We were fortunate enough yesterday to see a herd of fine deer and this morning we saw one or two which remained standing with heads erect and noses sniffing the air until we got tolerably near them and then they bounded off most beautifully. But our chief anxiety was to see a wolf in its native place and Basil offered a reward of a dollar to anyone who should first point out one of those animals. Accordingly, this afternoon whilst we all had our eyes on the stretch, Mrs. Cownie exclaimed, "What is that!" and there to be sure was a wolf not very far from us. We stopped to look at him and he remained still long enough to allow us to have a good look at him, and now we don't care tho' we see no more either deer or wolves. Most of this day's journey has been over prairie. Some beautiful touches of forest we have had likewise, of magnificent oaks and hickory, all in their original beauty without the barbarous mauling of "girdling", or burning of ugly stumps, and now I shall go to bed for we have been much jumbled to-day, in a most rude conveyance. We changed our carriage when we changed our horses to-day, and a strange looking vehicle we got instead, of the same form as the other but a mighty deal older, uglier, and more disagreeable in every respect, and my bones ache badly and then I have nothing to rest them upon but a feather bed, which only increases the evil. One of the things I miss most in this country is a comfortable sofa at the end of a fagging day's work. In the most luxurious houses there is never anything of the kind beyond one of horsehair, not such a one as Mr. Dowbiggin would make, but a miserable, nasty, narrow thing with wood on which to break your elbows at every corner and yet when you go to call upon an American lady she invariably begs you to take a seat on the "sofa" as if there were not more pain than pleasure in such promotion.

VINCENNES, STATE OF INDIANA, MAY 27:—Our last night's quarters were on the banks of the little Wabash, a river regarding which I have felt considerable interest merely because at the time when we first began to think of visiting America I read a book by an anonymous author who mentioned "Cat's Ferry on the Little Wabash," and the name tickled me so much that I was always in hopes it should fall in the course of our route to cross Cat's Ferry, but we only passed within three miles of it. However, we had the satisfaction to learn that it is no longer a ferry, a bridge having taken its place, so that the disappointment is not so great. Thirty-six miles from our starting point we stopped at the place where it was meant we should dine, but there was nothing but pork, and as it was only one o'clock we preferred waiting until we should reach the end of our journey, and whilst the driver ate his dinner and hitched his horses Basil and I walked on till we were brought up by the river Embarras, on the bank of which we waited till the carriage came up and then we were all ferried across, and after travelling over a road, whose character you may guess from its appellation of Purgatory, we crossed the great Wabash and arrived at Vincennes at five o'clock. The day has been actually cold and the road throughout rough and bad, but Eliza has been the best of children. The first two days of our journey she was somewhat fidgety and I was afraid she was going to lose her character as a good traveller but since then she has quite retrieved it, and she takes so much notice of everything as we drive along that she is quite an amusing little companion, but partly from real shyness and partly from imitating other children at times she now makes as bad a figure in company as any child who has never been out of the nursery, which is very annoying to her Mama's vanity. This is only occasional and is very short-lived for in half an hour she is good friends with anyone, and I hope she will soon get over this little folly. The accommodations on this road are on the whole better than those in the South but still they are rude enough. It is never for a moment supposed that our party is to occupy more than one sleeping room, and a chicken is all we get besides the eternal pork which makes its appearance on every American table, high and low, rich and poor. The people are very rough and disagreeable in manners, quite as much as the Southerners, but not like them, indo-lent. We have met many parties of immigrants going to the West, which is all the rage in this country. The rich soil and the lead-mines of Missouri hold out great inducements to settlers, and those from Kentucky in particular, because it is a slave State and they can carry along with them their slaves, whereas the two intervening States of Indiana and Illinois being free they could not bring their black property into them, at least not as slaves.

LOUISVILLE, KENTUCKY, MAY 30:—The last fortnight's rough-ing makes us enjoy returning to this comfortable house with a double relish. The road from Vincennes to Louisville is even worse than what preceded it. On the morning of the twenty-eighth we were roused up at half past three and by a few minutes after four we were off. The style of driving on that road we found augments its natural evils. The drivers universally drive smack along through holes, over stumps and stones, up hills, and across long pieces of corduroy in a manner that it is as impossible for me to describe as it is for you to imagine.

STEAMBOAT *Clinton* ON THE OHIO, MAY 31 :—Our first inquiry at Louisville was about the stage to Lexington, but it was so full, and several persons well acquainted with the road gave such discouraging accounts of it that tired as we were with the jolting we had experienced from St. Louis and our bones still aching we had little mind to encounter such another journey, we next walked down to the wharf to learn what steamboats were going to Cincinnati. We found that there were three named to start as yesterday so we stepped on board the *Clinton,* whose time of starting the clock told us would be four in the afternoon. She was already crammed full of passengers, and there seemed to be no way of stowing us so we walked off, not well knowing what to do. However, on a second visit Basil interested the clerk so much in us that he volunteered to give up his own little stateroom to Mrs. Cownie and Eliza whilst Basil and I were to be accommodated with two berths in the gentlemen's cabin, which we were to screen off as we best could. We were suffering under an attack of the travellers' fever and I believe would have taken our passage under any circumstances, so we dined, got ready, and were on board and off by half past four. The boat and its accommodations are of the same description of magnificence as in all the other much vaunted boats in these western waters. We were disturbed by the dressing bell at half past four this morning and to try to sleep longer was in vain for the passengers began walking and clattering like the hens and geese in a poultry yard roused by the first crowing of the cock. To be sure it was two hours and a half before we got breakfast and then not a drop of milk was there to be had altho' they had stopped several times in the night and might have procured it, I think, had they been desirous of doing so. But they are not anxious to provide any such luxuries, and it is not surprising that they should be indifferent when they find their passengers put up with anything they choose to give them. The Americans are the most extraordinary people in that respect I ever saw. I have seen them over and over again sit down and eat a dinner barely eatable as to cookery or diet and not above half sufficient for the size of the party without uttering a word of complaint or seeming to find out that anything was wrong.

CINCINNATI, JUNE 3:—We landed at Cincinnati yesterday and walked up to Mr. Watson's Hotel on the bank of the river. It is an immense establishment and we got rooms, but on proceeding to terms we did not much like the arrangements they wished to make and as they made difficulties about what we considered essential comforts we walked off in search of accommodation on the other side of the street at the Broadway Hotel where we got matters settled to our minds and immediately moved over. This house has only been opened for a fortnight and the old adage of "new brooms sweep clean" applies with greater force to an American Hotel than to anything else with which I am acquainted. In the first place the furniture is new and therefore it is to be hoped free of vermin, and then there is a certain wish to give satisfaction and gain custom which is entirely at an end after they are fairly established. Our next occupation was to read our letters, and without doubt by far the greatest pleasure experienced in travelling is receiving letters from home.

The first of June was Sunday and as a quiet Sunday is what we have not always in our power to enjoy, we delayed sending out our letters of introduction till the following morning and employed ourselves in going to church where we heard a most excellent preacher and in walking round the town and up to the top of one of the numerous beautiful hills in the neighbourhood from whence we had a fine view of this town and the surrounding country. Cincinnati is certainly an astonishing place. Ohio has not been a State much more than thirty years and the commencement of the town is of still more recent date and now it is an immense place with a greater appearance of bustle and business than any town we have seen since those in the Northern and Eastern States. The situation of Cincinnati is very beautiful and judiciously selected on this river, which is so apt to overflow its banks that except on a hill like this a town is liable to be under water many weeks at a time. Mr. Bullock of the Museum has a most beautiful place on the opposite bank of the river, consequently in Kentucky, about two miles down the river. Yesterday morning we sent out our letters, three in number, and in a couple of hours the results showed themselves in an importation of visitors and an invitation to spend the evening at Mrs. Ferbiger's. The breakfast hour of this house is seven o'clock and the dinner hour one. The early breakfast I can by no means submit to and so we have a separate meal for ourselves but we find it necessary to put up with the gothic time of dining as all appointments for sight-seeing are made in reference to it. At three o'clock yesterday we went out under the chaperonage of Dr. Drake to see all that we had left unseen of the town and its vicinity and had a very pleasant drive and got home just in time to escape a violent thunder storm. This morning we have been denied to all visitors as we wished to write and have engagements after dinner. A great many cards have been brought to me, which make me feel not a little thankful to have escaped the tiresome duty of receiving all those who left them.

ON THE STEAMBOAT *Waverley* ON THE OHIO, JUNE 4:—Well, we are once more in motion, much sooner than we intended. The fact is that now that we have got our faces turned homewards our impatience to get there and our want of patience with this country increases daily. So long as we were going *from* home we did not allow ourselves to confess the feeling of weariness and disgust that we felt. But now the spring after being wound up to the greatest possible tightness has suddenly been let go and rattles down with prodigious velocity. I believe we saw all that there really was to see at Cincinnati.

JUNE 5:—We are actually going home straightway and shall write from Wheeling to New York to secure accommodation in the London Packet of the first of July. We are sick of travelling, we are sick of America, and we are homesick, three diseases too powerful to be resisted. We have frequently of late hinted to each other how remarkably agreeable it would be to cut our task short and go home, but it was not until yesterday that we fairly took courage and spoke out. The proximate cause of our doing so was a slight attack Eliza had of a complaint incident to children in hot weather in this country. Of course, no consideration in the world could induce us to expose her to what might injure her health and every plan must yield to what is most beneficial for her, but in the present instance we wanted but a slight motive to do what we wished and this kind parental solicitude of our's is, I believe, quite uncalled for as the child is already rapidly recovering. Nevertheless, I own I should feel unhappy after this warning in exposing her to a second summer in this climate.

JUNE 7:—The monotony of a steamboat life offers but little subject for a journal. We go on day after day in the same routine, breakfast at seven, dinner between one and two, and supper at seven; between these intervals we, I mean Basil and myself, read, write, sleep if we can, nurse Eliza, and talk to Mr. Kilbee who is really a very agreeable addition to our party, he is always so good humoured. There is a friend of his, too, on board, a Swiss gentleman from the Havannah, who is a prodigious acquisition. He has so many little attentions to pay. He has on board with him claret, sherry, and champaign brandy, all of which he distributes most liberally. He gave me a box of Havannah sweet-meats too, and every time the boat stops he sends his servant on shore for butter-milk and fresh milk and he himself goes in search of bunches of roses. The river is very beautiful but we are almost tired of looking at its banks. We have seen them so long and their beauty is of that tame nature which does not bear very long contemplation. Besides, it is really difficult to admire anything from on board a steamboat. The days however, are delightful and comfortable in comparison of the nights which in this steamboat above all baffle description. The heat of the weather which since we came on board has been greater than any we experienced all last summer, combined with the heat of the cabin and stateroom which are placed directly over the fire and the boilers renders one's existence miserable as these outward circumstances have the power of doing. Two nights more and we shall have done with it and have no more steamboating in this country, I trust, except in the boat which takes us from New York to the packet *Corinthian* on the first of July. We have made up our minds to go through Pennsylvania from Pittsburgh to New York.

PITTSBURGH, PENNSYLVANIA, JUNE 9:—We got up to this port last night between eleven and twelve. Too late, of course, to come on shore, but this morning Basil sallied out whilst the rest of his party was still asleep and engaged rooms for us at Colonel Ramsay's Hotel. Yesterday there was a change of weather and from being oppressively hot it became very cool and pleasant, which was much in favour of Eliza who quite revived with the breeze, and to-day she is quite well. Last night we stopped at a place called Economy, one of those eccentric establishments of which there are so many in this country. The founder and manager of this one is a German of the name of Rapp. Daylight was dying fast when we stopped at Economy so that half an hour was all that the Captain would allow us to spend there, and it was impossible to see anything in that space of time of the establishment. All that we could view was the exterior of the buildings, which had a very cheerful appearance. I cannot pretend to tell you under what kind of management the place is, but I believe that Mr. Rapp is a clever man and tolerably despotic, so that it will probably continue to flourish during his life and fall to pieces at his death. When I took a view from the boat this morning I thought I had got somewhat near home, for on every side were manufactories

od natured and ann maled, and amuses me very much by her
long aristocratic feelings, of which I believe she is quite unconscious.
She has a little niece living with her, a child two years older
than Eliza, who I was requested to take along with us yesterday —
the little girl is a delicate fit of a thing, by no means a match for
my tomboy, which Miss Eliza soon found out, and when she
discovers that any child is afraid of her, from that moment she
tyrannises over her without mercy — So it was yesterday, and the
poor little Livingstone was thoroughly frightened by Eliza's roughness. We owe at least half our popularity in this country to Eliza
she is so perfectly at home with every one, so ready to laugh and
talk in her own fashion to those who will laugh & talk with
us, that her good humour is quite irresistible, and altho' she
is not what can strictly be called a pretty child, there is something in her long flowing hair, white skin, merry blue eyes and
round shoulders that attracts the attention of all strangers.
We went from the Governor's to a party at General Solomon
Van Rensselaer's the Post Master, & his two daughters. it
was very much of the same kind as that of the night before,
not so numerous, but the eatables were of the same quality
and quantity — The attendance was not so good, & was a
very tolerable specimen of how ill that branch of polite society
or at least of its accompaniment is understood — The first of
the train was a black man in white trousers, next followed
a lass, in a black stuff gown and white apron with not a few
holes, and last of all came a little girlie not more than ten or
twelve years old. One of my correspondents remarks that the
ladies in America must be very stupid not to arrange their
domestic concerns and their tables better, but it must be
remembered that such a luxury as a good servant is not
to be had; nothing but the very lowest riff raff of the
Irish; and the ease of getting another place, or doing for
themselves in some way in case of dismissal, is so great, that
if you venture to find fault with your housemaid or But
ler they will tell you that you may suit yourself elsewhere.
exactly the same thing happens in Canada, and from the
same reasons, so that the inconvenience need not be set
down as the result of republican principles, tho' they too
may have their share. You may remember that the beauty of the
ladies struck us very much at New York, I begin to suspect that

FACSIMILE OF LETTER WRITTEN BY
MRS. BASIL HALL

walked.

puffing volumes of black coal smoke. Pittsburgh is one of the greatest manufacturing places, especially in iron and glass, in the United States. After we had settled ourselves in our hotel we went out with the intention of demolishing some of the lions, and with this purpose we ⸳⸳⸳ᵈ first of all to the house of Mr. Bakewell, uncle to the gentleman of that name whom we met at Louisville and also to Mrs. Audubon and Mrs. Berthoud. Mr. Bakewell was at his glass factory, which was exactly what we wished, and we pursued our course in quest of him. We found him in his store, and he accompanied us to see not only his own manufactory but some iron works and a paper manufactory, which was as much as we could overtake before dinner which still continues at one o'clock. The glass is the best made in this country, but it is very inferior indeed to good English glass, so dark in the colour and the cutting is not nearly so good. I remember hearing some American ladies remarking one day that they thought the American glass quite as prettily cut as the English, which appeared to me a great stretch of national prejudice, but I forgot for the moment how inferior a quality of goods of every description is sent to this country. You cannot really form an idea of the trash that is to be found in the best shops and the extreme difficulty and often impossibility of procuring what we consider the most common articles is what you can form no idea of. But to return to our transactions here. At four in the afternoon we went with Mr. Kilbee and his obliging friend, Mr. Winter, to see the Penitentiary, which is conducted on a benevolent, Quakerish plan of solitary confinement and idleness. The building is an exceedingly expensive one, and they have found out, now that it is too late, that it is extremely ill-adapted for its purpose. Opposite to the Penitentiary there is a hill to the top of which we walked and had from thence an excellent view of the town and also of the three rivers on which I may say Pittsburgh is situated—the Monongahela, the Alleghenie, and the Ohio, which commences at the point of land where the other two meet. The situation of this town is altogether beautiful, surrounded by highly cultivated country and beautifully wooded hills which form an amphitheatre, but I have thought and feeling for nothing now except the delightful prospect of returning home.

PHILADELPHIA, JUNE 16:—What a round we have made since we left Philadelphia six months ago, and I must do Miss Boyd the justice to say that in all that time we have not been in so comfortable a house as this is. When we arrived here last evening we were a good deal disconcerted by Miss Boyd saying that her house was full. However, she was as anxious to take us in as we were to be accommodated by her and she said she could put a bed in a private parlour. This would do admirably, we said, and we felt our difficulties to be at an end, but not so Miss Boyd who remarked then, but what should she do for Mrs. Cownie and Eliza.

"Have you two beds?" said I. Yes, she said, she had two beds, but then she had but one room to put them both into and she could not possibly think of packing us all into that. This was a degree of scrupulosity so foreign to what our late habits have been that the circumstance never had presented itself to me as a difficulty, and I soon put our good landlady's mind at ease on this score, so here we are feeling as if we had already got home, and certainly quite in Paradise in as far as comfort and attention to our wishes goes. But, I must tell you somewhat of our journey from Pittsburgh. Our first days journey across the Alleghanies took us to Armagh and very pretty it was. The weather, too, was cool and pleasant, and every step that we receded from the river and advanced into the mountain air appeared to increase Eliza's returning health till now that she is as well and as merry as I ever saw her in my life. I must say this much for her, that whatever faults she may have, however inferior to other children she may be in good order or acquirements or anything else of that kind, as a traveller in a stage she has not her equal that I ever saw or heard of either of a child or of a grown up person. When we were all out of humour and tired and vexed with the bumping and thumping we had been undergoing for twelve or fifteen hours in the hardest and roughest of stages over the most jolting of roads there she sat, laughing and chattering and singing, looking as pleased as if she had been in the easiest of English post chaises driving over macadamised roads. To be sure, she suffered less than any of us because, of course, we took more care to save her from annoyance of every kind and she being so little she lay in anyone's arms clear of all the corners and hardness of the stage. There is one thing that we might all take a lesson from her and that is how to drink in a carriage, which those who have made the experiment must be aware is a most difficult thing to do. If any one of us held the cup to her mouth we invariably spilt part of the contents, but when she got it into her own hands she put merely the edge between her lips and sucked in the water, and this I have seen her do without spilling a single drop. You have no idea of the degree of fatigue we have endured during three days. We had rough conveyances, rough roads, and bad accommodation on each night. We had not more than between four and five hours' sleep and, as I have already said, I set out with a most severe cold which went on increasing and made me quite feverish. To stop anywhere for the sake of rest was out of the question in such inns as those where we lodged. We were only too glad to get out of them with all speed, the soft, buttery, feather beds we had to sleep upon but increased our fatigue and the aching of our bones. There was no comfort in the shape of attendance and no wish to oblige, so that there was nothing for it but to go on and get to the end of our troubles. The sole comfort that we experienced, and that most fully compensated for all our little discomforts, was the hourly improvement in the health and spirits of our little darling who altho' she had got quite over her complaint when I wrote from Pittsburgh had not then recovered her cheerful spirits and good temper, but each new jolt increased her health and her mirth and frequently when I was so tired that I could scarcely speak she sat singing so merrily that I could have envied her had I not preferred her comfort to my own. On the fourteenth we crossed the Susquehanna along the banks of which we drove to Harrisburg, the capital of this State, Pennsylvania, a pretty little town. We had proposed to remain here a day, but by this time we were just beginning to get over our fatigue, and our bones had so far recovered from the severe discipline they had undergone that we feared this little intermission would only cause us the misery of having to recommence all those sufferings again. For this reason we resolved to continue our journey and have done with it and, therefore, having merely dined and stayed an hour at Harrisburg we went on thirty-six miles further to Lancaster, another very pretty little town, with such a nice inn that I felt quite bewildered by the grandeur of it. The country between Lancaster and Philadelphia is from its beauty and richness termed the Garden of Pennsylvania and a very pretty garden it is. Philadelphia is an infinitely gayer-looking place than it appeared to us when we were here in December at a time when the rain never ceased to fall. Our passage is engaged in the *Corinthian* which sails from New York for London on the first of July.

JUNE 18:—Here is weather much hotter than any we experienced all last summer. The Philadelphians say they never felt it hotter; nevertheless, I am glad we came here now, otherwise we should have had a very inaccurate idea of how Philadelphia looked in favourable weather. You may remember, perhaps, that when we were here last December the rain never ceased, and I went away under impression of its being a dirty, gloomy place but not now; nothing can appear more lively and cheerful than it does, and the shops are, in my eyes, so splendid that either they must have improved or else, which I expect is the true reason, I have of late become accustomed to things in such a homely style that I am dazzled by the contrast. The dress of the ladies always struck me as being better than elsewhere in America and the manner of entertaining infinitely superior to what I had seen at New York or anywhere except at Boston, altho' there is more show here than at Boston. On the evening of the sixteenth we walked out to see our Quaker friends, Mr. and Mrs. Robert Vaux, who altho' of a different way of thinking upon the subject of prison discipline from us are nevertheless excellent and kind people, and I do not remember anywhere in this country to have met with so hearty a reception as from Mrs. Vaux. After sitting for some time with them we walked across the streets in a body to call upon Mr. and Madame Neiderstetter, the Prussian chargé d' Affaires, who make their home here and only go to Washington during the meeting of Congress. We learnt there that Mr. Baker, the English Consul-General, and his sister had just arrived at Philadelphia on their way to England. Yesterday we saw a good many of our former acquaintances here, and after dinner paid some visits and then went to tea to a small party at Dr. Hare's. The staple commodity in the eating line at parties just now is strawberries and cream which they have in great perfection. We took Eliza on a drive last night before going to the party and can do so to-night and every evening for it is too hot to admit of her walking and we wish to keep her in the admirable health she is now in by exercise.

JUNE 20:—We have been living a life of the greatest luxury since we came here. I am quite dazzled and ask myself ten times a day if there is anything in the world more comfortable and more magnificent than Miss Boyd's boarding house. It would stand comparison very well with most places but when contrasted with the style in which we have of late lived it is magnificent indeed.

Ever affectionately yours,

MARGARET HALL.

LETTER XXII

FAREWELL TO AMERICA

In spite of "the enmity" she was aware they had excited and "the ill-natured
stories told against them", Mrs. Hall felt more kindly towards America on
the eve of departure than she had done during the whole tour. After
a ball at Mr. Waddington's and a theatre party with Mr. Wilkes the
travellers board the *Corinthian* for home. Eliza turns into "a little sailor
boy," trots about the ship in all weathers and drinks cider with "the
mates". On the twenty-second day of the voyage they reached Cowes.
The "bustling dream" was over, and they awoke to the re-assuring sight of
footmen in red, blue, and yellow liveries. England was England yet.

NEW YORK, June 25, 1828.

MY DEAREST JANE,

We are once more in this bustling place and have since our
arrival on the evening of the twenty-third been in a perfect whirl.
I remember when we went from New York to Philadelphia last
year Philadelphia appeared to me in comparison so dull and inanimate that I thought it more like a city of the dead than of living,
stirring beings. When I returned there a few days ago after our
long exile in the wilderness of the West the comparison I had to
draw was so different that Philadelphia appeared to me entirely
changed in its character and to have acquired all the activity of
New York, and here again the bustle appears to have increased
ten-fold.

On the twenty-first Basil dined at a bachelor party and we
spent the evening in paying farewell visits to some few of our most
intimate acquaintances, particularly to the Vauxs and Neider-
stetters who were the only people I was really sorry to part with,
not that it afflicted me either, and do you know that altho' parting

with those we love is very painful there is a more disagreeable
feeling attending leaving a place altogether without regret, as I
fear I shall America, and yet it is ungrateful to do so, for in spite
of the enmity which we know to exist to us and the many ill-natured
stories told against us we should certainly leave some kind friends
in this country, which is proved to us by the letters full of regret
at the prospect of not seeing us again. To be sure, these regrets
are expressed chiefly by English persons, most of whom we hope
to see again elsewhere. I am very glad we paid this second visit to
Philadelphia for I left it with very different impressions as to the
beauty of the town and surrounding country than those which I
carried away with me on our former visit. The town is too regular
certainly, and too flat, but there are some very handsome streets
and an air of great cheerfulness and cleanliness. We were roused
from bed on the twenty-third at five o'clock, dressed leisurely, and
went down to the steamboat without hurrying ourselves, fancying
that we had plenty of time to spare and forgetting that we had
exchanged dilatory off-putting habits of the South for the anticipation in appointments of the North, so that altho' it still wanted
ten minutes of six, the hour named for starting, the last bell was
ringing, and it was with difficulty that we got ourselves and our
baggage huddled on board, in fact, Basil having to jump on shore
again for some of his boxes, the boat actually left the wharf without him, and it was only on Mr. Bankhead remonstrating that the
Captain put back for him. You cannot imagine how luxurious the
steamboats on these Northern rivers appear to us after the nasty
things in which we were so long cooped up on the western waters.
The large, wide space to walk upon was what we principally enjoyed
and everything, both on water and land, is in so superior a state of
comfort and elegance (two words I should not have thought of
applying to any part of the States a year ago) compared to what
we have of late been accustomed to, that my head is quite turned by
the grandeur with which I am surrounded. We made a very rapid
journey between Philadelphia and New York, the most rapid indeed
that we have made in any part of the States. The first part of it

was up the Delaware twenty-three miles to Trenton. There we landed and found an army of stages ready to carry us across part of New Jersey twenty-seven miles to the little town of New Brunswick when we took boat again down the Raritan whose turnings and windings you may remember I described as being quite tormenting when we went up it last year. At a little after five o'clock we landed near the Battery in New York. As I came up the bay some little recollections of the dreamy feeling I had when I first looked upon New York thirteen months ago crossed my imagination, but the feeling was very short; then all was imagination, now all was certainty and I walked up to the hotel almost as if I were at home. The "Adelphi" where we had secured accommodation is within two hundred yards of where we landed. It is a new house, new from top to bottom, a great advantage in this country. It is an immense establishment, but as yet it is well conducted. We have got good rooms and are well attended to. We had the advantage of a quiet evening and time to read an immense budget of letters.

At nine o'clock yesterday our *levée* began. It commenced with Mr. Wilkes whilst we were still at breakfast and continued till half past one o'clock, no less than seventeen persons in all at different times, but many of whom sat more than an hour. When we got quit of all our visitors we went to call upon some old Halifax friends of Basil's, Bishop Inglis and Judge Haliburton. The judge looks as young as himself altho' he was a lawyer in high practise when Basil knew him twenty-five years ago. All this business and dressing filled up our time till near four o'clock when we went to a family dinner at Mr. Wilkes's. In the evening we all went together to a party at a certain Mr. Waddington's, who appears to be a most hospitable man, for altho' none of us had ever seen him before that morning he had invited us all to dinner, and being engaged for that he asked us for an evening party. All the company were sighing and groaning on account of the heat, nevertheless the room appropriated for dancing was soon filled by melting ladies and gentlemen. I looked on with Captain Sheriff until a waltz was played and then we were both inspired. Another couple also showed themselves ready and a third young lady declared her willingness, provided they could procure for her as partner a married man or a cousin. I really did not think that any girl would have made such a fool of herself, but there she stood meditating her conditions whilst the room was searched by the mistress of the house demanding of each gentleman first if he were married and, secondly, if he could valse? "As if," said Captain Sheriff who, although married and having six children is the greatest flirt I have met with for long, "As if a man would not flirt if he had a mind to whether he were married or single." After a great deal of laughing and quizzing on the subject Mr. Bankhead was selected as a proper person and the scrupulous lady valsed. It was a very agreeable little party and we got home at eleven o'clock. To-day we have denied ourselves to visitors as we must put our things in order for our voyage.

JUNE 28:—It is rather severe to be obliged to be very busy in hot weather, at least, so everyone seems to feel except me. I bear the heat with the utmost philosophy simply because it does not affect me. I see everyone around me oppressed to the greatest degree whilst I am quite comfortable. Even Basil is quite done up by it. But there is another reason why I do not suffer when he does, I do nothing, he does all the work, except what Mrs. Cownie does in the way of packing. Last night I went with the Wilkeses and a large party to the theatre. It was a benefit so we had a prodigious dose of amusement and the heat was very great. That morning the captain of the packet in which we are to sail called to inform us that he had succeeded in exchanging our accommodation for the best on board the ship, a nice stateroom with four berths, and from which there is access to the Ladies' Cabin when we wish to go there. The cabins appear to me to be smaller than those on board the *Florida,* tho' they are neat and unpretending. Eliza went on board with us and was as much taken up with examining everything on board as we were. Whilst writing I have been interrupted by a visit from the Patroon, Mr. Van Rensselaer, whose son was in Edinburgh last winter. Both father and son are full of gratitude for the attention the young man met with from our friends there. Another one sails on the first of July for England and both of them are to pass next winter in Edinburgh. The one who has been there was extremely anxious that his brother should join him. He says that before going there he conceived himself to be a good scholar, but there he has learnt his mistakes. He thought also that he knew something of good society, but in that too he finds he erred; the society is so very different in Edinburgh from what it is in America. In short, there never was a more grateful or a more admirable youth, which is very pleasant, for one does not like one's friends' attentions to be thrown away upon thankless subjects.

NEW YORK, JULY 1 :—I am idle enough this morning to have time to write, altho' in little more than two hours we shall be aboard the steamboat that is to carry us to our ship. All our baggage except a few things of which it is impossible to divest oneself is gone on board. The day looks foggy and east-windy, which is a disagreeable prospect for us. I cannot say that I feel at all sorry or that I have the smallest regret on leaving New York, or indeed America. I feel nothing but unmixed pleasure at the thoughts of returning home. The only persons I am sorry to leave are the Coldens and Wilkeses and there is no bad chance that I shall see them again in England.

NEW YORK HARBOUR, ON BOARD THE *Corinthian*, JULY 1 :— Here we are on board, but not making any progress. The wind and the fog are both against us, and altho' we might get down to Sandy Hook Lighthouse we should be obliged to come to anchor there and should be exposed to a heavy sea instead of lying quietly here. We left the hotel to-day between nine and ten o'clock accompanied by several acquaintances. When we got on board the boat we were surrounded, and in coming down we met so many persons whom we know on the move, bound either for the Havre or Liverpool Packet that it appeared as if all New York was preparing to cross the Atlantic. We had quite a gay setting off as there was no one there whom it cost us a tear to part with. There are fourteen passengers in all, six ladies and eight gentlemen, besides Eliza. The captain appears to be a very obliging man and at present we are getting on all smoothly. We have arranged all our things comfortably in case of being incapacitated from doing so by and by. And now I must say my stay in America appears like a dream. I can hardly believe that I have been there and have left it, but I am not sorry that the dream is over tho' in spite of many disagreeable circumstances attending it it has not been a disagreeable one. We have seen much to interest us, have met, at least, hospitality everywhere, have made some good new friends, principally among our own countrymen.

JULY 20:—On the thirteenth we went so far as to dress ourselves a little more smartly, put on muslin collars, friz out our hair, and, in short, felt quite sure that we should never be sick any more. Such was our opinion on the fourteenth also. The fifteenth the wind came more to the north and the weather grew very cold. All this time, you will observe, we were getting on at the rate of eight or nine knots an hour. Basil expressed many a devout wish that we might not increase our speed, as he knew full well that the consequence would be an equal increase of motion with all its attendant evils to weak stomachs. The sixteenth wind increased very much. We bounded along at ten and eleven knots, the cold was extreme, frequent squalls of rain and such rolling and pitching as was only outdone by that of the seventeenth, when all our miseries were increased ten fold. Oh such pitching, such deathlike sickness; for the first time since we came on board, I did not stir from bed during the whole day. It was indeed a wretched day, even the strongest and best sailors were completely subdued, all excepting Eliza. She trotted about as stoutly and boldly as ever, not one bit sick, laughing and making others laugh in spite of their qualms. A more perfect recovery than she has made it is impossible to conceive. Her little face has resumed all its roundness tho' not yet its roses. She eats, drinks, and sleeps with a heartiness and soundness I never saw surpassed. All day long she is on her legs, running about and as busy as she can be. The passengers are everyone kinder than another to her. The captain is indefatigable in his attention. The mates, with whom she drinks cider at their dinner and tea in the evening, independently of her own meals, think her quite a wit and the steward says she is the nicest little girl that ever came in the ship. She calls herself a "little sailor boy" and, in truth, she has as good sea legs as if she really were so. Even a poor, sick, half-dying passenger lies on her mattress in fits of laughing at her funny ways. Of course, everyone spoils her, but when she is well as she is now she is so good-tempered naturally that the effects are not very visible. Such is Miss Eliza at the present time. The eighteenth things became a little less uncomfortable, altho' the cold and the rain squalls continued to be troublesome, but I came once more up on deck, and by the help of cloaks and umbrellas braved the elements pretty well, and then under all our discomforts we had the inexpressible satisfaction of knowing that every hour carried us ten or eleven knots nearer home, for since the moment that we sailed we have not had a bad wind for one single minute, and it is not to be told what a difference this makes in the patience with which one bears one's distresses. The nineteenth the weather became somewhat milder and we were amused about dinner time by the number of porpoises which came leaping and dancing along the side of the ship, very beautiful creatures indeed. To-day we go on smoothly again altho' still very fast, but the conversation now begins to be of what are the best hotels at Cowes, Ryde, or Portsmouth, the hour of coaches starting from Portsmouth for London, and all those subjects which show how near we are to home, tho' I still tremble lest the wind should change and leave us beating about in the Chops of the Channel for six weeks, as Basil did when he went home in the *Lyra*.

JULY 21:—An hour ago Captain Chadwick told me that we were just a hundred and eight miles from the Isle of Wight and assured me at the same time that we shall reach Cowes in time to put our letters into the Post Office for the mail of to-morrow. This is a very cheering piece of information and, in consequence of it, I have been writing my letters which are intended to announce our arrival.

FOUNTAIN HOTEL, COWES, ISLE OF WIGHT. JULY 22, 1828, 9 O'CLOCK P.M. :—There's a date for you, but I thought that the first lines I wrote when once more on English ground were well worthy of all particularity. Yes, here we are indeed, in old England after a bustling dream of fifteen months which has passed away as if it were only as many days, at least, so it appears to me at this moment, when I take a rapid glance in my mind over the whole, and I cannot yet realise it to myself that we have done so much and are really at home again. Perhaps a good night's rest may serve to clear my ideas a little, but that is a luxury which I have not enjoyed for many nights. Sleep seemed to have forsaken everyone on board of late, and last night especially the fever of expectation made us more wakeful than ever, all except Eliza. She, poor lamb, unconscious whether she were on the Mississippi or the Atlantic and neither knowing nor caring whether her destination were to Cowes or New Orleans. These sleepless nights make some of the ladies very hungry, and at four o'clock I was awakened from a very short sleep by peals of laughter from their cabin occasioned by the exploit of one of them, who, sallying forth in need of something to appease her hunger, returned in triumph with the skeleton of a goose. This noisy mirth completely banished any little inclination that I had had for repose and soon the bustle on deck and the wish to get the first sight of land induced me to begin to dress, but alas it was only a beginning, for presently the ship rolled and pitched and kicked in a more disagreeable fashion than anything we have experienced in crossing the Atlantic. The sea was extremely rough and we rounded to for a pilot and, in short, it was altogether very miserable and I was obliged to lie down for a couple of hours until things quieted a little, and then I went on deck and feasted my eyes with a sight of the rugged barren coast of Dorset and Hampshire. The day was clouded with frequent showers of rain, and at three o'clock we came to anchor in the harbour of Cowes in the midst of wind and rain mixed with a little sunshine that welcomed us home. Basil went on shore for letters and to secure lodgings, and by five o'clock we were snugly seated beside the fire in a nice parlour in the Fountain Hotel. As soon as we had dined we walked off to the public walk on the beach to see the world, and I must say that I find that all the bright images I had of England whilst I was in so different a country were to the full realised as far as there was scope for it in so short a time. Every house looked so neat and nice and beautiful that I longed to live in each one that I passed. The children, too, delight me, and there is an appearance of neatness and plainness about the ladies so unlike the gaudy overdressing of the American women which is very pleasing. But what do you think excites Basil's admiration most strongly? The footmen in livery! It is so long since we have seen a well dressed servant that those gay white, red, or blue and yellow coats delighted Basil as much as, I have no doubt, they will Eliza when she sees them. The town of Cowes is not pretty, but the houses around it have all the beauty and taste of every English sea-bathing place that I have seen. The yachts of the gentlemen of the Yacht Club are lying here preparatory to the Regatta, which is to take place shortly. And so here ends my story and,

I remain, my dearest Jane,

Ever affectionately yours,

MARGARET HALL.

INDEX

INDEX

INDEX

INDEX

Lomond, Loch, 31
Long Island, 28
Louisville, 267, 271, 273
Lowell, 91
Lyceum, The, New York, 26
Lynd, Captain, 32, 109

MacAlan, Mrs., 14
MacKennèy, Colonel, 185
Maclean, Mr., 207
Maclure, The Misses, 253
Macon, 237, 238
Macready, Mr., Mrs. and Miss, 29
MacTavish, Mrs., 158, 159
Malibran, Madame, 23
Mallet, Mr., 205
Maltity, Baron, 177
Manchester, 48
Manlius Fourcorners, 48
Mareuil, Baron de, 170
Marshall, Miss, 88, 93
Mayo, Mr., 199
Mease, Dr., 152
Menou, Count, 171, 194
Middleton, Mr., 148, 237
Middletown, 112, 113
Minot, Mrs., 98
Mitchell, Mr., 19
Mobile, 243, 244, 245
Molyneux, 225, 226
Monroe, Mrs. James, 22, 28
Montgomery, 227, 241, 243
Montmorenci, Count Henri de, 171
Montpellier, 206
Moore, Mrs. Clement, 128
Morse, Mr., 69
Mount Pleasant School, Amherst, 83
Mount Vernon, 195
Murat, Prince, 133
Murray, Mrs. and the Misses, 121
Musignano, Prince and Princesse de,
127, 177, 178, 186, 200

Natchez, 262
National Gallery, New York, 26
Neiderstatter, Mr. and Mrs., 142, 152,
170, 193, 293
Nelson, Mr., 206
Newark, 29
Newfoundland, 14
New Haven, 83, 112, 113
New Orleans, 246
New York, 10, 14, 15, 17–30, 31, 35, 37,
54, 86, 99, 113, 116, 134
Niagara, 56, 57, 68
Nicklin, Mr. and Mrs., 141

Niskayuna, 43, 44
Nolte, Mr. Vincent, 257
North, Mr., 112
Northampton, 80, 82, 83, 88, 115
Nott, Mrs., 211, 212

Obregon, Mr., 183
Ochando de la Banda, Mr., 194
O'Fallon, Colonel and Mrs., 278, 279
Oglethorpe, General, 230
Old Creek Agency, 237
Oliver, Mr., 163
Olney, Mr. and Mrs., 149
Oneida Indians, 48
O'Neill, Mrs., 236, 237
Ontario, Lake, 57
Otis, Mrs., 90
Ouseley, Mr., 166, 197, 198
Owen, Mr. Robert, 253

Paddock, Mrs., 138
Palmer, Mrs., 138
Panorama of Athens, 26
Parma, 55
Parsons, Mrs., 112
Partridge, Captain, 112
Passaic, Falls of, 29, 30
Paterson, 29, 30
Paulus Hook, 29
Pawtucket, 106
Peale, Mr., 143
Penn, John, 145
Penn, William, 145
Perkins, Colonel, 87, 94, 100
Perkins, Miss, 120
Pettigrew, Attorney General and Mrs.,
211, 212, 216
Philadelphia, 67, 132, 133–152
Philosophical Society, 137
Pilié, Surveyor General, 256
Pillans, Mr., 27
Pillsbury, Mr., 109, 111
Pine Orchard, Catskill, 26
Pittsburgh, 288, 289
Pleasanton, Mrs., 169
Pocahontas, 199
Pole, Mr. and Mrs., 247, 248
Pooley, Captain, 120
Portage des Sioux, 276, 277
Porter, Judge, 254, 257
Powhatan, 198
Pratt, Mr., 87
Prescott, Judge, 95
Prescott, Mr. W. H., 96
Proctor, Mr., 121
Providence, 106, 113

306

INDEX

307

INDEX

504 EY
OP - PLUG?